eBay Auction Templates Starter Kit

Michael Miller

QUe®

800 East 96th Street, Indianapolis, Indiana 46240 USA

eBay Auction Templates Starter Kit

Copyright © 2006 by Que Publishing

International Standard Book Number: 0-7897-3563-6

Library of Congress Catalog Card Number: 2006920310

Printed in the United States of America

First Printing: June 2006

09   08   07   06   4   3   2   1

Trademarks

Warning and Disclaimer

Bulk Sales

Que Publishing offers excellent discounts on this book when ordered in quantity for bulk purchases or special sales. For more information, please contact

U.S. Corporate and Government Sales

1-800-382-3419

corpsales@pearsontechgroup.com

For sales outside of the United States, please contact

International Sales

international@pearsoned.com

Associate Publisher
Greg Wiegand

Acquisitions Editor
Michelle Newcomb

Senior Development Editor
Rick Kughen

Managing Editor
Charlotte Clapp

Project Editor
Dan Knott

Indexer
Chris Barrick

Proofreader
Kathy Bidwell

Technical Editor
Michelle Brantner

Publishing Coordinator
Sharry Lee Gregory

Multimedia Developer
Dan Scherf

Book Designer
Ann Jones

Page Layout
Nonie Ratcliff

Contents at a Glance

Table of Contents

About the Author

Michael Miller is a top eBay seller and a successful and prolific author. He has a reputation for practical, real-world advice and an unerring empathy for the needs of his readers.

Mr. Miller has written more than 75 nonfiction books since 1989, for Que and other major publishers. His books for Que include *Easy eBay, Absolute Beginner's Guide to eBay, Making a Living with Your eBay Business*, and *Tricks of the eBay Masters*. He is known for his casual, easy-to-read writing style and his ability to explain a wide variety of complex topics to an everyday audience.

You can email Mr. Miller directly at ebay-templates@molehillgroup.com. His website is located at www.molehillgroup.com, and his eBay user ID is trapperjohn2000.

Dedication

To Sherry. Of course.

Acknowledgments

Thanks to the usual suspects at Que, including but not limited to Greg Wiegand, Michelle Newcomb, and Rick Kughen. Additional thanks go to the book's technical editor, Michelle Brantner, who verified the technical accuracy of all that lies within. Thanks as well to Dan Scherf for wrangling all the software and templates on the accompanying CD, and to all the companies and individuals who kindly granted permission for us to include their products.

We Want to Hear from You!

As the reader of this book, *you* are our most important critic and commentator. We value your opinion and want to know what we're doing right, what we could do better, what areas you'd like to see us publish in, and any other words of wisdom you're willing to pass our way.

As an associate publisher for Que Publishing, I welcome your comments. You can email or write me directly to let me know what you did or didn't like about this book[md]as well as what we can do to make our books better.

Please note that I cannot help you with technical problems related to the topic of this book. We do have a User Services group, however, where I will forward specific technical questions related to the book.

When you write, please be sure to include this book's title and author as well as your name, email address, and phone number. I will carefully review your comments and share them with the author and editors who worked on the book.

Email: feedback@quepublishing.com

Mail: Greg Wiegand
            Associate Publisher
            Que Publishing
            800 East 96th Street
            Indianapolis, IN 46240 USA

Reader Services

Visit our website and register this book at www.quepublishing.com/register for convenient access to any updates, downloads, or errata that might be available for this book.

Introduction

Have you ever wondered how some sellers create those colorful, well-designed, professional-looking auction listings? Especially when your standard-issue eBay listings look so...well, so boring?

It's all about auction templates. A template is a building block you can use for all your auction listings. A good template includes a combination of fonts, colors, pictures, and page layout that does a good job of presenting the items you're selling in a visually interesting fashion. Once you have a template you like, you can apply it to any new eBay auction by inserting specific item information and photos. You can use the same template for all your listings, or use different templates for different types of products—or different seasons of the year.

There are many different ways to obtain great-looking auction templates. You can use eBay's own Listing Designer feature; you can use third-party websites to create your own templates online; you can download pre-designed auction templates from a variety of different websites; or you can create your own custom templates using HTML code.

If any of the above sounds too complicated, then you've turned to the right place. *eBay Auction Templates Starter Kit* is your guide to all the different types of eBay auction templates—from easy-to-use pre-designed templates to the kinds of HTML-based templates you create on your own. Whichever way you want to go, this book will help you get there.

What's in This Book

This book consists of 10 chapters and 2 appendixes, organized into 4 major sections:

- We'll start out in Part I, "Creating More Effective Auction Listings," by examining some design guidelines that should apply to all eBay auction listings.

- Then, in Part II, "Using Predesigned Auction Templates," we'll take a look at various types of template-creation services, as well as a variety of predesigned download-able templates.

- In Part III, "Creating Your Own Auction Templates," we'll work through a crash course in HTML coding, complete with ready-to-use code you can use for your own eBay templates and special effects.

- Finally, the book's two appendixes detail special HTML code you can use in your About Me and eBay Stores pages, as well as describe the contents of the CD that accompanies this book.

And the good thing is, what you read in this book is supplemented by the materials on the accompanying CD-ROM. The CD includes ready-to-use HTML code for all the templates and special effects presented in this book, as well as hundreds of other predesigned auc-tion templates from a variety of third parties. There's even a selection of HTML and photo editing software you can use to help create your own auction templates. Like the title says, this truly is a "starter kit" for creating all different types of eBay auction templates!

Who Can Use This Book

eBay Auction Templates Starter Kit can be used by any level of eBay seller. If you want an easy solution, read the first two sections of the book and use the ready-to-use templates included on the accompanying CD. If you're a bit more adventurous, read the third section and learn how to create your own auction templates using simple HTML code. This is a lot easier than it sounds, thanks to the ready-to-run HTML code included on the accompany-ing CD. You don't have to be an experienced HTML programmer to get started—although there are plenty of tips and tricks that even veteran HTML coders will find useful. There's something for everyone!

How to Use This Book

I hope that this book is easy enough to read that you don't need instructions. That said, there are a few elements that bear explaining.

First, there are several special elements in this book, presented in what we in the pub-lishing business call "margin notes." There are different types of margin notes for different types of information, as you see here.

NOTE This is a note that presents information of interest, even if it isn't wholly relevant to the discussion in the main text.

TIP This is a tip that might prove useful for whatever it is you're in the process of doing.

CAUTION This is a caution that something you might accidentally do might have undesirable results.

You'll also find several icons scattered throughout the margins of the text. These icons alert you to special information, as follows:

CD-ROM This icon tells you that the template, special effect, or software program under discussion can be found on the CD-ROM that accompanies this book.

This icon tells you that the program or template under discussion is available free of charge.
Free

This icon tells you that the program or template under discussion costs money to use.
Pay

There are also lots of web page addresses in the book, like this one: www.molehillgroup. com. When you see one of these addresses (also known as a URL), you can go to that web page by entering the URL into the address box in your web browser. I've made every effort to ensure the accuracy of the web addresses presented here, but given the ever-changing nature of the web, don't be surprised if you run across an address or two that's changed. I apologize in advance.

The other thing you'll find a lot of in this book is HTML code. A snippet of code might look like this:

```
<p>
This is a line of text.
</p>
<img src="URL">
```

You should be able to enter this code, exactly as written, into eBay's HTML editor on the Describe Your Item form (when you're creating a new auction listing). You can also enter this code into any text editor or HTML editor program, for further editing.

When part of the code is italic (such as the *URL* in the previous example), this means that you need to replace the italicized code with your own individual information. In the previous example, you would replace *URL* with the full URL and filename of an image file you want to include in your auction template.

And if you don't want to enter all the code by hand, the HTML code for all the templates and special effects included in this book can be found on the accompanying CD-ROM. See Appendix B, "Contents of the eBay Auction Templates Starter Kit CD," for more information on how to use the contents of the CD.

Ready, Get Set, Go!

With all these preliminaries out of the way, it's now time to get started. While I recommend reading the book in consecutive order, feel free to skip around, especially if you're a more experienced seller. And definitely feel free to visit my website at www.molehillgroup.com, for more information on this book and other books I've written. You'll even find an errata page for this book, in the inevitable event that an error or two creeps into this text. (Hey, nobody's perfect!)

So get ready to turn the page and learn more about creating better-looking eBay listings with auction templates. Not only will your auction listings look better, they'll also be more effective—which means selling more items at higher prices. What's not to like?

Creating More Effective Auction Listings

The Good, the Bad, and the Ugly: Do's and Don'ts for Effective Auction Listings

This book is all about creating better-looking eBay auction listings. Looks are important, because the better-looking your listings, the more effective they'll be—you'll attract more potential buyers and get them to bid more aggressively. It's not that you can't sell items with plain-looking listings, it's that you'll have better luck if your listings look more attractive and more professional.

Have you ever been online shopping and visited a new website that looked garish and unprofessional? How did you feel about purchasing something from that site? Not too confident, I bet.

And have you ever been online shopping and visited a new website that was well-designed and very professional-looking? How did you feel about purchasing something from *that* site? Fairly confident, I'd wager.

You see, a well-designed website or web page tells you something, at least on an unconscious level, about the person or store doing the selling. A cheap-looking site makes you wonder about the reliability of the merchant. A professionally designed, easy-to-navigate site makes you more confident about placing your order. Maybe both merchants are equally solid, but the one that *looks* more solid will get your order, all other things being equal.

It's the same thing in the world of eBay auctions. A well-designed, visually appealing auction listing not only attracts more buyers, it makes them feel more confident about buying from you. A poorly designed listing will turn off some potential buyers. Since you never want to turn away any potential business, you want your listings to do as effective a sales job as possible.

All of which means that you need to design the look of your listings with every bit as much care as you choose the products that you sell. The better the job you do, the more successful auctions you'll have.

Essential Elements of an Effective eBay Auction Listing

It doesn't matter if you're selling $10 trinkets or $1,000 antiques, an effective eBay auction listing contains the same essential elements. You *must* incorporate these elements in your listings, or you risk losing potential buyers.

What are these elements? Let's take a quick look—going pretty much from top to bottom in your listings.

Title

Every auction listing starts with a title. Actually, two titles—the official 55-character title that eBay uses to index your auction (and is included at the top of the listing page), and the title that you place above the text description in the body of your auction listing. These two titles can be the same, although they don't have to be. That's because the title you include within the body of your listing doesn't have a character limit; it can be as long and descriptive as you want it to be.

Since you want the title to stand out from the body of your description, you probably want to format it somewhat differently. That means using a larger type size, boldface type, a different type face, or a different color. (Figure 1.1 shows a typical title, using larger, boldface type.)

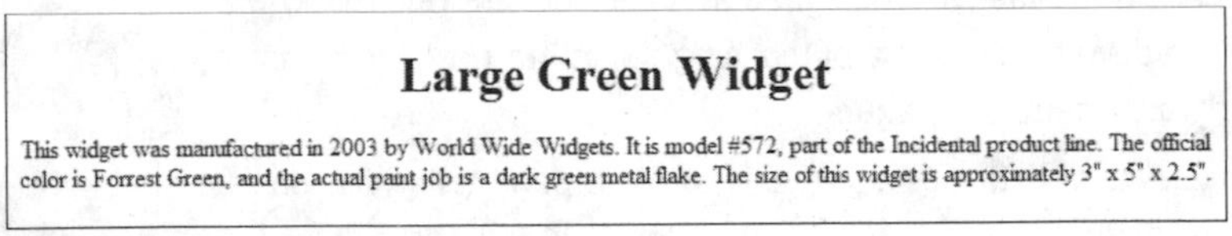

Large Green Widget

This widget was manufactured in 2003 by World Wide Widgets. It is model #572, part of the Incidental product line. The official color is Forrest Green, and the actual paint job is a dark green metal flake. The size of this widget is approximately 3" x 5" x 2.5".

FIGURE 1.1

A typical listing title—the type is larger and bolder than the rest of the listing.

The key thing is to treat the title as you would the headline in a newspaper. It needs to attract the attention of potential buyers, and include all the keywords that touch the buyers' hot buttons.

That said, the title—while theoretically of unlimited length—shouldn't be *too* long. There's no need to limit yourself to just 55 characters, but you shouldn't let the title stretch more than two lines. Titles are for grazing, not for prolonged reading. If the title can't be absorbed in a single glance, it's too long.

If you need to go to a third (or fourth) line of type, consider breaking the title into a title and a subtitle, with the subtitle in slightly smaller, perhaps different-colored type. (Figure 1.2 shows a listing with both title and subtitle; note the type size difference.)

> **TIP** Including all essential keywords is even more important in eBay's official listing title. That's because most buyers use eBay's search function to find items to buy, so the title has to include the keywords that they're likely to search for.

Large Green Widget

Slightly used, in original box

This widget was manufactured in 2003 by World Wide Widgets. It is model #572, part of the Incidental product line. The official color is Forrest Green, and the actual paint job is a dark green metal flake. The size of this widget is approximately 3" x 5" x 2.5".

FIGURE 1.2

A listing with both a title and a subtitle; the subtitle is slightly smaller than the main title.

General Description

Below the title, we get to what I like to think of as the introduction to your listing—the first paragraph of your item listing. This first paragraph serves as the introduction to the detailed item description.

Note that I treat the first paragraph separate from all subsequent paragraphs. That's because many people only read so far before they lose interest. You see this in the construction of newspaper articles, where the main topic is overviewed in the initial paragraph. Newspaper people call this first paragraph the *lede*, and it always contains the most important information about the story that follows. If the reader reads nothing but that first paragraph, he gets a general overview of what the story is about. It's

> **NOTE** Many laypeople unknowingly misspell the newspaper's *lede* as *lead* (both pronounced as "leed"). The misspelling makes sense since the lede is the "lead paragraph" of the story, but it's still incorrect. Interestingly, the word *lede* was originally spelled this way to prevent confusion with the metal *lead* (pronounced "led"), which was used to make the individual letters in the old typesetting days, and with the similarly pronounced *lead* that refers to the spacing of lines in printed text. Too many leads led to the word lede!

obviously not as detailed as the rest of the story, but it does the job of keeping the reader informed at a glance.

For our purposes, the overview paragraph needs to tell the potential buyer *just enough* about the item you're selling to keep him or her reading. This paragraph should be relatively short (no more than 3 to 4 sentences), and use short sentences. It should tell the equivalent of the newspaperman's "who, what, why, when, and where"—the basics of what you're selling, and perhaps why. Not a lot of detail, just the gist of the story.

Design-wise, this overview paragraph can be in the same font and type face as the rest of the description, or you can use a *slightly* larger typeface, as shown in Figure 1.3. The advantage of using slightly larger type is to make the initial paragraph easier to read. If you go this route, don't go more than 2 points larger. For example, if the main description text is in 12-point type, make the initial paragraph 14 point.

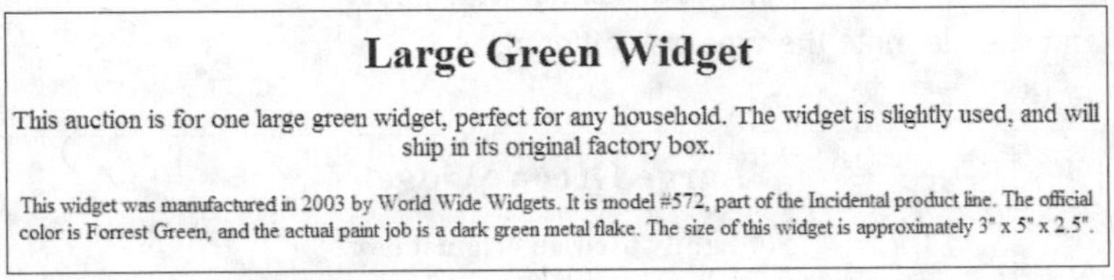

Large Green Widget

This auction is for one large green widget, perfect for any household. The widget is slightly used, and will ship in its original factory box.

This widget was manufactured in 2003 by World Wide Widgets. It is model #572, part of the Incidental product line. The official color is Forrest Green, and the actual paint job is a dark green metal flake. The size of this widget is approximately 3" x 5" x 2.5".

FIGURE 1.3

The overview paragraph of the item description, formatted 2 points larger than the body text.

Detailed Description

Now we come to the meat of your auction listing—the detailed description of the item you're selling. This is where you tell potential buyers all they want to know about what you want to sell. There's no need to scrimp on the description; take all the space you need to provide an appropriate amount of accurate and detailed information.

When you write your description, it helps to think like a copywriter for one of the big catalog or direct mail firms. Take a look at how L.L. Bean and Lands End do it, and emulate that style and level of detail. You should not only describe the item, you should *sell* the item. That means listing not only the item's features, but also its benefits. It's not enough to say that this widget includes a 1/4" blowhole; you need to tell the buyer what that blowhole will do for him.

The details to provide should include any and all of the following:

- Manufacturer name
- Item name
- Model number
- Product line
- Year manufactured or sold

- Approximate age of the item
- Condition—new, used, like-new, mint, fair, in original box, and so on
- Color
- Size
- Dimensions
- Included accessories

Now stop for a minute and take a look at how I presented the previous information. Instead of listing all those details about the details in a long, hard-to-read text paragraph, I broke them out into a bulleted list. This is a good technique to apply in your auction listings, too. When you have a lot of details to include, turn them into a list. Bulleted lists are easier for the reader to absorb than are long paragraphs, which is why you see them used quite often in catalog copy.

Along the same lines, consider other formatting options that can make a long description easier to read. This might mean putting the information in a table (as shown in Figure 1.4) or using a two- or three-column design to separate the details from the descriptive text (as shown in Figure 1.5). The goal is to present as much information as necessary, but in a way that's easy for the potential buyer to grasp. Don't make the buyer work for it; use good page design to make your listing as easy to read as possible.

Large Green Widget

This widget was manufactured in 2003 by World Wide Widgets. It is model #572, part of the Incidental product line. The official color is Forrest Green, and the actual paint job is a dark green metal flake. The size of this widget is approximately 3" x 5" x 2.5".

Feature	Benefit
Scaled gearing	Quick shifting with no missed shifts
Synchromesh transmission	Automatic shifts with no manual interaction
Lubricoat coating	Smooth operation with no maintenance required

FIGURE 1.4

Item details presented in a table.

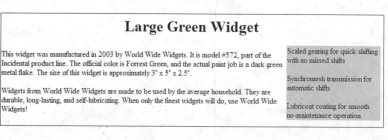

Large Green Widget

This widget was manufactured in 2003 by World Wide Widgets. It is model #572, part of the Incidental product line. The official color is Forrest Green, and the actual paint job is a dark green metal flake. The size of this widget is approximately 3" x 5" x 2.5".

Widgets from World Wide Widgets are made to be used by the average household. They are durable, long-lasting, and self-lubricating. When only the finest widgets will do, use World Wide Widgets!

Scaled gearing for quick shifting with no missed shifts

Synchromesh transmission for automatic shifts

Lubricoat coating for smooth no-maintenance operation

FIGURE 1.5

Item details presented in a separate column.

Photos

A text description is important, but a photograph is, in almost all cases, mandatory. Potential buyers need to know what an item looks like before they make a bid, and the only way to do that is to show them a picture. Or two. Or three. Or as many as it takes to accurately present the item.

The pictures you include should be large enough to show off the appropriate level of detail, but not so large that they're slow to download. (Something in the 400 x 400 pixel range is good, give or take a hundred pixels either direction.) The pictures should be well-lit, well-focused, and well-framed. You should include at least one large photo of the entire item, plus additional photos of important details or alternate sides or angles. And it's okay to make a scan instead of take a photo, if you're dealing with a flat item (like a book or CD).

Where should you place the photos(s) in your listings? That's a matter of taste and some debate. Some sellers like the pictures on top, either before or just after the title, as shown in Figure 1.6. Other sellers like the pictures after the description, as shown in Figure 1.7. Still other sellers are savvy enough to create a multiple-column layout that places the photos on either the left or right side of the description, as shown in Figure 1.8. There's no absolute right or wrong when it comes to picture placement.

Large Green Widget

This auction is for one large green widget, perfect for any household. The widget is slightly used, and will ship in its original factory box. This widget was manufactured in 2003 by World Wide Widgets. It is model #572, part of the Incidental product line. The size of this widget is approximately 3" x 5" x 2.5".

FIGURE 1.6

A photo placed at the very top of a listing.

FIGURE 1.7

The same photo, placed at the bottom of the listing.

FIGURE 1.8

An alternate approach, with the photo to the left of the item description.

Terms of Service

Now we come to the end of your item description, after which it's appropriate to talk a little bit about how you conduct your business. What I'm talking about here is your *terms of service* (sometimes called the *terms of sale*, or just *TOS*), or what some folks refer to as the "fine print." It's important to include your TOS in your item listing, but not so important that it draws attention to itself. Hence the position at the bottom of the listing instead of the top; it's there for potential buyers to read, but not positioned as a key selling point for your auction.

Your TOS can also be formatted in a way that separates it from the item description (which is a good thing), without making it appear too important. Different tricks including using a smaller or different-colored type face, as shown in Figure 1.9; placing a different-colored background behind the TOS, as shown in Figure 1.10; or putting the TOS in a text box or surrounding it with a border, as shown in Figure 1.11. Either of these approaches has the desired effect.

Large Green Widget

This auction is for one large green widget, perfect for any household. The widget is slightly used, and will ship in its original factory box. This widget was manufactured in 2003 by World Wide Widgets. It is model #572, part of the Incidental product line.

Terms of Service
I accept payment via PayPal, money order, cashier's check, or personal check. (Personal checks may delay shipment for up to 10 business days.) I ship via USPS Priority Mail. Shipping/handling fee is $5.00 anywhere in the continental United States. Email me for shipping charges outside the U.S.

FIGURE 1.9

A TOS with smaller type than the preceding description.

Large Green Widget

This auction is for one large green widget, perfect for any household. The widget is slightly used, and will ship in its original factory box. This widget was manufactured in 2003 by World Wide Widgets. It is model #572, part of the Incidental product line.

Terms of Service
I accept payment via PayPal, money order, cashier's check, or personal check. (Personal checks may delay shipment for up to 10 business days.) I ship via USPS Priority Mail. Shipping/handling fee is $5.00 anywhere in the continental United States. Email me for shipping charges outside the U.S.

FIGURE 1.10

The same TOS, separated out with a different colored background.

Large Green Widget

This auction is for one large green widget, perfect for any household. The widget is slightly used, and will ship in its original factory box. This widget was manufactured in 2003 by World Wide Widgets. It is model #572, part of the Incidental product line.

Terms of Service
I accept payment via PayPal, money order, cashier's check, or personal check. (Personal checks may delay shipment for up to 10 business days.) I ship via USPS Priority Mail. Shipping/handling fee is $5.00 anywhere in the continental United States. Email me for shipping charges outside the U.S.

FIGURE 1.11

Another way to segregate the TOS, using a border.

And just what should you include in your terms of service? Here's a short list:

- What payment methods you accept, and which you prefer
- Any restrictions for different payment methods (such as waiting 10 days for personal checks to clear)
- Which shipping services you use
- Your shipping/handling charge

- Whether or not you offer insurance or delivery confirmation, and if so, how much you charge
- Your returns policy, if any
- Which countries you do or don't ship to
- Any other bidder restrictions
- After-the-auction checkout instructions

In short, any details that potential buyers need to know before they place a bid should be spelled out in your TOS.

Cross-Promotions

If you're a heavy seller, you want to use any particular auction listing to cross-promote other items you have for sale, either in other auctions or in an eBay Store. This can be accomplished with simple text links, or with pictures of some of the other items, as shown in Figure 1.12. This type of cross-promotion section is typically placed at the very bottom of your listing, after your TOS.

FIGURE 1.12

Cross-promoting other items you have for sale.

Employing Good Listing Design

Now that we've covered what elements you need to include in your auction listings, let's take a quick look at the best ways to present those elements. It all boils down to effective and tasteful web page design—and employing that design to your eBay auction listings.

- **Subtle design**—First, know that an effective web page (or auction listing) uses subtle design elements. The design itself shouldn't knock you over the head; it should be noticeable without calling attention to itself. That means not using design elements for design's sake. The layout should be practical without being showy, and the font and color choices should be understated.

- **Logical page structure**—The structure of the page should work to draw the reader's eyes to the most important elements on the page. That might be the item's title or photo, or (ultimately) to the "Bid Now" button. There shouldn't be any speed bumps in the way from top to bottom. Subsidiary elements should be sectioned off, accessible but not mandatory in the reading scheme.

- **Columns and tables**—Multiple columns and tables should be used when necessary, but not overused. It's okay to place bulleted lists or photos in a separate column, but don't put the main description in a two- or three-column layout.

- **Flush left or justified text**—Text reads best when it's flush left or justified. Right-justified text is darned-near unreadable, and you don't want to center large blocks of text. (Centering is okay for titles and subtitles, however.)

- **High contrast color scheme**—The whole design should work toward readability. That typically means dark text on a light background, like the black text against white pages of this book. Some reverse text can be used, for effect, but know that it's difficult to read large blocks of light text against a dark background.

- **Understatement**—Nothing in the listing should scream at the potential bidder. That means no over-large fonts, no overly-bright colors, no flashing graphics or animations. Pictures should be large enough without dominating the page. Fonts should be large enough to be readable, but not so large that body text looks like a headline.

In short, use design to help sell your item, not to draw attention to itself. As you'll learn throughout this book, there is a lot of neat stuff you can do with HTML—but that doesn't mean you should do all of it in a single auction listing. Use discretion and subtlety to work toward readability and emphasis on the key features of what you're selling.

Ten Ways to Create a More Effective Auction Listing

With the principles of good web page design now lodged in your head, let's get down to brass tacks—and go through a short list of ways to improve your auction listings.

1. **Prioritize your information.** It's always good to assume that potential bidders are in a hurry. Make it easy for people to graze your listing without having to read every single word. Put the most important information at the beginning, and the least important at the end. Don't make the bidder read through to the end of the listing before placing a bid. Grab their attention and convince them to *bid now!*

2. **Organize your content on the page—break it into sections.** Organization is different from prioritization, although it has the same goal—to make your listing easy to read. Not only should the most important information be the first thing on the page, it should also be the most dominant thing. Use various page design

techniques to separate out different types of information and put them in different sections on the page. Make it easy for potential bidders to find the item overview, detailed description, and your terms of service.

3. **Present complete information, in a logical order.** Your item description should say more than "Here's a green widget." It should fully describe what you're selling—which means including manufacturer information, model number, production year, size or dimensions, and a full list of features and benefits. Include all relevant information, and organize that information logically. When you're presenting a lot of details, consider using a bulleted list instead of long text paragraphs. Make the description flow, from start to finish.

4. **Use text formatting to emphasize important words or phrases.** Not every part of your item listing is of equal importance. Don't hide the most important stuff; put key words and phrases in boldface or in a different color. Force the reader's eyes to focus on what's important.

5. **Identify important keywords and use them in your title and item description.** Remember, most eBay users search for what they want to buy. Make sure you include the most likely search keywords in the formal listing title, as well as the title in your item description—and in the description itself. And don't forget alternate phrasing and spelling; not every buyer will search in the "correct" way.

6. **Include at least one product photo—and put the most informative photo first.** Item listings with photos sell much better than those without. Potential buyers need visual reinforcement in order to bid with confidence; since they can't see the item in person, your photos have to substitute for the "in-person" experience. Make sure your photos are well-focused, properly framed and cropped, and present the subject in appropriate detail. If the buyer needs to see more than the front of the item, use multiple photos—but always lead with the most informative photo.

7. **Include a detailed terms of service—*after* your product description.** It's important to include the fine print of how you conduct business—what methods of payment you accept, which shipping services you use, your shipping/handling charges, whether you offer a returns policy, and so on. But don't place undue emphasis on this section; place it at the bottom of your listing, after the main description. Remember, your TOS doesn't entice people to buy; it's necessary, but not the most important part of your listing.

8. **Use proper page design to enhance the eye-appeal of your listing.** There's nothing wrong with a plain-text listing—assuming you include photos, of course. But there's also nothing wrong with including a little eye candy, in the form of background color or graphics, a variety of fonts, and an attractive page organization. This is where it pays to know a little HTML—or to use an attractive listing template.

9. **Cross-promote other items you have for sale.** If you're an active seller, there's not reason not to promote your other auctions (or eBay Store) in all your auction listings. Yeah, eBay includes that little "View my other auctions" link, but some pretty pictures of your other auction items will do a much better job of cross-selling.

10. **Spell check your listings.** Successful online selling is all about establishing buyer confidence. When your auction listing includes gross misspellings, that confidence is eroded. Do yourself a favor; use a spell checker before you list!

Ten Things *Not* to Do in Your Auction Listings

Okay, it's only fair. We just discussed ten things you *should* do in your auction listings. Now let's look at ten things you *shouldn't* do—at the risk of decreasing your sales!

1. **Don't make your listing too long.** Yeah, I know I said that you need to include all the necessary details in your item description. But the important word is "necessary," not "all." Don't force potential buyers to scroll through multiple screens of unnecessary information. Put the important stuff up-front and get to the end as quickly as you can. Two screens worth of info is more than enough for most listings. Anything longer will cause potential buyers to click away to another auction.

2. **Don't use large, slow-loading graphics.** Not every buyer is on an ultra-fast broadband Internet connection. A good 40% of your potential customers still use old-fashioned dial-up connections—and these connections, in case you forgot, are *slow*. If you pack your pages with a half-dozen extra-large photos, it might take a minute or more for your entire page to load on a dial-up connection. Many potential buyers simply won't wait that long, which means they click away before the page is done loading. Make sure you resize your graphics to minimize download times, and use just enough photos to enhance the sale.

3. **Don't make your listing too wide.** Web users hate to scroll sideways. While some users with older PCs are still running at 480 x 640 resolution (that's just 640 pixels wide), most users today have at least a 600 x 800 display. So figure that you have a maximum of 800 pixels to work with, in the width direction, and format your text and graphics to be no wider than this.

4. **Don't use too many different font, type size, and color combinations.** I remember back in the early 1990s when desktop publishing programs first hit the mainstream. All of a sudden everyone thought they were expert page designers—but they weren't. The upshot of PageMaker and similar programs was a profusion of poorly designed newsletters and reports, most of which used too many different fonts. Unfortunately, this same type of poor design is all too common in eBay auction listings, and too many fonts and type sizes make your listings hard to read. You should limit yourself to no more than two type faces, one for the title and one

for the descriptive text—although it's more than okay to use the same font for both. You should also limit yourself to no more than five type sizes—for the title (largest), subtitle (next-largest), first paragraph (next-largest), main description (regular), and terms of sale (smallest). And limit yourself to no more than two or three different type colors throughout the entire listing—one for your title/subtitle, another for your body text, and a third for emphasized text within the listing body.

5. **Don't use color combinations that are hard to read.** Along the same lines, keep the color combinations down to a reasonable number, and make sure the colors are easy for anyone to read. That probably means dark type on a light background; reverse type (light text on a dark background) is much, much harder to read. You should also avoid garish color combinations, like orange and green, or purple and red. And remember that your eye automatically goes to the brightest color—so don't use the brightest color for the least important information!

6. **Don't confuse the buyer with an overly-busy layout.** Back to the PageMaker example, it's way too easy to create a page layout that is overly busy and often-times confusing. Try to lead the user's eye down the page in a natural manner, don't force the eyes to jump all over the page. That means going light on the random text boxes, graphics, and tables, all of which can serve as speed bumps for anyone trying to read from top to bottom.

7. **Don't overuse animations and other flashy special effects.** Most users hate, hate, *hate* flashy graphics and animations on a web page. Yeah, they attract attention—but not in a good way. Unless you have a really good reason for including these types of special effects, avoid animations and flashing graphics like the plague. Just because you *can* do something (using HTML), doesn't mean you *should* do it.

8. **Don't subject the buyer to automatically playing background music.** Equally annoying is background music that plays as soon as the listing page is loaded. Not only is background music normally unwanted, it'll drive some potential customers away—particularly those who are browsing on their work computers. If you must include sound in your auctions, make the sound play only after the customer clicks a button. Optional sound is okay; forcing users to listen isn't.

9. **Don't overwhelm the buyer with too many details and restrictions.** Some sellers focus too much on the negative. There is nothing that turns off potential buyers faster than reading line after line of what the seller *won't* do. No personal checks; no foreign bidders; no bidders with negative feedback; no returns allowed; no this and no that. All that negativity drives customers away. It's okay to have a reason-able terms of sale (more than okay, actually; it's a good idea), but don't let the details get in the way of selling your item. Along the same lines, don't put your TOS at the top of your listing; keep it at the bottom, in the fine print, where it belongs.

10. **Don't lie**. This should go without saying. You should never misrepresent the items you sell on eBay. That means telling the truth, the whole truth, and nothing but the truth about the item being listed. And part of the truth is being honest about any defects or damage. Along the same lines, don't use keywords in your title that don't apply to your item; you won't win over any buyers by describing your item as "NOT a green widget."

Different Ways to Create Better-Looking eBay Listings

The essentials of good design and effective listings apply no matter what tools you use to create your eBay auction listings. Throughout this book we'll discuss several different ways to create your eBay listings; each approach has its own pros and cons, which often revolve around ease-of-use and desired effect. Here's what we'll discuss:

- For the ultimate in ease of use, you can create simple text listings (with basic formatting) by using eBay's standard text editor. We'll discuss this approach in Chapter 2, "Using Standard Text Formatting and eBay's Listing Designer."

- Also high on the ease-of-use scale is eBay's Listing Designer, which offers some very basic auction templates (which eBay calls "themes") for 10 cents a pop. We'll discuss this approach in Chapter 2, as well.

- Many third-party sites offer listing services and standalone software that let you create your own fancy-looking eBay listings, no HTML coding required. We'll discuss this approach in Chapter 3, "Using Auction Listing Services and Software."

- Still more sites offer pre-designed auction templates into which you can insert your own auction information and photos. I've included dozens of these templates on this book's CD, and discuss this approach in Chapter 4, "Using Third-Party Auction Templates."

- Then there's HTML. When you create your own HTML code, you can manipulate the look and feel of your eBay listings to an astonishing degree. To that end, the rest of the book—from Chapter 5 on—is all about using HTML to create your own auction templates. It's a little work, but for many sellers, it's worth the effort.

This should set the stage for what comes next. So turn the page and let's get started with creating fancy eBay listings the easy way—on eBay's standard sell your item form.

Using Predesigned Auction Templates

Using Standard Text Formatting and eBay's Listing Designer

When it comes to creating great-looking eBay auction listings, you can do it the hard way or you can do it the easy way. My motto is to try the easy way first; you never know, it might just be good enough. So that's what this chapter is about—the easy way to create formatted auction listings.

And the easy way, in this case, means sticking to the standard auction listing process on eBay's website. Believe it or not, there's a lot you can do to make your auctions stand out from the crowd, using the simple tools provided in eBay's standard sell your item process.

Formatting a Normal Auction Listing with the Text Editor

If you don't care about fancy background colors and graphics, you can perform a fair amount of text formatting for your item description using nothing more than eBay's standard text editor. As you can see in Figure 2.1, when you click the Sell link to enter the sell your item process, the Describe Your Item page contains the familiar Description section. As you no doubt know (or have quickly figured out), this is a text box where you enter your item description. What's neat about the Description box is that it functions as a WYSIWYG (what you see is what you get) text editor, thanks to the formatting commands available just above the text box. All you have to do is enter your description, highlight the text you want to format, and then click the appropriate formatting command.

The result can be as visually interesting as you like, as you can see from the example in Figure 2.2. You can format the text's font, size, color, justification, and other attributes. Read on to learn more.

> **NOTE** eBay is constantly updating its forms and tools to improve the user experience. With that in mind, it's possible that the text editor and other tools discussed in this chapter might look different from what is presented here.

FIGURE 2.1

eBay's standard text editor in the Description section of the Describe Your Item page.

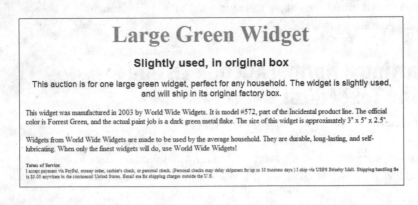

FIGURE 2.2

An item description formatted with the commands available in the standard text editor.

Available Formatting Commands

Just what formatting commands are available in the standard text editor? Table 2.1 provides a complete list.

Table 2.1   Text Editor Formatting Commands

Formatting Command	Description
Font	Selects from four type families: Arial, Courier, Times, and Verdana
Size	Selects from seven type sizes, from 8 pt. to 36 pt.
Color	Changes the color of the selected text; available colors include Black, Blue, Red, Green, Brown, Gold, Purple, Pink, and Orange
Bold	Displays the selected text in bold
Italic	Displays the selected text in italics
Underline	Underlines the selected text
Flush left	Aligns the current paragraph to the left border
Center	Centers the current paragraph on the page
Flush right	Aligns the current paragraph to the right border
Bulleted list	Displays the current paragraph as a bulleted list item
Numbered list	Displays the current paragraph as a numbered list item
Decrease indent	Moves the selected paragraph further to the left
Increase indent	Moves the selected paragraph further to the right

You can use the various text formatting commands to create different formatting for different parts of your item description. For example, you can use a larger type face in bold to create a separate title, then a smaller type face (non-bold) for the main description. You can also highlight important words and phrases in bold or with a different color, or break out long lists of features into a bulleted list.

> **TIP**
> The text editor also includes its own built-in spell checker. Just click the Check Spelling button to ensure that no embarrassing spelling mistakes creep into your item listing.

Adding Inserts

eBay's text editor also includes some predesigned HTML code, in the form of *inserts*, for some of the most popular additional functions. To insert an insert, all you have to do is position your cursor within the text where you want the item to appear, and then select the insert from the pull-down menu.

Table 2.2 details the available inserts.

Table 2.2   Text Editor Inserts

Insert	Example
Sellers Other Items	Check out my <u>other items</u>!
Add to favorites list	Be sure to add me to your <u>favorites list</u>!
My Stores Logo	stores
eBay stores logo	eb Y stores
My Store newsletter	<u>Sign up for my email newsletters</u> by adding my eBay Store to your Favorites

Creating Your Own Inserts

The use of inserts presents a great way to include repeating text or graphics in all your eBay listings. To that end, eBay lets you create your own inserts, which you can then insert from the Inserts list in the text editor.

To create a new insert, follow these steps:

1. From the Description section of the Describe Your Item page, pull down the Inserts list and select Create an Insert.

2. When the Create an Insert window opens, as shown in Figure 2.3, enter a name for your insert.

3. Enter the text or HTML for your insert into the appropriate text box.

4. Click the Save button.

> **TIP**
>
> To create an insert for a graphic, use the HTML <img> code, as explained in Chapter 5, "Learning How to Code with HTML."

Your newly created insert should now appear in the Inserts list, along with eBay's default inserts.

Previewing Your Listing

When you're done formatting the text of your item description (and adding any desired inserts), you can preview how it will look on screen. Just click the Preview Description button, and a new window will open on your desktop, with the description section of your listing displayed, as shown in Figure 2.4.

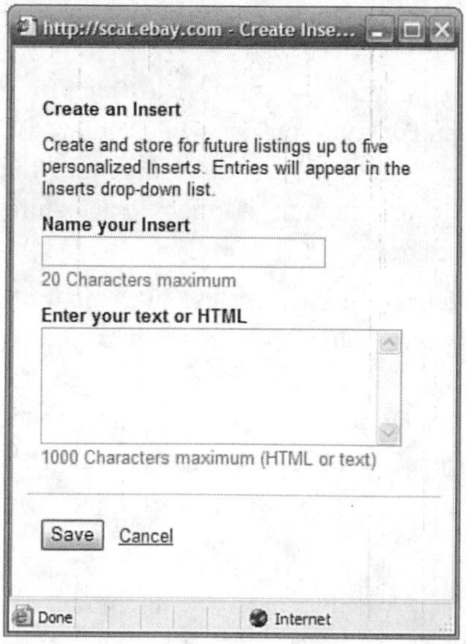

FIGURE 2.3

Creating a new insert for the text editor.

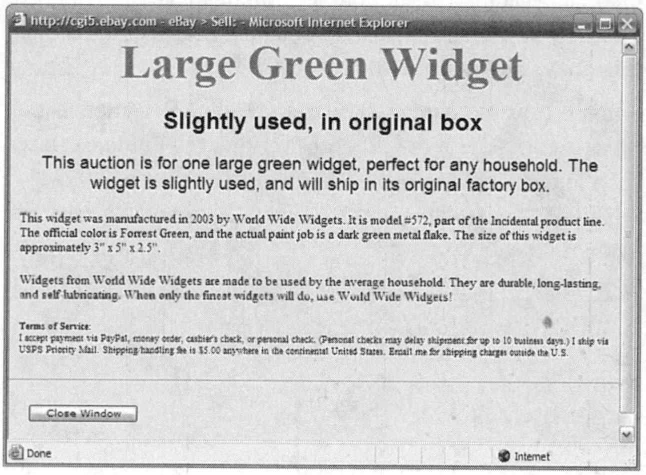

FIGURE 2.4

Previewing your item description in a separate window.

Enhancing Your Listing with Listing Designer

$ Pay

eBay's text editor lets you format your listing text, but doesn't let you add anything in the way of graphic interest. For that you need to use eBay's Listing Designer, also accessible from the Describe Your Item page. Listing Design lets you apply predesigned templates, which it calls *themes*, to your item description. This feature isn't free; you pay 10 cents per listing to use Listing Designer.

Listing Designer also lets you customize the placement of the photos in your item listing. Normally, eBay sticks your photos below the listing; you don't have a choice in the matter. But when you use Listing Designer, you now can choose to put your photos at the top, bottom, left, or right of your item description. For many sellers, the customized photo placement alone is worth the 10-cent price of using Listing Designer.

Choosing a Theme

As just discussed, Listing Designer lets you apply one of more than 200 different visual themes to your listing. While these themes aren't near as sophisticated or versatile as a full-featured listing template, they do add a little visual spice to your listings.

A theme typically consists of some sort of background color or graphic, typically surrounded by a graphic border of some sort. The theme does *not* include any text formatting; you'll still need to format your item description text in the text editor. But by combining some simple text formatting with a colorful Listing Designer theme and custom photo layout, you can create listings that stand out from the standard eBay text-only listings.

Selecting a theme is as easy as scrolling to the Listing Designer section (under the Description section, as shown in Figure 2.5) and checking the Enhance Description with a Theme and Layout option, pulling down the Theme list to select a category, and then selecting a specific theme within that category. A thumbnail of the selected theme is displayed next to the pull-down list.

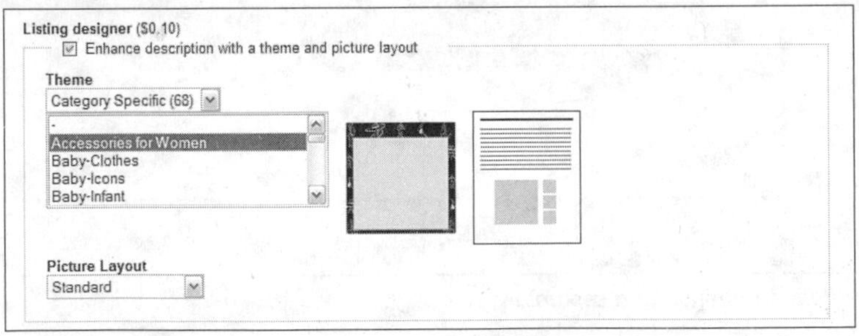

FIGURE 2.5

Selecting a Listing Designer theme.

eBay organizes its Listing Designer themes into seven major categories:

- **New**, which features the latest themes—such as the Night Driving theme, shown in Figure 2.6.
- **Special Events**, which features themes for anniversaries and other celebrations—such as the Celebration - Glasses theme, shown in Figure 2.7.
- **Category Specific**, which features themes designed for specific product categories—such as the Coins - Red theme, shown in Figure 2.8.
- **Patterns/Textiles**, which features themes with patterned borders or backgrounds—such as the Elegant Floral theme, shown in Figure 2.9.
- **Holiday/Seasonal**, which features a variety of holiday-based themes—such as the Christmas Tree theme, shown in Figure 2.10.
- **eBay Stores,** which features themes of interest to eBay Stores sellers—such as the Stores Awning theme, shown in Figure 2.11.
- **Miscellaneous**, which features themes that don't fit in any of the other categories—such as the Flags theme, shown in Figure 2.12.

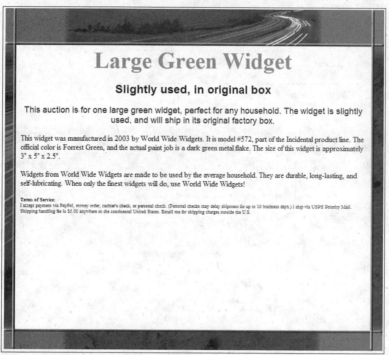

FIGURE 2.6

eBay's Night Driving theme.

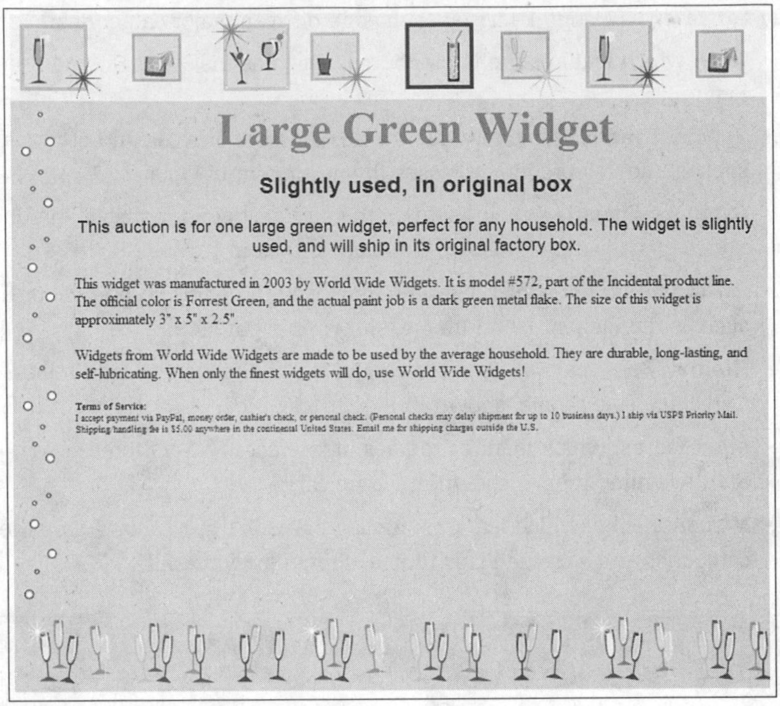

FIGURE 2.7

eBay's Celebration - Glasses theme.

FIGURE 2.8

eBay's Coin - Red theme.

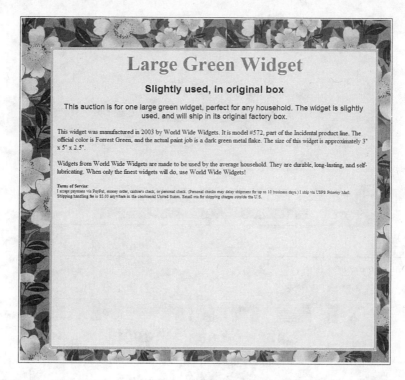

FIGURE 2.9

eBay's Elegant Floral theme.

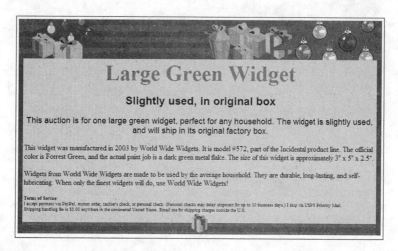

FIGURE 2.10

eBay's Christmas Tree theme.

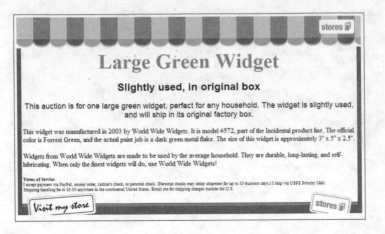

FIGURE 2.11

eBay's Stores Awning theme.

FIGURE 2.12

eBay's Flags theme.

Selecting a Picture Layout

Once you've selected a Listing Designer theme, you can select how you want your photo(s) to appear in your listing. All you have to do is pull down the Picture Layout list and select one of the following options:

- **Standard**, which displays your photos in the default position underneath the item description, as shown in Figure 2.13. With this option, multiple photos appear as one big photo and a series of smaller thumbnails; visitors have to click a thumbnail to view the full-size picture.

- **Photo on the left**, which displays your photos on the left side of your listing, with the item description text to the right, as shown in Figure 2.14.

- **Photo on the right**, which displays your photos on the right side of your listing, with the item description text to the left, as shown in Figure 2.15.

- **Photo on the bottom**, which displays your photos below the item description text, as shown in Figure 2.16. This option differs from the Standard layout in that all photos are displayed full size, stacked one on top of another.

- **Photo on the top**, which displays your first photo at the very top of the listing and the others below the description text, as shown in Figure 2.17.

FIGURE 2.13

eBay's Standard photo layout.

FIGURE 2.14

Photos displayed on the left of the item description.

FIGURE 2.15

Photos displayed on the right of the item description.

Large Green Widget

Slightly used, in original box

This auction is for one large green widget, perfect for any household. The widget is slightly used, and will ship in its original factory box.

This widget was manufactured in 2003 by World Wide Widgets. It is model #572, part of the Incidental product line. The official color is Forrest Green, and the actual paint job is a dark green metal flake. The size of this widget is approximately 3" x 5" x 2.5".

Widgets from World Wide Widgets are made to be used by the average household. They are durable, long-lasting, and self-lubricating. When only the finest widgets will do, use World Wide Widgets!

Terms of Service:
I accept payment via PayPal, money order, cashier's check, or personal check. (Personal checks may delay shipment for up to 10 business days.) I ship via USPS Priority Mail. Shipping/handling fee is $5.00 anywhere in the continental United States. Email me for shipping charges outside the U.S.

FIGURE 2.16

Photos displayed below the item description.

FIGURE 2.17

Multiple photos displayed above and below the item description.

Previewing Your Listing

Unfortunately, you can't preview how your listing will look with the Listing Designer theme directly from the Describe Your Item page. You have to click the Continue button at the bottom of the page to advance to the Review and Enhance Your Listing page. Scroll down to the Review Your Listing section, and you'll see your listing displayed within the short scroll box, as shown in Figure 2.18. This probably won't give you a good idea of how the listing will really look in a web browser, so click Preview in a Window to open a full-size preview of your listing in a new browser window, as shown in Figure 2.19.

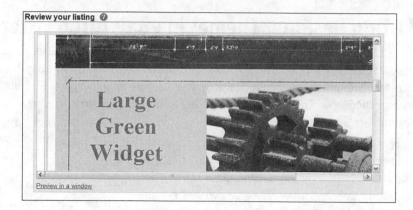

FIGURE 2.18

Your themed listing displayed in the middle of the Review and Enhance Your Listing page.

FIGURE 2.19

The same listing, previewed full-size in a separate window.

Using Listing Designer Themes in eBay Turbo Lister

eBay's Listing Designer themes are also available in eBay's Turbo Lister program. Turbo Lister, if you're not aware, is a free bulk listing creation tool offered by eBay. It's a nice program that integrates well with the eBay site, as you might expect. And all the Listing Designer themes and picture layouts available on the eBay site are also present in Turbo Lister

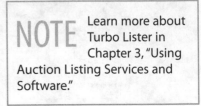

> **NOTE** Learn more about Turbo Lister in Chapter 3, "Using Auction Listing Services and Software."

To apply a theme within Turbo Lister, you have go to the listing you want to format and click the Change button in the Description section. This opens the Enter Your Description window, shown in Figure 2.20. Click the Use Designer option on the left side of the page, and then select a theme from the Themes list and a photo layout from the Layout list. You can preview how the listing will look with the theme applied by selecting the Preview tab.

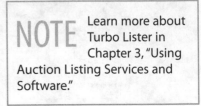

FIGURE 2.20

Applying a Listing Designer theme from within eBay's Turbo Lister program.

Use Other Programs to Create Fancy eBay Listings

Like I noted at the start of this chapter, using standard text formatting and Listing Designer themes is the easy way to enhance the look of your auction listings. This approach is limited, however, not only to a set number of themes but also in the sophistication of the designs.

That said, there are lots of other websites and software programs you can use to create eBay auction listings, and some of these offer some pretty cool-looking listing designs. That's what we'll discuss in the next chapter—so turn the page to learn more about these third-party listing creation services and programs.

Using Auction Listing Services and Software

Practically every eBay seller starts out by using eBay's default sell your item form. As we discussed in the previous chapter, that form allows a good bit of listing customization, thanks to the Listing Designer feature, but it's certainly not the most robust way to create fancy-looking auction listings.

That's probably why so many third parties have entered the market for creating eBay auction listings, with a variety of listing creation services and software. Some of these services/software are freestanding, dedicated only to the creation of auction listings; some are part of a more comprehensive auction management package that also offers end-of-auction emails, checkout services, bulk feedback listing, and so on. Most of these sites and programs come with a fee, although a few are free to use. Almost all let you create listings that are somewhat more sophisticated than those you can create with eBay's Listing Designer.

Should you avail yourself of one of these third-party listing services or programs—and if so, which one? That's what this chapter is all about, so read on to become more informed.

Using Auction Listing Services

An auction listing service is, quite simply, a website that lets you create eBay auction listings from within your web browser. You create the listings, apply some sort of predesigned template (or perform your own custom formatting), and then have the service upload the listing to the eBay auction site. Depending on the service, your listings may be free; you may be charged a per-listing fee; or you may pay a

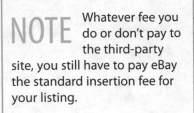

NOTE Whatever fee you do or don't pay to the third-party site, you still have to pay eBay the standard insertion fee for your listing.

flat monthly subscription charge. And, as part of the package offered by the site, you may have other auction management services available to you.

That's it in a nutshell—although the specific features offered will differ from site to site.

Why Pay for an Auction Listing Service?

If eBay lets you create basic auction listings for free (aside from the normal insertion fee, of course), why would you pay money to do the same thing at a different site?

That's a good question, with a few good answers.

First, remember that eBay listing creation is free only if you want a standard text-based listing. If you include more than one photo, you have to pay extra. And if you want to use the fancy Listing Designer background themes, you pay an extra dime for that service. So listing creation on eBay isn't always free.

Second, there's the matter of variety and flexibility. As you learned in Chapter 2, "Using Standard Text Formatting and eBay's Listing Designer," the themes that eBay offers aren't that spectacular, really. And there's only so much customization you can do; eBay's themes don't automatically create separate sections or formatting for different parts of your listing. So if you want a wider variety of better-looking predesigned templates, you have to look outside of eBay.

Which is why all these listing-creation services exist.

Popular Auction Listing Services

There are a number of sites that offer auction management services, and almost all of them include fancy listing creation as part of those services. In addition, there are a handful of sites that offers standalone listing-creation services, without all the other auction management stuff. We'll look at the major ones next.

TIP You have lots of choices when it comes to choosing a third-party listing-creation tool. Don't assume that the most expensive tools are the best—or that the most affordable ones lack features. Most of these tools are offered with some sort of preview plan, so take advantage of the offer and give 'em a trial run!

Ándale

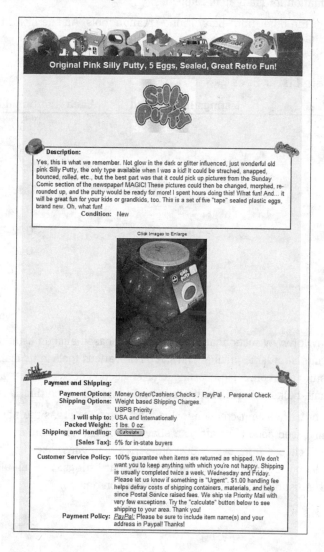

Ándale (www.andale.com) is a site that offers various services for eBay sellers. Chief among these tools is the Ándale Lister bulk listing creation tool.

Ándale Lister lets you create good-looking listings, working from a catalog of more than 100 professionally created listing templates. (Figure 3.1 shows a typical Ándale listing template.) You also get a built-in HTML editor, so you can customize the existing templates or create your own custom listings.

FIGURE 3.1

A listing created with Ándale Lister.

You can create your listings in bulk and then upload them according to your designated timetable. You can even program a series of listings to launch on a regularly occurring schedule—or until your inventory runs out. Other listing features include a built-in spell checker, delayed launch scheduling, inline images (and an image hosting service), and pre-filled information for many item categories.

> **NOTE** Ándale also offers the Ándale Lister Pro software-based listing tool, discussed later in this chapter.

Like most of the other third-party listing creation tools, Ándale Lister isn't free; Table 3.1 details the tiered pricing schedule.

Table 3.1   Ándale Lister Fees

Monthly Fee	Listings Included	Each Additional Listing
$2.00	10	$0.50
$7.50	40	$0.30
$16.95	110	$0.20
$33.95	275	$0.18
$56.95	550	$0.15
$89.95	1,100	$0.12
$149.95	2,750	$0.10
$224.95	5,600	$0.08

Auction Hawk

($) **Pay**

Auction Hawk (www.auctionhawk.com) is a web-based auction listing/management service with quite affordable pricing. The site offers various tools in its main service, including built-in listing creation, image hosting, end-of-auction checkout with automated winning-bidder email, bulk feedback posting, and profit-and-loss reporting.

The site's primary listing-creation tool is the 1-Page Lister. As the name implies, it uses a single form-based page to create your eBay auction listings. More important, 1-Page Lister lets you use choose from over 2,000 pro-series templates (like the one shown in Figure 3.2), or use your own image backgrounds for your listings. You can also include up to 50 of your other listings in a scrolling cross-promotion gallery.

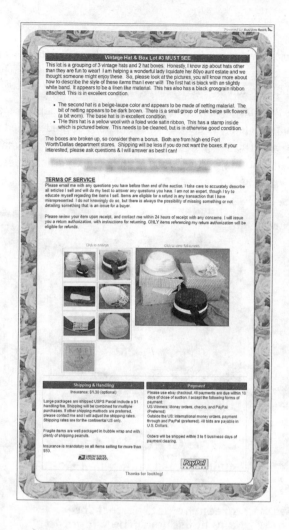

FIGURE 3.2

A listing template created with Auction Hawk's 1-Page Lister.

Auction Hawk offers a five-level flat pricing scheme, as detailed in Table 3.2.

Table 3.2   Auction Hawk Fees

Level	Monthly Fee	Number of Listings Included
Basic	$12.99	110
Power	$21.99	250
Preferred	$29.99	550
Professional	$44.99	1,100
Unlimited	$89.99	Unlimited

Auctiva

Free

Auctiva (www.auctiva.com) offers a variety of different auction listing/management services, all of which are completely free of charge. Free is good, which explains Auctiva's newfound popularity among eBay sellers.

Auctiva's One-Page Listing Tool (this one-page thing is a popular marketing angle, in case you haven't noticed) lets you choose from hundreds of predesigned templates, such as the one in Figure 3.3. The templates are pretty basic, similar to what you get with eBay's Listing Designer, but they cost 10 cents less than eBay's templates. (They're free, in case you forgot.)

FIGURE 3.3

One of Auctiva's free predesigned auction templates.

ChannelAdvisor

ChannelAdvisor (www.channeladvisor.com) offers a variety of auction and retail management tools—most of which are targeted at larger online merchants. The service you want to look at is ChannelAdvisor Pro, which is actually HammerTap Manager in disguise. (We'll get to HammerTap next.) This service is a surprisingly easy-to-use collection of auction management tools, quite reasonably priced at a flat fee of just $29.95 per month.

With ChannelAdvisor Pro you can choose from a variety of predesigned templates or write your own HTML. You also get delayed scheduling, image hosting, and the other expected listing-creation features.

HammerTap

Next, we come to HammerTap (www.hammertap.com). HammerTap sells various auction management software and services, all offered with a la carte pricing. The tool you're interested in is HammerTap Manager, the kissing cousin of ChannelAdvisor Pro, which offers web-based listing creation. As noted in the ChannelAdvisor Pro discussion, HammerTap Manager offers both predesigned templates and do-it-yourself HTML listing creation. Pricing is on a tiered schedule, as shown in Table 3.3.

Table 3.3   HammerTap Manager Fees

Level	Monthly Fee	Number of Listings Included
Standard	$29.95	500
Gold	$54.95	1,000
Platinum	$99.95	2,000

inkFrog

inkFrog (www.inkfrog.com) is a cute name for some heavy-duty web-based auction management services. The one we're interested in is the i-Lister, which lets you create your own custom-built auction listings, based on a variety of predesigned templates. (Figure 3.4 shows a typical inkFrog auction template.) You also get bulk listing, delayed auction launching, free image hosting, and the i-Showcase cross-promotion tool. Various pricing plans are offered, starting at $7.95 per month.

SpareDollar

SpareDollar (www.sparedollar.com) is a top choice of frugal eBay sellers. This popular site offers a complete package of auction management services—including the sdLister bulk upload tool—for just $8.95 per month. No extra charges, just a flat $8.95, no matter how many listings you create. Not a bad deal!

Description

This auction is for one large green widget, perfect for any household. The widget is slightly used, and will ship in its original factory box.

This widget was manufactured in 2003 by World Wide Widgets. It is model #572, part of the Incidental product line. The official color is Forest Green, and the actual paint job is a dark green metal flake. The size of this widget is approximately 3" x 5" x 2.5". Widgets from World Wide Widgets are made to be used by the average household. They are durable, long-lasting, and self-lubricating. When only the finest widgets will do, use World Wide Widgets!

Click to Enlarge

Payment Terms

I accept payment via PayPal, money order, cashier's check, or personal check. (Personal checks may delay shipment for up to 10 business days.)

Shipping Terms

I ship via USPS Priority Mail. Shipping/handling fee is $5.00 anywhere in the continental United States. Email me for shipping charges outside the U.S.

FIGURE 3.4

A listing template created with inkFrog's i-Lister.

The sdLister tool is a web-based editor complete with a variety of predesigned listing templates, like the one shown in Figure 3.5. You can schedule your listings to start hours, days, or even weeks in advance, and you even get the ability to relist unsold items in bulk. It's a pretty good deal—especially when you consider the other tools (auction tracking, image management, and so on) you get as part of the package.

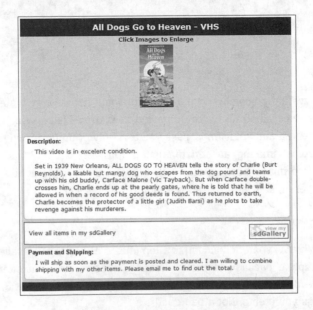

FIGURE 3.5

A listing template created with SpareDollar's sdLister.

Vendio

Vendio (www.vendio.com) claims to be the largest third-party supplier of services to eBay sellers, used by tens of thousands of sellers each month. The company offers the Sales Manager service, which is a powerful set of listing creation and auction management tools. You can use Sales Manager not only to create new item listings, but also to manage all of your current and post-auction activity.

You can actually choose from two versions of Sales Manager. Sales Manager Merchandising Edition is designed for sellers who sell a lot of unique items; Sales Manager Inventory Edition is designed for sellers who sell multiple quantities of similar items. Both versions let you create listings based on predesigned templates (and customized with your own HTML), such as the one in Figure 3.6.

FIGURE 3.6

A listing template created with Vendio's Sales Manager service.

Whichever version you choose, the pricing is the same, using a combination of monthly fees, per-item listing fees, and per-item final value fees. It's all a little complicated, especially when you consider that Vendio offers both variable rate and flat rate plans. Table 3.4 details Vendio's current pricing.

Table 3.4   Vendio Sales Manager Fees

Plan	Monthly Fee	Listing Fee	Final Value Fee
Pay as You Go Plan	none ($2.95 monthly minimum)	$0.10	1%
Variable Rate Premium Plan	$12.95	$0.05	1%
Variable Rate Power Plan	$29.95	none	1.25%
Flat Rate Premium Plan	$12.95	$0.20	none
Flat Rate Power Plan	$39.95	$0.10	none
Annual Listing Plan	$250 (yearly)	$0.06	none

If you're interested in using Vendio primarily for its listing creation services, you probably want to sign up for one of the flat rate plans, which don't take a hunk out of your final sales price. Or, if you just want to check things out, perhaps the Pay as You Go Plan is the best way to go, as you don't have a hefty up-front monthly charge. I don't know; all these pricing variations are probably good, but they confuse me.

Using Auction Listing Software

All of the services we've discussed so far in this chapter are just that—services, based on the company's website. To create an auction listing, you use your web browser to access the website, log in, and then get to work.

But many sellers prefer to do their listing creation offline, at their own pace. For these sellers, a listing creation program is the preferred tool, like the ones we'll discuss next.

Why Use Listing Software Instead of a Web-Based Service?

There are a few advantages to using a listing program instead of a web-based service. For one, using a software program lets you work offline, at your own pace; you can create your listings at any time of day or night, and upload them at your leisure.

Second, since you work offline, all your auction information is stored on your own computer—not on somebody else's website. That makes it easier to access past information when you're not online, and to manage it as you see fit. (Many sellers like to create their own sales reports using Excel or Access, which isn't always doable with web-based management services.)

Third, most web-based listing services charge you money for each listing you create—or sale that you make. That's not always the case with listing creation software; while some programs come with subscription plans, many are available as simple one-time purchases, just like most of the other software you have installed on your PC.

Popular Listing Creation Programs

If the software route sounds like the way you want to go, then here are the programs to check out. It's important to note that several of these listing creation programs are offered by eBay, which doesn't make them any better or any worse than the other programs; it only makes them "official," whatever that is worth.

Ándale Lister Pro

Earlier in this chapter we discussed the web-based Ándale Lister service. Ándale also offers a software-based listing-creation tool, called Ándale Lister Pro (www.andale.com), which provides the option of creating all your auction listings offline, at your leisure. The software is free to download, although Ándale still charges fees for all listings you upload.

> **NOTE** There's no need to repeat Ándale's fee structure here. Refer to Table 3.1 for all the details.

Auction Lizard

Auction Lizard (www.auction-lizard.com) is an easy-to-use listing-creation software program. It creates simple auction listings using forms and templates; you can also format your auctions using a WYSIWYG HTML editor. (Figure 3.7 shows one of many Auction Lizard auction templates.) Auction Lizard is shareware, with a $29 registration fee.

Native American Teal and Black Beaded Earrings

▶ Description
Beautifully hand beaded Silver-lined Teal, Silver and black earrings created in Marybeth's own caring and unique design.
Marybeth (Ombaashi) has been beading for over 35 years. Within this time she has discovered that her father's mother was from the Iroquois nations (Seneca). With this knowledge beading has become her way to connect to her Ancestors (including the grandmother she never had the chance to meet). Many of her pieces reflect her spiritual understanding of the 13 Original Clan Mothers (the feminine aspect of First Nations spirituality), the Sioux Nations and traditions passed on by Elders and Medicine People of the First Nations. She has been fortunate to have received the teachings of a Blackfoot Artist who in turn was taught the traditions of beading by his Elders. Marybeth began to travel to Alberta, Wyoming, Montana, South Dakota and North Dakota. Wherever she went she would research local museums that featured First Nations Art (specifically the beaded items). Frequently her family would be left waiting as she sketched a Lakota Pony Blankets or teepees being set up for a local PowWow. Much of her larger pieces can be found at Whetung's Art Gallery at the Curve Lake Reserve.

▶

Accepted Payment:
PayPal, Money Order/Cashiers Check, Personal Check,

FIGURE 3.7

A listing template created with Auction Lizard.

Auction Wizard 2000

Auction Wizard 2000 (www.auctionwizard2000.com)—that's *wizard*, not *lizard*—is an auction management software program that includes a listing creator, an image editor, a report generator, an FTP manager, and an auction database. It costs $75 for the first year (and $50 for each subsequent year) with no monthly subscription fees.

Auction Wizard's strength is as a bulk listing tool. It does offer predesigned listing templates, and lets you do a variety of formatting within the templates; a typical auction template is shown in Figure 3.8.

FIGURE 3.8

A listing created with Auction Wizard 2000.

AuctionSage

AuctionSage (www.auctionsagesoftware.com) is a software program that lets you post and manage your eBay auction transactions. It includes a basic listing creation tool, capable of

CD-ROM creating auctions like the one shown in Figure 3.9. The program is available on a subscription basis—$29.95 for 3 months, $49.95 for 6 months, or $79.95 for a year.

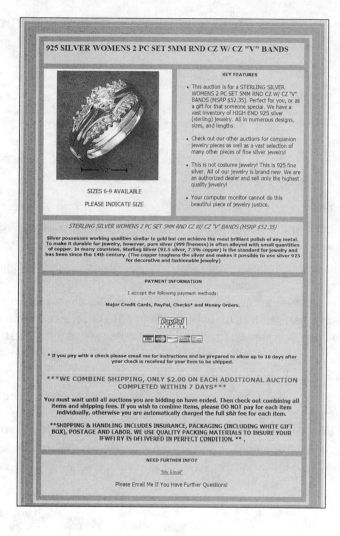

FIGURE 3.9

An auction listing created with AuctionSage.

AuctionTamer

AuctionTamer (www.auctiontamer.com) is an all-in-one auction management software program for both sellers and bidders. For sellers, it features an WYSIWYG HTML editor with a handful of simple templates, like the one in Figure 3.10. Cost is $12.95 per month or $99.95 for a year.

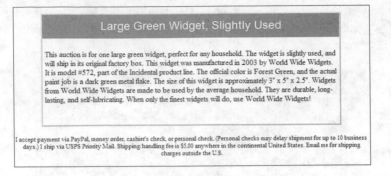

Large Green Widget, Slightly Used

This auction is for one large green widget, perfect for any household. The widget is slightly used, and will ship in its original factory box. This widget was manufactured in 2003 by World Wide Widgets. It is model #572, part of the Incidental product line. The official color is Forest Green, and the actual paint job is a dark green metal flake. The size of this widget is approximately 3" x 5" x 2.5". Widgets from World Wide Widgets are made to be used by the average household. They are durable, long-lasting, and self-lubricating. When only the finest widgets will do, use World Wide Widgets!

I accept payment via PayPal, money order, cashier's check, or personal check. (Personal checks may delay shipment for up to 10 business days.) I ship via USPS Priority Mail. Shipping/handling fee is $5.00 anywhere in the continental United States. Email me for shipping charges outside the U.S.

FIGURE 3.10

An auction listing created with AuctionTamer.

eBay Blackthorne Basic

eBay Blackthorne (previously known as Seller's Assistant) is an auction listing/management program offered by eBay. It comes in two variations: Basic and Pro.

Blackthorne Basic (pages.ebay.com/blackthorne/basic.html), shown in Figure 3.11, is the best program for casual and small-volume sellers, offering HTML-based listing creation (using forms and templates), auction tracking, and basic post-auction management. The software is available on a per-month subscription; you'll pay $9.99 each month, no matter how many listings you create. (Figure 3.12 shows a fancy listing created with Blackthorne Basic.)

eBay Blackthorne Pro

eBay Blackthorne Pro (pages.ebay.com/blackthorne/pro.html) is essentially Blackthorne Basic on steroids, with many more post-auction management features for high-volume sellers. It also includes free Listing Designer templates, which (if you like them) are worth 10 cents a pop. Other than the Listing Designer templates, the listing-creation functions are identical to those in Blackthorne Basic. The program costs $24.99 per month.

eBay Turbo Lister

eBay Turbo Lister (pages.ebay.com/turbo_lister/) is eBay's official software program for the bulk uploading of multiple auctions. Although Turbo Lister doesn't offer any auction tracking features, it excels at bulk uploading—and it's free, with no monthly subscription fees.

> **TIP**
>
> If you're an Apple user, check out eLister (www.blackmagik.com/elister.html), a Macintosh-only listing creation program. The subscription fee is $19.95 for three months.

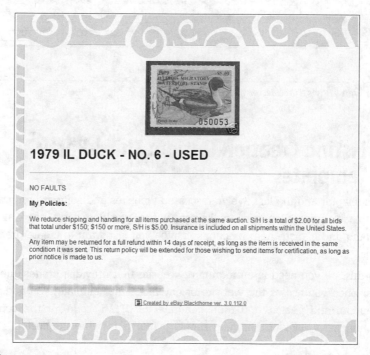

FIGURE 3.11

eBay's Blackthorne Basic program.

1979 IL DUCK - NO. 6 - USED

NO FAULTS

My Policies:

We reduce shipping and handling for all items purchased at the same auction. S/H is a total of $2.00 for all bids that total under $150; $150 or more, S/H is $5.00. Insurance is included on all shipments within the United States.

Any item may be returned for a full refund within 14 days of receipt, as long as the item is received in the same condition it was sent. This return policy will be extended for those wishing to send items for certification, as long as prior notice is made to us.

Created by eBay Blackthorne ver. 3 0 112 0

FIGURE 3.12

An auction listing created with Blackthorne Basic.

The Turbo Lister software is quite easy to use. As you can see in Figure 3.13, it uses a series of forms to request information about your listings. You can format your listings with the built-in WYSIWYG text editor, a raw HTML editor, or just apply a Listing Designer theme. (You'll get charged the standard 10 cents per theme when you upload your listings.) In short, using Turbo Lister is like using eBay's web-based sell your item pages, but it works offline, on your own PC.

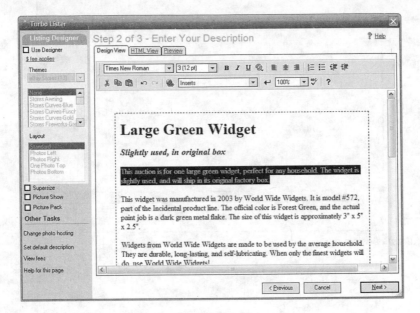

FIGURE 3.13

Creating a listing with eBay's Turbo Lister program.

Another Listing Creation Option: Third-Party Auction Templates

In this chapter and the last, we've discussed websites and software programs that create and upload entire eBay auction listings. But maybe you don't need all those auction launching and management functions; maybe you just want to create great-looking eBay listings.

To do this, all you need is a program or website that provides predesigned auction templates. Once you access the website or download the template, you add your own title, description, and photos, and then generate the HTML code for the completed listing. Launching your auction, then, is a simple matter of copying the custom HTML code into eBay's sell your item page.

This process is a lot easier than it sounds, since you don't have to write the HTML code yourself; the template provides the code for you, no coding required. Some of these templates are free, some aren't, and some are provided for your use on this book's included CD. Learn more when you turn the page and read Chapter 4, "Using Third-Party Auction Templates."

Using Third-Party Auction Templates

In the last two chapters we've looked at different ways to create eBay auction listings, using eBay's sell your item feature and third-party services that help to automate the listing creation process. Most of these third-party services package their listing creation tool with other auction management tools—to which you might not need or want to subscribe. Sometimes all you really want is a way to create great-looking eBay listings, without all the other frills and trappings.

When it comes to creating fancy eBay listings, without coding your own HTML, nothing beats a predesigned auction template. Creating eBay auction templates is a big business, with dozens of sites offering templates and template generators either for free or for a modest charge. There are even a lot of web page design firms who've entered the template creation business, offering their services to help you design truly custom eBay listing templates—for a price, of course.

This chapter is all about where to find these predesigned auction templates, and how to add them to your standard eBay listings. For your shopping convenience, I've noted which of these services are free, and which charge a fee—and don't assume the free templates are any less attractive than the ones you have to pay for!

How to Use Auction Templates

There are two types of auction template services available on the web. The first type features a web-based form (sometimes called a *code generator* or *code generating website*) that you complete with the information for your particular auction. The second type features pre-written code that you download to your computer for editing. In both cases, the final HTML code that is generated has to be inserted (by you) into the description of your eBay listing.

NOTE To insert pictures into an auction template, you'll need to upload your product photos to an image hosting website. Learn more in Chapter 7, "Adding Pictures to Your Auction Templates."

Using a Code Generating Website

There are a surprising number of third-party websites that offer code generators for eBay auction templates. Even more surprising, most of these code generators are free for you to use, with no fees whatsoever.

While each code generator is slightly different in implementation, they all work in pretty much the same fashion. For example, K&D Web Page Design's Custom Auction Creator (www.kdwebpagedesign.com/tutorials/tut_template.asp), shown in Figure 4.1, starts with a listing of the available backgrounds and colors for your template. Click the background and colors you want, then scroll down to the form at the bottom of the page (shown in Figure 4.2). Enter the auction title, description, payment info, and so on, as well as the URLs for your photos, and then click the Show Me My Auction button. The next page, shown in Figure 4.3, shows you what your listing will look like, and displays the HTML code for your template in a separate text box. It's this code that you'll copy into your eBay listing.

Other code generators use more of a WYSIWYG approach to creating templates. For example, Auction Writer (www.auctionwriter.com) starts by showing you thumbnails of the available template designs, as shown in Figure 4.4. Click the template you want, and you're presented with a full-page version of the template, with placeholder text and graphics, as shown in Figure 4.5. Click a piece of text and a pop-up box appears, as shown in Figure 4.6; enter your own text, and then click the Update button. The same thing with pictures; click a placeholder graphic, and then enter the URL for your own photo. When you're done customizing the template, click the Download button, and the generated code will be downloaded to your PC in a TXT file. You can view this code with any text editor program, such as Windows Notepad.

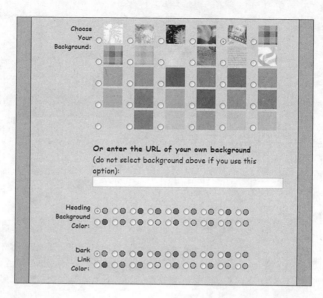

FIGURE 4.1

K&D Web Page Design's Custom Auction Creator—start by choosing your template's background and colors.

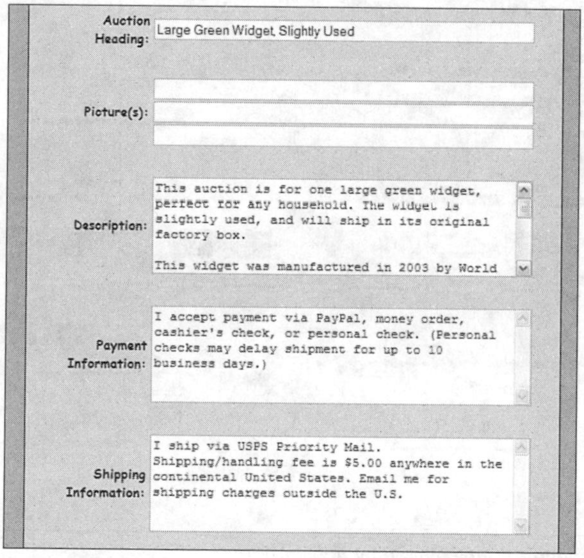

FIGURE 4.2

Fill in the blanks with your auction title, description, and other information.

FIGURE 4.3

After you've filled in the blanks, the HTML code for your template is automatically generated.

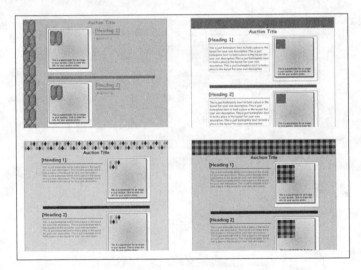

FIGURE 4.4

Some of the auction template designs offered by Auction Writer.

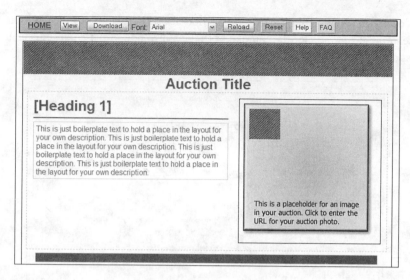

FIGURE 4.5

The auction template displayed with placeholder text and graphics.

FIGURE 4.6

Replacing placeholder text with your own auction information.

Using a Downloadable Auction Template

In some ways, using a downloadable auction template is even simpler than using a code generator website—if only because you don't have as many choices. The template layout and color scheme is already predetermined, so all you have to do is replace the placeholder text with your own auction information.

For example, when you choose one of the free templates available from AuctionSupplies. com (www.auctionsupplies.com), the site displays the full HTML code for the template on a separate web page, as shown in Figure 4.7. You can then copy this code into your own text editor (such as Notepad or WordPad), and edit the appropriate sections to include your own text description and picture URLs. (You'll also need to download the accompanying background graphics for the template.) Once you've edited the code with your own information, you can then copy the edited code into your eBay item listing.

```
<!--Start template-->
<!--Your background color image's URL on the next line-->
<table background="http://www.your_colored_image's_URL_here.jpg" width="100%" border="1"
bordercolorlight="#a52a2a" bordercolordark="#a52a2a" cellpadding="0" cellspacing="0">
  <tr>
    <td>
      <table width="100%" border="0" cellpadding="0" cellspacing="0">
        <tr>
<!--Your butterfly border image's URL on the next line-->
          <td background="http://www.your_butterfly_image_URL.jpg" width="58">

          </td>
          <td>
<table width="100%" border="0" cellpadding="20" cellspacing="0">
  <tr>
    <td>
    <div align="center">
<!--Your item's picture URL on the next line-->
<img src="http://www.your_item_picture's_URL.jpg">
<p>
        <table border="1" bordercolorlight="#a52a2a" bordercolordark="#a52a2a" bgcolor="#ffffff" width="80%"
cellpadding="15">
          <tr>
            <td align="center">
<font face="arial,verdana,helvetica,sans serif" color="mediumvioletred">
<!--Description text on the next line-->
Description text here
</font>
            </td>
          </tr>
        </table>
    </div>
    </td>
  </tr>
</table>
<br>
<table width="100%" border="0" cellpadding="0" cellspacing="0">
  <tr>
    <td>
    </td>
  </tr>
</table>
          </td>
        </tr>
      </table>
    </td>
  </tr>
</table>
```

FIGURE 4.7

The HTML code for an AuctionSupplies.com auction template.

Other sites provide their template code in a downloadable TXT file, which saves you the bother of copying the code from their web page. Just open the TXT file in your text editor and edit in your own information. You can then copy the edited code into your eBay item listing.

Still other sites make you do a little more work. Instead of downloading the HTML code in a TXT file, they download the template itself (with placeholder graphics) as an HTML page, typically included along with the necessary graphics in a ZIP file. UnZIP the ZIP file and you have an HTML file and one or more JPG graphics files. What you'll need to do here is open the downloaded HTML page in your web browser, then view the page's source code. (In Internet Explorer, pull down the View menu and select Source.) This opens the HTML code for the page in a text editor, typically Windows Notepad. You can then edit the file in Notepad, to replace the placeholder text with your own text and URLs. Then you can copy the edited code into your eBay auction listing.

Inserting Auction Template Code into an eBay Auction Listing

Once you've generated the final HTML code for your listing, it's a simple matter to insert this code into eBay's sell your item form. As you've just learned, you'll be presented with the final code for your template, either in a text box of some sort on the service's web page or in a text editor on your computer. You then have to do the following:

1. Begin the process of creating a new item for sale on eBay, and proceed to the Describe Your Item page.

2. On the code generator's web page or in the text editor program, select the entire code listing by holding down the Shift key while you move your cursor from beginning to end.

3. Copy the code listing by pressing Ctrl+C.

4. Return to eBay's Describe Your Item page and scroll down to the Description section.

5. Click the View HTML link to display the HTML editor.

6. Position your cursor in the empty Description text box, as shown in Figure 4.8, and insert the copied code by pressing Ctrl+V.

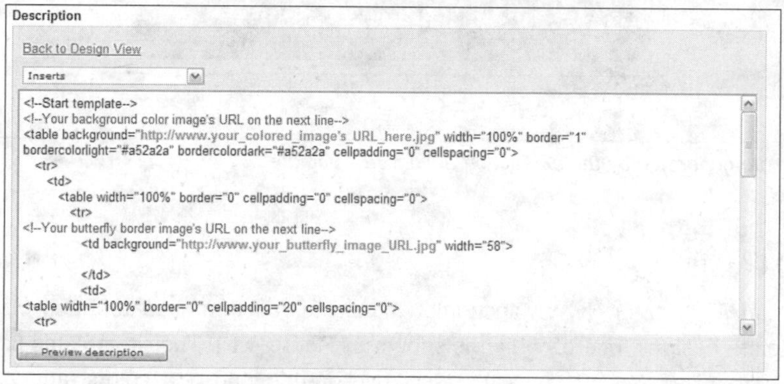

FIGURE 4.8

Inserting the HTML code for an auction template into the Description box in eBay's Describe Your Item page.

It's that easy. Just copy the code that was generated and paste it into the Description box in HTML view. You can preview how it looks by clicking the Preview Description button, and then proceed to complete the rest of your new item listing.

Using Create-Your-Own Template Websites

We'll start our tour of third-party templates by examining some of the most popular create-your-own template websites. These sites are often referred to as code generators, since that's what they do—generate HTML code that you then insert into your eBay item listing.

Antique Central eZ Auction Advanced Template

Antique Central's eZ Auction Advanced Template (www.antique-central.com/eztemplate. html) offers simple text-based templates, like the one in Figure 4.9. There is no provision for adding images, although you can enter your own HTML image codes into the final generated code.

FIGURE 4.9

A sample template generated by the eZ Auction Advanced Template.

Auction AD Creator

Auction AD Creator (www.auctionlotwatch.co.uk/auctionadcreator.html) offers four basic template designs, one of which is shown in Figure 4.10. Their templates use tables for a well-organized layout; you can select background and text colors, and insert a single photo.

Auction Insights Free Auction Template & Ad Creator

The Auction Insights code generator (www.auctioninsights.com/practice/auction-template.html) offers a simple single-column design, as shown in Figure 4.11, with your choice of six color schemes. You can add up to three photos, as well as a separate section for shipping terms.

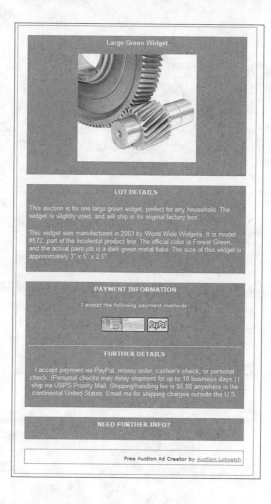

FIGURE 4.10

One of the four template designs offered by Auction AD Creator.

Auction Riches Free Auction Ad Creator

Free

Auction Riches (www.auctionriches.com/freead/create.pl) offers a very simple code generator. The generated template is a basic single-column design, as shown in Figure 4.12, with a single photo and your choice of border and background color.

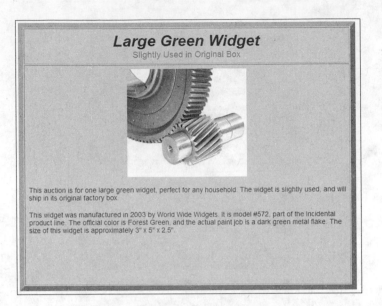

FIGURE 4.11

A simple single-column auction template from Auction Insights.

FIGURE 4.12

The basic auction template generated by Auction Riches' Free Auction Ad Creator.

Auction Writer

Free

Auction Writer (www.auctionwriter.com) is one of the more full-featured free code generators. It uses a WYSIWYG approach to generate a variety of different templates, using various layouts and color schemes. Just click on the placeholder text to add your own item description and details; you can include up to three photos, as shown in Figure 4.13.

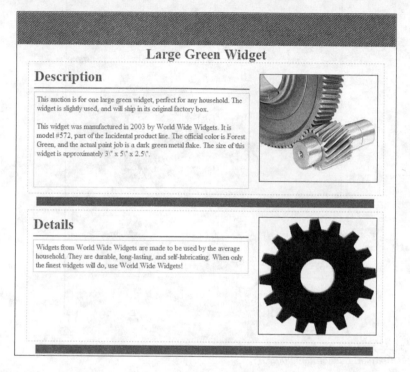

FIGURE 4.13

One of the better-looking auction templates created with Auction Writer.

AuctionFlash Code Generators

Free

AuctionFlash (www.auctionflash.com) offersthree different code generators—Basic, Basic Plus, and Detailed, each more sophisticated than the last. (Figure 4.14 shows a Detailed template, with two pictures.) The page also includes code generators for special auction effects, such as thumbnail image selection, slideshows, specifications tables, and so on.

FIGURE 4.14

AuctionFlash's Detailed auction template.

AuctionSpice

AuctionSpice (www.auctionspice.com) offers four free auction templates, all rather sophisticated in their design, as you can see in Figure 4.15. You can include up to 10 pictures in your listings, with your choice of background colors. (The site also offers a Professional membership for $4.99 per month, with access to a wider selection of template designs.)

Bay Dream Design

Bay Dream Design (www.bay-dream.com) lets you choose from nine different layouts, like the one in Figure 4.16. You can change the page background and border colors, and add up to three product photos.

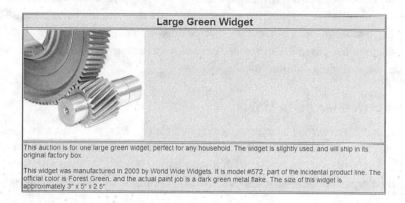

Large Green Widget

This auction is for one large green widget, perfect for any household. The widget is slightly used, and will ship in its original factory box.

This widget was manufactured in 2003 by World Wide Widgets. It is model #572, part of the Incidental product line. The official color is Forest Green, and the actual paint job is a dark green metal flake. The size of this widget is approximately 3" x 5" x 2.5".

Click To Enlarge

Shipping and Contact Information

Shipping on this item will be $5.00 via USPS Priority Mail. I accept payment via PayPal, money order, cashier's check, or personal check. (Personal checks may delay shipment for up to 10 business days.) I ship via USPS Priority Mail. Shipping/handling fee is $5.00 anywhere in the continental United States. Email me for shipping charges outside the U.S. If you have any questions or comments about this auction, feel free to e-mail me at . Thank you and good luck bidding!

Product and Bidding Disclaimer READ!!

Please remember that bidding is a **contract**. Please do not bid if you do not intend on completing the transaction. I do my best to post all information I know about an item in my auction descriptions. If there is something you are unclear about please ask me before you place your bid. Thank you.

This Auction Template was created FREE at www.AuctionSpice.com

FIGURE 4.15

One of AuctionSpice's four free auction templates.

Large Green Widget

This auction is for one large green widget, perfect for any household. The widget is slightly used, and will ship in its original factory box.

This widget was manufactured in 2003 by World Wide Widgets. It is model #572, part of the Incidental product line. The official color is Forest Green, and the actual paint job is a dark green metal flake. The size of this widget is approximately 3" x 5" x 2.5".

FIGURE 4.16

One of the nine different template layouts offered by Bay Dream Design.

BiggerBids

Pay

CD-ROM

BiggerBids (www.biggerbids.com) lets you choose from six professional-looking templates, like the one in Figure 4.17. The first five auctions are free; after that, pricing is tiered from $5.95/month (for 50 auctions) to $44.95/month (for 2,000 auctions).

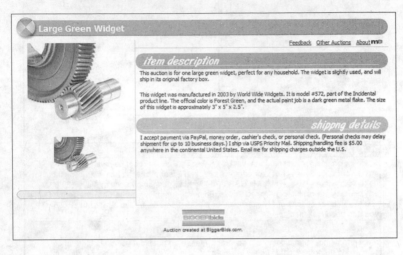

FIGURE 4.17

A very professional auction template from BiggerBids.

Birddogs Garage Basic Template Generators

Free

Birddogs Garage (www.birddogsgarage.com/bdg_2/modules.php?name=Template_Generators) offers separate code generators for six different template layouts—no text, one picture, two pictures, three pictures, four pictures, and five pictures. (Figure 4.18 shows the one-picture template.) Different sections of your listing are displayed in separate text boxes, for a slightly different design.

DeadZoom Auction Template Maker

Free

DeadZoom (www.deadzoom.com/auction-template/) lets you create fully-customizable templates—you choose the number of pictures, background color/image, borders, fonts, and so on. You can even add tables, background music, and a USPS rate calculator. (Figure 4.19 shows a typical DeadZoom-generated auction template, complete with rate calculator.)

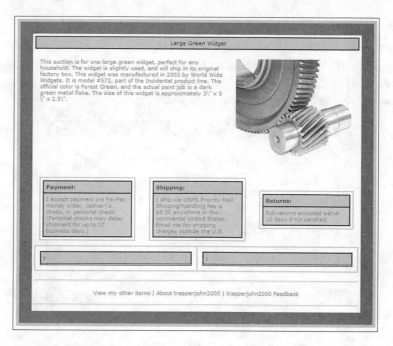

FIGURE 4.18

A one-picture template from Birddogs Garage.

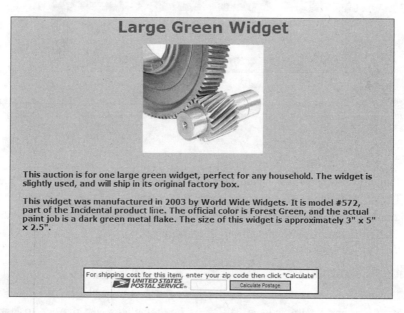

FIGURE 4.19

Just one of the infinite number of fully-customizable DeadZoom auction templates.

K&D Web Page Design Custom Ad Creator

Free

The Custom Ad Creator offered by K&D Web Page Design (www.kdwebpagedesign. com/tutorials/tut_template.asp) creates simple single-column auction templates, with your choice of background image and text color, and up to three product photos. Figure 4.20 shows what one of these templates looks like.

FIGURE 4.20

A simple eBay template generated by K&D Web Page Design's Custom Ad Creator.

ListTailor

Free

ListTailor (www.listtailor.com) lets you choose from seven basic layouts, like the one shown in Figure 4.21. The initial templates come with placeholder text, which you can then edit; depending on the design, you can include up to two product photos. (The site is free, but a 10-cent donation per template use is encouraged.)

Nucite Auction Templates

Free   Pay
CD-ROM

Nucite (members.nucite.com) offers a variety of auction selling tools on its site, including both free and paid templates. The three free templates, like the one in Figure 4.22, are well-organized and let you include up to seven photos. For $4.95 per month you get access to 16 additional templates, which include cross-selling links and up to 12 product photos.

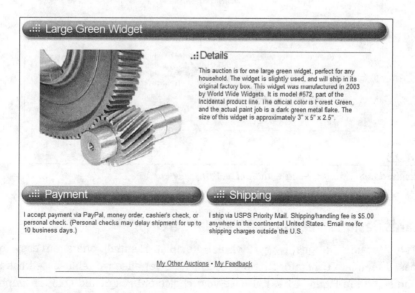

Large Green Widget

This auction is for one large green widget, perfect for any household. The widget is slightly used, and will ship in its original factory box.

This widget was manufactured in 2003 by World Wide Widgets. It is model #572, part of the Incidental product line. The official color is Forest Green, and the actual paint job is a dark green metal flake. The size of this widget is approximately 3" x 5" x

Widgets from World Wide Widgets are made to be used by the average household. They are durable, long-lasting, and self-lubricating. When only the finest widgets will do, use World Wide Widgets!

I ship via USPS Priority Mail. Shipping/handling fee is $5.00 anywhere in the continental United States. Email me for shipping charges outside the U.S.

I accept payment via PayPal, money order, cashier's check, or personal check. (Personal checks may delay shipment for up to 10 business days.)

There is no reserve on this auction. Don't hesitate to contact me if you have any other questions.

Happy Bidding

Free Auction Templates & Image Hosting by ListTailor.com

FIGURE 4.21

One of the seven different auction templates offered by ListTailor.

.::: Large Green Widget

.::Details

This auction is for one large green widget, perfect for any household. The widget is slightly used, and will ship in its original factory box. This widget was manufactured in 2003 by World Wide Widgets. It is model #572, part of the Incidental product line. The official color is Forest Green, and the actual paint job is a dark green metal flake. The size of this widget is approximately 3" x 5" x 2.5".

.::: Payment

I accept payment via PayPal, money order, cashier's check, or personal check. (Personal checks may delay shipment for up to 10 business days.)

.::: Shipping

I ship via USPS Priority Mail. Shipping/handling fee is $5.00 anywhere in the continental United States. Email me for shipping charges outside the U.S.

My Other Auctions • My Feedback

FIGURE 4.22

One of Nucite's three free auction templates.

RobsHelp.com FreeForm Builder

The FreeForm Builder code generator at RobsHelp.com (www.robshelp.com) lets you create very sophisticated eBay auction listings; it is perhaps the most customizable of all these form-based listing creators. You can customize virtually every piece and part of your item listing, just by clicking on the appropriate buttons and making the necessary option choices. (Figure 4.23 shows a sample listing created with FreeForm Builder.) RobsHelp.com also offers an advanced version of FreeForm that lets you add a variety of special features to your auctions, including background music, no right-click images, and more sophisticated customization. Both the basic and advanced versions of FreeForm are free to use, although donations are encouraged.

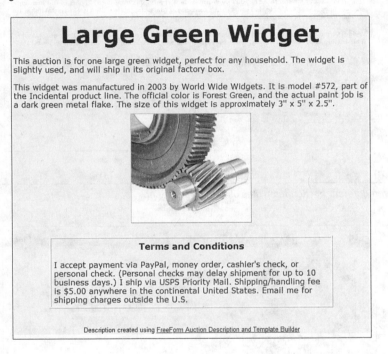

Large Green Widget

This auction is for one large green widget, perfect for any household. The widget is slightly used, and will ship in its original factory box.

This widget was manufactured in 2003 by World Wide Widgets. It is model #572, part of the Incidental product line. The official color is Forest Green, and the actual paint job is a dark green metal flake. The size of this widget is approximately 3" x 5" x 2.5".

Terms and Conditions

I accept payment via PayPal, money order, cashier's check, or personal check. (Personal checks may delay shipment for up to 10 business days.) I ship via USPS Priority Mail. Shipping/handling fee is $5.00 anywhere in the continental United States. Email me for shipping charges outside the U.S.

Description created using FreeForm Auction Description and Template Builder

FIGURE 4.23

A fully customized item listing created with the FreeForm Builder.

Two Wizards Designs Free Auction Template Creator

Two Wizards Designs (www.2wiz.net/dtemplates1.shtml) offers an easy-to-use form-based template generator that produces simple yet effective table-based listings, like the one shown in Figure 4.24. You have your choice of background color or graphic, and can insert up to two product photos.

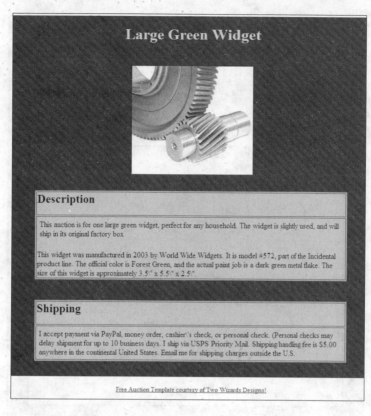

FIGURE 4.24

A simple table-based template from Two Wizards Designs.

Wizard's Free Auction Template Creation Form

Free

The Wizard's Free Auction Template Creation Form (www.ambassadorboard.net/hosting/ free-form.php) is another simple-to-use form-based code generator. You can choose background and border images, and include up to three photos, as shown in Figure 4.25.

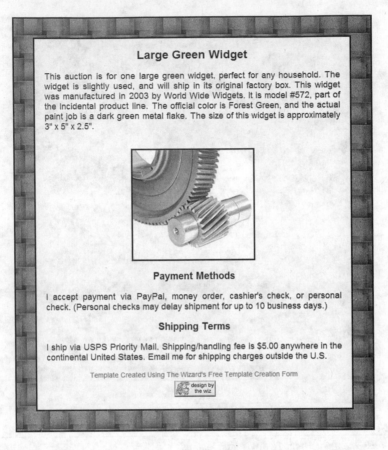

FIGURE 4.25

One of many custom templates you can create with Wizard's Free Auction Template Creation Form.

Using Downloadable Auction Templates

Online HTML code generators are great, but what if you don't want to go to somebody else's website to design your eBay auction listings? If you prefer to work within the comfort and safety of your own computer desktop, consider using a downloadable auction template. These templates feature predesigned color schemes and layouts; you have only to open them in any text editor program (such as Windows Notepad or WordPad) to insert your own auction information, and then copy the final code into your eBay item listing.

You can find all manner of both free and paid templates for your auction use. I'll point out some of the most popular ones next.

Alou's 20 Free eBay Auction Templates

 Alou Web Design (www.alouwebdesign.ca/free-ebay-templates.htm) offers 20 templates you can download for free from its website. These are nice-looking but relatively simple templates; the main difference between the themes is the color scheme and border image.

AuctionSupplies.com Free Auction Templates

 The folks at AuctionSupplies.com (www.auctionsupplies.com/templates/) offer a handful of free downloadable templates. Most of these templates come in variations based on number and layout of product photos.

Auction Template Central

 Auction Template Center (www.auctiontemplatecentral.com) offers more than a hundred different downloadable auction templates, all in the country (or "primitive," as they call it) style. Most templates sell for $15.00 apiece.

AuctionWraps

 AuctionWraps (www.auctionwraps.com) offers 75 or so downloadable auction templates, including one for each Major League Baseball team. You get access to all their templates for $7.97 per month.

DeSa C.S. Auction Templates

 DeSa C.S. (www.desacs.com) offers a variety of auction templates for sale, as well as a few sample templates, for free download. Templates are organized into sets of 15, which sell for $5 per set.

Free Auction Help Auction Templates

 Free Auction Help (www.freeauctionhelp.com/free_auction_template.htm) offers two auction templates for free download.

K&D Web Page Design Custom Ad Creator

 K&D Web Page Design (www.kdwebpagedesign.com/auction_templates.asp) offers several auction templates for free download. These are very professional-looking designs, created with sophisticated Cascading Style Sheet code. The site also sells a variety of other auction templates, priced between $3.99 and $12.99 apiece.

Pace Computing Limited Auction Templates

 Pace Computing Limited (www.pc-limited.com/web-design-templates.htm) offers a variety of web design services and also sells some cool-looking eBay auction templates. Prices run from $24.95 for pre-designed templates, or you can contact them to create your own custom templates.

SaverSites Custom eBay Auction Templates

Pay

SaverSites (www.saversites.com/services_ebay_auction_templates.htm) sells custom eBay templates. Their services include custom logo design, custom layout, dynamic rollover effects, and other advanced features. Prices run from $25 (for the Economy Solution) to $295 (for the Power Seller Auction Template).

The Ultimate eBay Resource eBay Templates

Pay

The Ultimate eBay Resource (www.sellingonebay.info/templates.html) sells a handful of simple auction templates for $1.99 apiece. There's nothing fancy about these templates, although you can use your own HTML to customize them.

Xample.net Free eBay Auction Templates

Free

Xample.net (www.xample.net/templates.htm) offers a few dozen auction templates for free download. These range from fairly simple templates to more sophisticated table-based templates.

Woo Woo Designs Auction Templates

Free

Woo Woo Designs (www.woowoodesigns.com) offers a dozen or so free templates for download. These are fairly simple templates that you can spruce up with your own custom HTML.

Using the Auction Templates on the CD

To supplement to all the templates that you can create or download from the web, I've included a sampling of free templates on the accompanying CD. These templates come from many of the same sites I talked about in this chapter, as you can tell from the CD icon next to some of the site listings.

The templates on the CD work just like the templates I talked about in the beginning of this chapter, except you don't have to download them; you only have to copy them from the CD to your computer's hard disk. Once copied, you can edit them using Windows Notepad or a similar text editor, and then copy the edited HTML code into your eBay item listings. It's as easy as that—copy (from the CD), edit (in your text editor), and copy again (to your eBay item listing). It's a great way to spruce up your eBay auctions, without having to learn HTML code.

Of course, if you want even better-looking listings, the HTML thing becomes necessary. That's what the rest of the book is all about, so if you're interested, turn the page to start learning how to code HTML!

Creating Your Own Auction Templates

Learning How to Code with HTML

As I noted in the first chapter of this book, there's the easy way to create fancy item listings, and then there's the hard way. So far we've discussed the easy way—using tools like eBay's Listing Designer, web-based code generators, and pre-designed auction templates. But the problem with doing things the easy way is that you're limited to the designs that are presented to you; there's only so much customization allowed.

If you want to create a truly custom item listing, you have to design it yourself. This approach is doing it the hard way, as you create your listing from the ground up using HTML codes.

If you're unfamiliar with HTML (short for *Hypertext Markup Language*), it's the engine behind every web page you've ever viewed. HTML is also used to create every single eBay auction listing, even the ones that aren't that visually exciting. It's a coding language that lets you turn on and off all sorts of different text and graphic formatting and effects.

So if you want to build your own eBay auction templates from scratch, you have to know a little HTML. We'll get into specific applications of HTML in subsequent chapters; right now, it's time to learn how HTML works.

Understanding Basic HTML

HTML coding might sound difficult, but it's actually surprisingly easy. Really. It's not near as complicated as a fancy computer programming language, such as BASIC or C++; coding in HTML is something anyone can do, with just minimal training. That's because HTML is nothing more than a series of hidden codes that tell a web browser how to display different types of text and graphics. The codes are embedded in a document, so you can't see them; they're only visible to your web browser.

How HTML Works

The first thing you need to know is that HTML consists of text surrounded by instructions, in the form of simple codes. These codes are distinguished from normal text by the fact that they're enclosed within angle brackets. Each particular code turns on or off a particular attribute, such as boldface or italic text. Most codes are in sets of "on/off" pairs; you turn "on" the code before the text you want to affect and then turn "off" the code after the text.

For example, the code <h1> turns specified type into a level-one heading; the code </h1> turns off the heading type. The code <i> is used to italicize text; </i> turns off the italic. (As you can see, an "off" code is merely the "on" code with a slash before it, </like this>.)

Any text not surrounded by code uses HTML's default formatting—normal Times Roman text. It's the same with tables and other elements; if no code is applied, they default to standard formatting.

There are several different types of HTML codes, used to format different elements on a web page—text effects, fonts, graphics, and so on. We'll examine each category of codes individually.

Codes for Text Formatting

Using HTML text formatting is the fastest and easiest way to add spice to your item listings. If you do nothing else, boldfacing important words in your description will add selling power to your ad—and you can do that with a pair of simple HTML codes.

Table 5.1 presents some of the common HTML codes that format the way selected text looks in your listing.

Table 5.1   Common HTML Text Formatting Codes

On Code	Off Code	Description
<h1>	</h1>	Formats text as a level-one heading
<h2>	</h2>	Formats text as a level-two heading
<h3>	</h3>	Formats text as a level-three heading
<h4>	</h4>	Formats text as a level-four heading

On Code	Off Code	Description
`<h5>`	`</h5>`	Formats text as a level-five heading
`<h6>`	`</h6>`	Formats text as a level-six heading
`<b>`	`</b>`	Boldfaces text
`<strong>`	`</strong>`	Another way of boldfacing text
`<i>`	`</i>`	Italicizes text
`<em>`	`</em>`	Another way of italicizing text
`<u>`	`</u>`	Underlines text
`<tt>`	`</tt>`	Creates monospaced typewriter-style text
`<center>`	`</center>`	Centers text (and other page elements)
`<pre>`	`</pre>`	Displays "preformatted" text to preserve line breaks and such
`<big>`	`</big>`	Increases text by one type size
`<small>`	`</small>`	Decreases text by one type size

Insert the "on" code right before the text you want formatted, and insert the "off" code right after the selected text. For example, if you want to boldface a single word in a sentence, make it look just like this:

This is the `<strong>`highlighted`</strong>` word.

It's really that simple; just add the **`<strong>`** and **`</strong>`** codes around the text you want boldfaced. The rest of your item description looks as normal as it did before.

> **TIP**
> eBay now prefers the use of the **`<strong>`** tag in place of the older **`<b>`** tag for boldfacing text, and the **`<em>`** tag in place of the older **`<i>`** tag for italicizing text—although both older tags continue to work.

Codes for Font Type, Size, and Color

You can also use HTML to specify a particular font type or size, using the **`<font>`** code.

To specify a font type for selected text, use the **`<font>`** code with the **face** attribute, like this:

`<font face="`*xxxx*`">text</font>`

> **NOTE**
> Learn how to apply text, font, and paragraph formatting in Chapter 6, "Creating Text-Based HTML Auction Templates."

Replace the *xxxx* with the specific font, such as Arial or Times Roman—in quotation marks.

Another common use of the **`<font>`** code is to specify type size. You use the **size** attribute, and the code looks like this:

`<font size="`*xx*`">text</font>`

Replace the *xx* with the size you want, from –6 to +6, with –6 being the smallest, +6 being the biggest, and 0 (or no size specified) being "normal" size type.

You can also use the **<font>** code to designate a specific text color. In this instance, you use the **color** attribute, like this:

<font color="#*xxxxxx*">text</font>

Replace the *xxxxx* with the code for a specific color. Table 5.2 lists 20 of the most common color codes, for those colors referred to as "web-safe" colors—meaning that they're apt to reproduce safely and similarly in all web browsers.

Table 5.2   Common HTML Color Codes

Color Name	Color Code
Black	000000
White	FFFFFF
Gray	808080
Silver	C0C0C0
Yellow	FFFF00
Orange	FFA500
Brown	A52A2A
Red	FF0000
Maroon	800000
Olive	808000
Fuchsia	FF00FF
Chartreuse	7FFF00
Green	008000
Lime	00FF00
Teal	008080
Aqua	00FFFF
Navy	000080
Blue	0000FF
Purple	800080
Violet	F080F0

As an example, suppose you want to color some text red. You use this code:

<font color="#FF0000">red text</font>

If you don't want to bother with learning hexadecimal color codes, you also have the option of simply entering the actual name of the color (still within quotation marks, of course). While this limits you to a handful of primary colors, it's easier than remembering all the detailed codes. For example, to rewrite our previous red text example, you use the following simplified code:

<font color="red">red text</font>

By the way, the 20 colors listed in Table 5.2 are just a fraction of the available colors you can use in your auction listings. To view all available colors, consult one of the many web-based HTML color charts, such as the ones at www.immigration-usa.com/html_colors.html and html-color-codes.com. Just choose a color and view the corresponding color code!

Codes for Paragraphs

When it's time to start a new paragraph, you start the paragraph with a **<p>** code. Then, when the paragraph is done, you close it with a **</p>** "off" code. The code looks something like this:

<p>
This is a normal text paragraph. It consists of
multiple sentences. Like these.
</p>

The **<p>** code can also contain the **align** attribute, which indicates how the paragraph is aligned—left, center, or right. Paragraphs are left-aligned by default, so if you want to center a paragraph, you'd use the following code:

<p align="center">
This is the paragraph to be centered. All the
text in the paragraph is aligned as indicated.
</p>

> **NOTE** Earlier versions of HTML let you use the **<p>** tag to indicate the start of a new paragraph, without requiring the corresponding **</p>** "off" code at the end the paragraph. Current HTML standards encourage the use of the **<p>** and **</p>** codes as proper containers for the paragraph text. That said, you can probably get by without the **</p>** "off" code, although it's good practice to include it.

Codes That Insert Things

So far, I've shown you codes that format text and paragraphs. There are a few other codes that insert items into your document. These codes include the following:

- **
** inserts a line break
- **<hr>** inserts a horizontal rule or line

Note that these insertion codes do not have corresponding "off" codes. You just insert the item, and be done with it.

Codes for Lists

If you have a lot of features to list for your item, you might want to format them in a bulleted list. Using HTML codes, it's easy to create a neatly bulleted list for your ad.

First, you enclose your bulleted list with the **<ul>** and **</ul>** codes. Then, you enclose each bulleted item with the **<li>** and **</li>** codes.

The code for a typical bulleted list looks like this:

```
<ul>
  <li>item one</li>
  <li>item two</li>
  <li>item three</li>
</ul>
```

Bulleted lists are great ways to run through a list of attributes or specifications; it's a lot cleaner than just listing a bunch of stuff within a long text paragraph.

You can also included a numbered list within your item listing. The approach is similar, except that you use the **<ol>** and **</ol>** container codes, instead of the **<ul>** and **</ul>** codes. The code for a typical numbered list looks like this:

```
<ol>
  <li>item one</li>
  <li>item two</li>
  <li>item three</li>
</ol>
```

Codes for Graphics

Adding pictures and other graphics to your auction templates really brings some excitement to the normally plain-text world of eBay. You can add pictures the eBay way (using eBay's Picture Manager on the Describe Your Item page), which puts all your pictures at the end of your text description, or you can put a picture *anywhere* in your text, using HTML.

Before you can insert a graphic into your listing, you need to know the address of that graphic (in the form of a web page URL). Then you use the following code:

```
<img src="URL">
```

No "off" code is required for inserted graphics. Note that the location is enclosed in quotation marks—and that you have to insert the http:// part of the URL.

As an example, if your graphic is the file **graphic01.jpg** located at www.webserver.com/ mydir/, you insert this code:

```
<img src="http://www.webserver.com/mydir/graphic01.jpg">
```

The nice thing about inserting graphics this way is that you can include more than just pictures—you can add logos, starbursts, you name it. (And you can put the graphics *anywhere* in your text description.) You use the same technique to link to any graphic image anywhere in your item listing.

> NOTE   Learn how to apply graphics in your auctions in Chapter 7, "Adding Pictures to Your Auction Templates."

Codes for Links

Web pages are all about hyperlinks to other web pages. Why should your eBay item listing be any different?

If you want to include a hyperlink to another web page, use the following code:

```
<a href="URL">this is the link</a>
```

The text between the on and off codes will appear onscreen as a typical underlined hyperlink; when users click that text, they'll be linked to the URL you specified in the code. Note that the URL is enclosed in quotation marks and that you have to include the http:// part of the address.

> CAUTION   eBay prohibits linking to other "sell" pages outside the eBay community. You can, however, link to pages that provide more information on the item you're selling.

Here's what a representative hyperlink code looks like:

```
<a href="http://www.webserver.com/mydir/mypage.htm">
Click for my Web page</a>
```

Working with HTML Tables

In addition to making pretty text and inserting links and graphics, one of the other interesting things you can do with HTML is add a table to your item listing. While tables sound complicated (and they are, to a degree), they're necessary for both formatting your listing's background and borders, and for organizing the content in your listing. Mastering tables gives you a powerful tool to use when creating your eBay auction templates.

> NOTE   Learn more about using tables in your auctions in Chapter 8, "Working with Tables, Borders, and Backgrounds."

Creating Simple Tables

Creating a table starts with a pair of container tags. That is, you enclose your table within matching **<table>** and **</table>** codes. Then you enclose each individual row in the table with **<tr>** and **</tr>** codes, and each cell in each row with **<td>** and **</td>** codes.

That's right—you create each row of your table one at a time. And each row can have different numbers of cells; you don't define the total number of columns for your table as a whole. If you want to create a table where the first row has a single cell, the second row has two cells, and the third row has four cells, you can do it. (And quite easily, too.)

But let's get back to basics. We'll start with a simple table that contains a single row that itself contains a single cell. The code for this table looks like this:

```
<table>
 <tr>
  <td>This is the text for the cell</td>
 </tr>
</table>
```

> **NOTE** To make this complex code easier to read, I'm offsetting the code for each subsequent section of the table, much as you would in a typical outline. This type of code offsetting is helpful, but not necessary; it doesn't change how the table actually appears.

The resulting table should like the one in Figure 5.1.

This is the text for the cell

FIGURE 5.1

A table with one row and one column.

Now let's take that same table and give it two cells in the solo row instead of one. Here's the new code:

```
<table>
 <tr>
  <td>This is the text for the first cell</td>
  <td>This is the text for the second cell</td>
 </tr>
</table>
```

Figure 5.2 shows the resulting table.

This is the text for the first cell	This is the text for the second cell

FIGURE 5.2

A table with one row and two columns.

Getting the idea? Now let's add a second row, also with two cells. Here's the code:

```
<table>
 <tr>
  <td>row 1 cell 1</td>
```

```
    <td>row 1 cell 2</td>
    </tr>
    <tr>
    <td>row 2 cell 1</td>
    <td>row 2 cell 2</td>
    </tr>
    </table>
```

Figure 5.3 shows what the table looks like.

row 1 cell 1	row 1 cell 2
row 2 cell 1	row 2 cell 2

FIGURE 5.3

A table with two rows and two columns.

Now, to show that you can have different numbers of cells in each row, let's take the same table but make it so the first row has a single cell, and the second row has three cells. Here's the code:

```
<table>
  <tr>
  <td>row 1 cell 1</td>
  </tr>
  <tr>
  <td>row 2 cell 1</td>
  <td>row 2 cell 2</td>
  <td>row 2 cell 3</td>
  </tr>
</table>
```

Figure 5.4 shows what this table looks like.

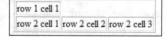

row 1 cell 1		
row 2 cell 1	row 2 cell 2	row 2 cell 3

FIGURE 5.4

A table with a single-cell first row, and a three-cell second row.

Within any individual cell in the table, you can insert any type of item—plain text, formatted text, bulleted lists, background shading, and even graphics. Just make sure that the contents of the cell are enclosed with the **<td>** and **</td>** tags.

Aligning and Sizing Your Table

The <table> tag can contain various attributes that affect the placement and formatting of the table. The two attributes we'll examine first are the **align** and **width** attributes.

Not surprisingly, you use the **align** attribute to determine how the table will be aligned—to the left margin, the right margin, or centered on the page. By default, the table will be aligned to the left margin, so it's only the other two options you need to worry about. For example, the code to center align a table is this:

```
<table align="center">
```

Note that the **center** (or **right** or **left**) parameter is in quotation marks.

To determine the total width of your table on the page, you use the **width** parameter within the <table> tag. You can specify the width as either a percent of the total page width, or as a specific width in pixels. To specify a percentage, enter the attribute as "*xx*%" (within quotation marks, with the percent sign); to specify a specific pixel width, enter the attribute as "*xx*" (within quotation marks, but without the percent sign).

For example, to specify a table 400 pixels wide, you'd use the following code:

```
<table width="400">
```

Or to specify a table that occupies 75% of the total page width, you'd use this code:

```
<table width="75%">
```

Of course, you can gang the **align** and **width** attributes together, like this:

```
<table align="center" width="75%">
```

Adding Table Borders and Backgrounds

A white table on a white page doesn't look much like a table at all. (Although it can help you align text in columns, by putting each column of text in a separate table cell.) One way to set your table off from the rest of the page is to put a border around it.

Not surprisingly, you add a border to your table by using the **border** attribute within the <table> tag. You specify the width of the border in pixels (surrounded by quotation marks). For example, here's the code to add a 2-pixel border around the outside of a table:

```
<table border="2">
```

By default, the border will pick up the color scheme of the page, which is typically a gray color. To create

> NOTE Alert readers will note that the tables in Figures 5.1 through 5.4 had borders around them. I did this by adding the **border** attribute to the example code, to make the table cells easier to discern.

a colored border, use the **bordercolor** attribute, followed by the hexadecimal code or color name (within quotation marks).

For example, to create a 2-pixel blue border, use this code:

```
<table border="2" bordercolor="blue">
```

You can also add a background color or graphic to your entire table. You do this with the **bgcolor** and **background** attributes.

You add the **bgcolor** attribute to the <table> tag, and then specify the color number or name, like this (for a light gray background):

```
<table bgcolor="#CCCCCC">
```

To use a graphic as a background image for your table, you employ the **<background>** attribute. Just set the value for the attribute to the full URL of the image file you want to use, like this:

```
<table background="URL">
```

Naturally, you can combine all the <table> attributes into a vary long tag, to create tables with sophisticated formatting. For example, here's the code for a table that's 500 pixels wide, centered on the page, with a 1-pixel blue border and a light gray background:

```
<table align="center" width="500" border="1"
bordercolor="blue" bgcolor="#CCCCCC">
```

When you take it one piece at a time, it's pretty easy.

Sizing and Formatting Individual Cells Within a Table

Not only can you format your table as a whole, you can also format each cell within the table individually. This is how you put borders around specific sections of your listing, or shade the background of selected sections.

We'll start with the simple act of sizing a cell. You do this by employing the **width** attributed within the <td> tag. You follow the same rules as with <table> sizing, specifying either a specific width in pixels, or the width as a percentage of the total table. For example, to size a cell as 50% of the total table width, you use this code:

```
<td width="50%">
```

To add a border to a table cell, you first have to specify a border width for the entire table. Then you can change the color of the border for the specific cell, by using the **bordercolor** attribute within the <td> tag, like this:

```
<table border="1">
<td bordercolor="green">
```

Shading the background of a cell is as simple as adding the **bgcolor** attribute to the **<td>** tag, like this:

<td bgcolor="*color*">

Finally, you can use a graphic image as the background for any single cell by using the **background** attribute to the **<td>** tag, and then specifying the full URL and filename of the image file, like this:

<table background="*URL*">

How does this work in practice? Figure 5.5 shows a single-row, two-column table where one of the cells has a shaded background and the other doesn't. Here's the code for the complete table:

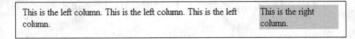

FIGURE 5.5

Shading just one cell in a table.

```
<table align="center" width="75%">
<tr>
  <td width="75%">
  This is the left column. This is the left column.
  This is the left column.
  </td>
  <td width="25%" bgcolor="#CCCCCC">
  This is the right column.
  </td>
</tr>
</table>
```

HTML Codes You *Can't* Use in Your eBay Listings

All of the HTML codes we've discussed so far are codes that fit within the body area of an HTML page. In proper HTML coding, this area is enclosed within the **<body>** and **</body>** tags. But the body isn't the only area of the page; there is also a head area, enclosed within **<head>** and **</head>** tags.

I haven't mentioned anything about the **<body>** tag yet, because you don't have to include it in your HTML code. In fact, you *can't* include it in your HTML code. That's because eBay provides its own HTML code for rest of the item listing page (including the head), and automatically inserts the code you provide into its pre-existing **<body>** section. If you were to include a **<body>** tag in your HTML code, that would create a page with two **<body>** tags—which could result in all manner of HTML confusion, and probably not display correctly on all web browsers.

To that end, you should only use those HTML codes that normally reside between the **<body>** and **</body>** tags. Any codes that need to be inserted into the **<head>** area are not allowed. For example, all **<meta>** and **<style>** tags, all embedded style sheets, and most JavaScript code work within the head section of the page, and thus can't be used in an eBay listing.

Prohibited HTML Code

So what codes can't you use in your auction templates? Here's a short list:

<base>
<basefont>
<body>
<head>
<html>
<link>
<meta>
<style>
<title>

Note that these are all valid HTML tags used when creating full web pages—but not when creating eBay listings.

The thing to remember is that you can only insert that HTML code that exists between the **<body>** and **</body>** tags—without including the **<body>** and **</body>** tags themselves. So if you're copying code from an HTML editor (which we'll discuss later in this chapter), copy only that code between these two **<body>** tags.

Prohibited JavaScript Code

In addition to straight HTML, eBay also doesn't allow use of many JavaScript functions. While eBay's HTML editor won't stop you from inserting the JavaScript code (and, in fact, the code might actually work within your eBay listing), if eBay catches you at it—and they will—you're likely to get your auction cancelled and your account suspended.

The particular types of scripts that eBay prohibits include the code used to do the following:

- Redirect the user to a page outside of the eBay site

NOTE   JavaScript is a special scripting language used to create various types of web page effects.

- Drop or read a cookie on any eBay page
- Calls remote scripts and pages
- Changes registry entries on the user's computer
- Writes data to the user's hard drive
- Launches pop-up windows
- Automatically posts to scripts in eBay
- Loads any binary program on the user's computer (with the notable exception of Flash content)
- Overwrites any area on the eBay listing page outside of the item description area

CAUTION This last prohibition also affects use of a second **<body>** tag or CSS **<style>** tags in an attempt to override the item page's default background color and fonts.

Why doesn't eBay like this type of JavaScript code? It's simple; these particular scripts can be used for malicious purposes. eBay wants to keep users on the eBay site, and not subject them to unwanted pop-ups and spyware. So don't do it!

Applying Advanced Formatting with Cascading Style Sheets

The HTML standard is continually evolving, and in fact has evolved far beyond simple **<b>** and **<p>** tags. One of the newer extensions to the HTML language is called *extensible HTML* or *XHTML*. What's cool about XHTML is that it uses something called *cascading style sheets*, or CSS, to more fully describe the appearance of web pages. And, not surprisingly, you can use CSS code to create your eBay item listings—within certain limits.

How CSS Works

The way CSS works is to universally define the look of specific elements on a page, so that whenever you use an element (such as an **<h1>** tag), the predefined attributes are applied. When you define a page element with CSS, that definition overrides the default page settings in the user's web browser. By using CSS, you don't have to apply the **<font>** tag and its associated attributes every time you want to format text on the page; just apply a predefined CSS element, instead.

Attributes are defined in CSS by means of a *rule.* Each rule includes the name of the attribute followed by a property and the value for that property.

For example, you might want to define an attribute so that all paragraph text consists of 8 point type. The rule for that attribute would be as follows:

font-size: 8pt

Note how the value for each property follows a colon (:). You can put a space between the colon and the value, as I've done here, or close up the space; either approach is allowed. Once you define the attribute in this fashion, all text enclosed within the attribute containers will be 8 point type.

> **NOTE** The properties and values assigned to an attribute are called the *declaration*.

You can also declare multiple properties within a single rule. Just make sure you separate each property with a semicolon (;). For example, to define an attribute as both 8 point and red, you use this code:

font-size: 8pt; color: red

Three Ways to Apply a Style Sheet

The CSS standard defines three different ways to apply a cascading style sheet, only one of which can be used in your eBay listings. That's because one of the methods uses the **<head>** of the HTML document (which eBay won't let you do), and a second references a separate style sheet file (which eBay also won't let you do).

The method of defining a style sheet within the **<head>** of an HTML page uses what is called a *global* or *embedded style sheet*. With this approach, all the attribute declarations are placed in the **<head>** of the document, within **<style>** and **</style>** container tags. If you remember, the **<style>** tag is one of those tags that is prohibited by eBay; this is why. So using an embedded style sheet is out of the question.

> **NOTE** Some sellers like to employ the **<style>** tag to universally change the attributes on the entire eBay listing page. While this technically will work, if eBay catches you they'll cancel your listing—and possibly bring disciplinary action against your account.

Also out of the question is using a *linked style sheet*. This approach requires the creation of a separate .CSS file that contains all the attributes and declarations, and is called from within the main HTML page by the **<link>** tag. Once again, sharp-eyed readers will recall that the **<link>** tag is banned by eBay, because it refers to a page (actually, the .CSS file) that is stored outside the eBay system. So you can't used linked style sheets.

This leaves us with the final, not quite so versatile method of defining styles that employs *local* or *inline style sheet* declarations. These inline declarations apply only to specific text on the page, and are used in place of **<font>** tags to specify font size, color, and so on.

You create an inline style sheet declaration by using the **style** attribute within any attribute tag, such as the **<p>**, **<h1>**, and **<img>** tags. The declarations are treated as attribute values, and placed within master quotation marks.

For example, let's say you want to format an **<h1>** heading with centered alignment. You could simply surround the heading with **<center>** and **</center>** tags, or you could use the following CSS code:

```
<h1 style="text-align: center">
This is the centered heading</h1>
```

All text within the **<h1>** and **</h1>** container tags would thus be centered on the page.

You can, of course, gang multiple CSS rules together in a single **style** attribute. Suppose that you wanted to format a particular paragraph with green 12-point boldface Arial type. Here's how you'd do it with CSS:

```
<p style="font-size: 12pt; color: green; font-weight: bold;
font-family: Arial">This is the text to format.</p>
```

Note that each declaration includes a separate "property: value" combination, and that the declarations are separated by semicolons.

CSS Properties

So what are the CSS properties you can declare using the **style** attribute? Table 5.3 presents some of the most common CSS properties.

Table 5.3 CSS Properties

Property	Description
background-color	Specifies a color for the background of a page or page element
background-image	Specifies an image file used for the background of a page or page element
border-color	Sets the color of a border
border-style	Sets the style of a border, from the following list: **none**, **hidden**, **dotted**, **dashed**, **solid**, **double**, **groove**, **ridge**, **inset**, and **outset**
border-width	Sets the width of a border, as either **thin**, **medium**, or **thick**; can also be used to set a precise width, in pixels
color	Specifies the color of selected text
font-family	Specifies the type face
font-size	Specifies the type size, in points
font-style	Sets the style of a font, as either **normal**, **italic**, or **oblique**
font-weight	Sets the weight of a font, as either **normal**, **bold**, **bolder**, or **lighter**
height	Specifies the height of an element

Property	Description
margin-bottom	Sets the bottom margin of an element, in pixels or as a percentage
margin-left	Sets the left margin of an element, in pixels or as a percentage
margin-right	Sets the right margin of an element, in pixels or as a percentage
margin-top	Sets the top margin of an element, in pixels or as a percentage
padding-bottom	Sets the bottom padding of an element, in pixels or as a percentage
padding-left	Sets the left padding of an element, in pixels or as a percentage
padding-right	Sets the right padding of an element, in pixels or as a percentage
padding-top	Sets the top padding of an element, in pixels or as a percentage
text-align	Specifies the alignment of selected text: **left**, **right**, **center**, or **justify**
text-decoration	Adds the following decoration to selected text: **none**, **underline**, **overline**, **line-through**, or **blinking**
text-indent	Specifies how much the first line of a paragraph is indented, in pixels or as a percentage
text-transform	Used to control the case of selected text: **none**, **capitalize**, **uppercase**, or **lowercase**
width	Specifies the width of an element

These are just a few of the many CSS properties that you can employ when creating HTML auction templates—but they're enough to do pretty much all we'll need to do. We'll discuss any additional properties that come up throughout the book if and when they arise.

> **NOTE** Want to learn more about CSS? Then check out *Sams Teach Yourself HTML and CSS in 24 Hours, 7th Edition* by Dick Oliver and Michael Morrison (Sams, 2005), available wherever computer books are sold.

Why Use CSS Instead of Straight HTML?

Given the limitations that eBay forces on the use of CSS (inline only), what advantages are there to using CSS over traditional HTML tags?

Well, in many instances, there is no benefit. If all you're doing is changing font size or color, you might as well use the old-fashioned <font> tag instead of the CSS **style** attribute approach. That's why a lot of the template code you'll find in this book is basic HTML, nothing fancy.

That said, CSS does allow some more sophisticated formatting that you can't do with straight HTML. For example, with CSS you can define the **margin-left** property, which helps to distance text from the left margin. You can't do this with the <font> tag, and it's useful for positioning text on the page. As another example, CSS lets you define specific font size in points, where you only get relative sizing with the **size** attribute in the **<font>** tag. Again, if you need a more precise design, CSS is the way to go.

How to Create Your HTML Code

Okay, so you think you know how to write some basic HTML code. The question is, what program do you use to write that code—and how do you get the code into your eBay item listing?

Using eBay's HTML Editor

If you're inserting a small amount of HTML code, there's no reason not to use the HTML editor included as part of eBay's sell your item process. Just go to the Describe Your Item page, scroll down to the Description box, and click the View HTML link. When the box changes to the HTML editor view, as shown in Figure 5.6, enter your code in the box. You can switch back to normal text editing mode to view the results of your code.

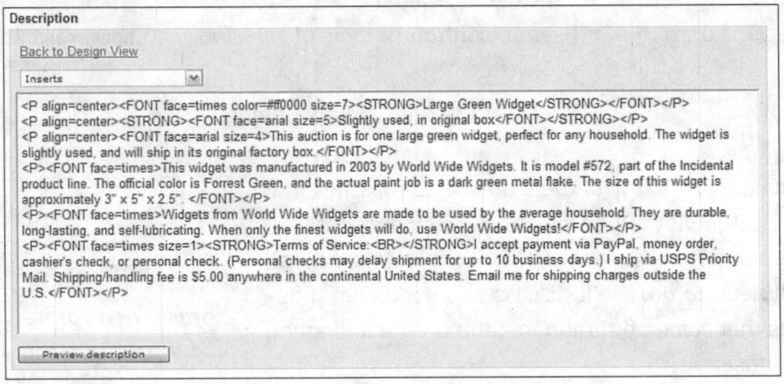

Description

Back to Design View

Inserts

<P align=center><FONT face=times color=#ff0000 size=7><STRONG>Large Green Widget</STRONG></FONT></P>
<P align=center><STRONG><FONT face=arial size=5>Slightly used, in original box</FONT></STRONG></P>
<P align=center><FONT face=arial size=4>This auction is for one large green widget, perfect for any household. The widget is slightly used, and will ship in its original factory box.</FONT></P>
<P><FONT face=times>This widget was manufactured in 2003 by World Wide Widgets. It is model #572, part of the Incidental product line. The official color is Forrest Green, and the actual paint job is a dark green metal flake. The size of this widget is approximately 3" x 5" x 2.5". </FONT></P>
<P><FONT face=times>Widgets from World Wide Widgets are made to be used by the average household. They are durable, long-lasting, and self-lubricating. When only the finest widgets will do, use World Wide Widgets!</FONT></P>
<P><FONT face=times size=1><STRONG>Terms of Service:
</STRONG>I accept payment via PayPal, money order, cashier's check, or personal check. (Personal checks may delay shipment for up to 10 business days.) I ship via USPS Priority Mail. Shipping/handling fee is $5.00 anywhere in the continental United States. Email me for shipping charges outside the U.S.</FONT></P>

Preview description

FIGURE 5.6

Entering simple HTML code into eBay's HTML editor.

Even if you're creating more complex code, you still need to use eBay's HTML editor. That's because the HTML editor is how you get your HTML code into your item listing. You'll want to copy the code from whatever HTML editing program you're using, and paste it into the HTML editor box on the Describe Your Item page.

Using Text Editors for HTML

That said, when you're creating a lot of HTML code—or want to reuse your code in multiple auctions—using the HTML editor won't get the job done. Instead, you'll want to use a dedicated text editing or HTML editing program.

The advantage of using a text editor—such as Windows Notepad or WordPad—is that it's free and relatively easy to do. You'll have to enter all your HTML code by hand, as shown in Figure 5.7, and then save the resulting file as a normal .TXT file. Once your code is complete, highlight it all and copy it; you can then paste it into eBay's Describe Your Item page, as previously discussed.

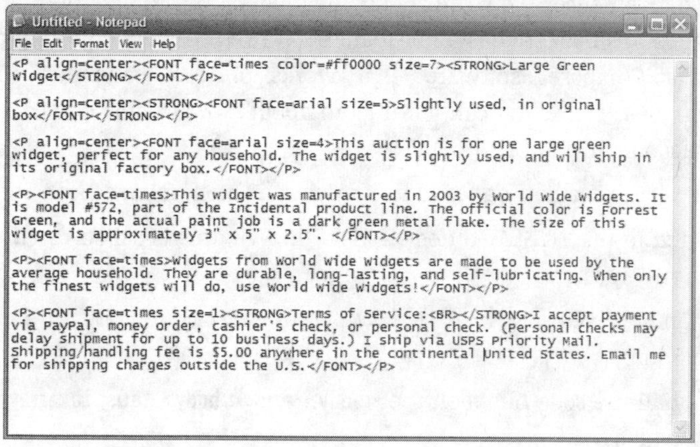

FIGURE 5.7

Using Windows Notepad to write HTML code.

Note that you need to save your HTML code in a .TXT file, not in a .DOC format file, like Microsoft Word uses. That's because Word files contain hidden formatting commands that play havoc with the basic text you need for HTML. This is why I don't recommend using Microsoft Word to write your HTML; while it's doable (assuming you save your results in a .TXT file) it's just too tempting to save your code in Word's default .DOC format, which is a no-no.

Once you save your code in a .TXT file, it's easy enough to reopen the .TXT file to reuse the basic code for future auctions. When you do this, you've created a reusable auction template—which is the best way to ensure consistently great-looking eBay auction listings over time.

Using Third-Party HTML Editors

Of course, entering all that HTML code by hand is a lot of hard work. That's why some eBay sellers prefer to use a dedicated HTML editing program to do the coding for them. These programs let you design your page or eBay listing in a WYSIWYG (What You See Is What You Get) environment, and then automatically generate the necessary HTML code behind the design.

CD-ROM There are lots of HTML editing programs you can use for this purpose. They range from free or low-cost programs such as 1st Page 2000 (www.evrsoft.com) and AceHTML (software.visicommedia.com/en/products/acehtmlfreeware/), to high-priced, high-end programs such as Microsoft FrontPage (www.microsoft.com/frontpage/) and Macromedia Dreamweaver (www.macromedia.com/software/dreamweaver/).

For your convenience, we've included the Nvu HTML editing program on the CD that accompanies this book. Nvu is a full-featured WYSIWYG web authoring program, based on the Mozilla Composer software, that works on any computer platform—Windows, Macintosh, even Linux. You can learn more about Nvu at www.nvu.com, or just start it up from the accompanying CD.

To use Nvu (or any other) editor to design your auction, follow these steps:

1. Switch to the WYSIWYG design view (in Nvu, this is called the Normal view) to design your listing.

2. When your design is complete, switch to HTML code view (in Nvu, this is called the Source view).

3. Copy all the code between the **<body>** and **</body>** tags, but not including those tags.

4. Paste this code into the Description box (in HTML view) on eBay's Describe Your Item page.

It's Step 3 that's the important one. When you use a freestanding HTML editor, you have to take care to copy only that code in the **<body>** section of the document. You should also avoid any special effects, JavaScript code, or CSS code that requires code within the **<head>** section of the document. Remember—you're inserting your code into eBay's pre-existing **<body>** section. Any code that falls outside the body is unusable!

Testing Your HTML Code

It's happened to all of us. You spend an hour or so designing a great-looking HTML template, but when you paste it into your eBay Describe Your Item page, it doesn't look the way you planned. Something is wrong with your code!

I won't go into the complex issue of debugging HTML code (that's for a dedicated HTML book!), but I will show you how to find out if your code works before you paste it into your eBay description. The key is to use an HTML practice board—a website that lets you paste in your HTML code and then displays the results of that code. If your code works, great; if not, it's time to do a little editing.

There are many practice boards on the web, including the aptly named Practice Board (www.practiceboard.com) and Zoicks HTML Practice Board (www.zoicks.com/practice.htm). But the one I really like is the auctionSupplies.com Practice Board (auctionsupplies.com/practice/ebay.shtml), shown in Figure 5.8. That's because this practice board not only shows you the results of your HTML code, it places those results within a mock eBay item listing, as shown in Figure 5.9. This way you'll know if your code interferes in any way with the display of the basic eBay listing page. It's a great approach, and (like all the other practice boards) totally free for you to use.

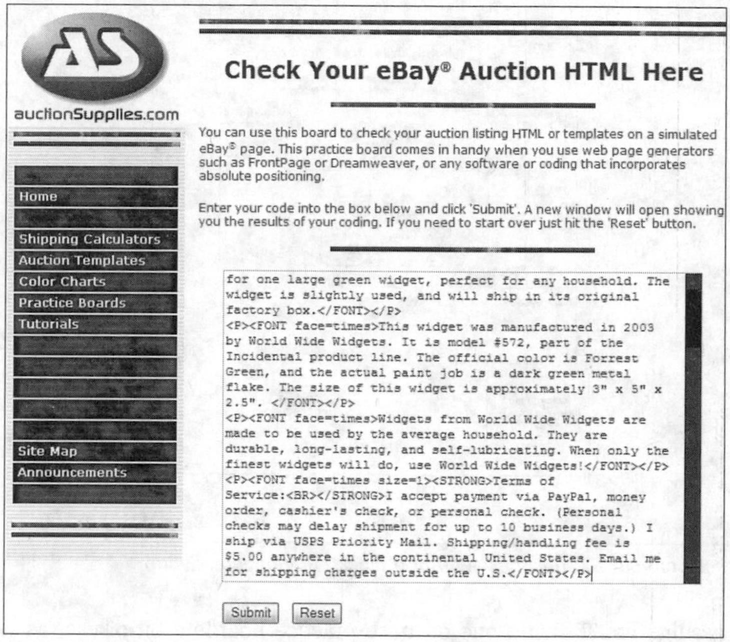

FIGURE 5.8

Test your HTML at the auctionSupplies.com Practice Board.

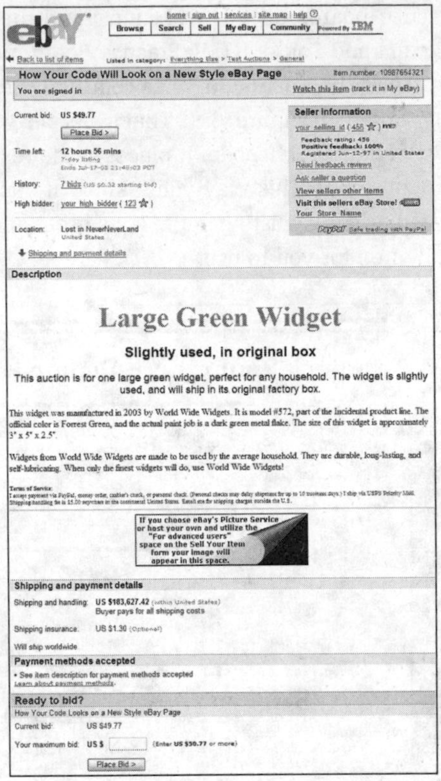

FIGURE 5.9

Displaying the results of your HTML codes—within a mock eBay auction listing.

And I assume you'll giving one of these practice boards a bit of use, as we move toward designing all manner of HTML auction templates. We'll start in the next chapter, where you'll learn how to create a variety of text-based templates—using the very same HTML codes you learned earlier in this chapter.

Creating Text-Based HTML Auction Templates

We'll begin our foray into HTML auction templates by presenting a variety of text-based templates. We start with the all-text approach for two reasons. First, it's relatively simple—at least compared to later templates that feature graphics, links, tables, and such. Second, you'll use the techniques presented here to create more sophisticated templates; consider these text-based templates to be the building blocks for the fancier templates you'll create in later chapters.

In this chapter and throughout the rest of the book, I'll show an example of the template being presented, and follow that with the HTML code to create the template. You can type the code directly into your text editor or eBay's Description form, replacing the default text with your own item description. And, to make things even easier, the code for all these templates is available on the accompanying CD; just copy the code into your text editor and you're good to go.

Creating Simple Text Descriptions

For now, I'll assume that you can insert simple text formatting commands, like **<strong>** or **<b>** for boldface or **<em>** or **<i>** for italic. You can use these simple tags to highlight important words and phrases within your main description text.

That assumed, we'll jump right in and create some text descriptions (no titles yet) with very simple formatting.

Template 6.1: Centered Text

CD-ROM We'll start with a very simple all-text template, with centered default Times Roman text, as shown in Figure 6.1. This template is identical to the standard text-based eBay item description, except that the text is centered instead of being left-aligned. Some people prefer item listings to be centered on the page, which is why this is a popular approach.

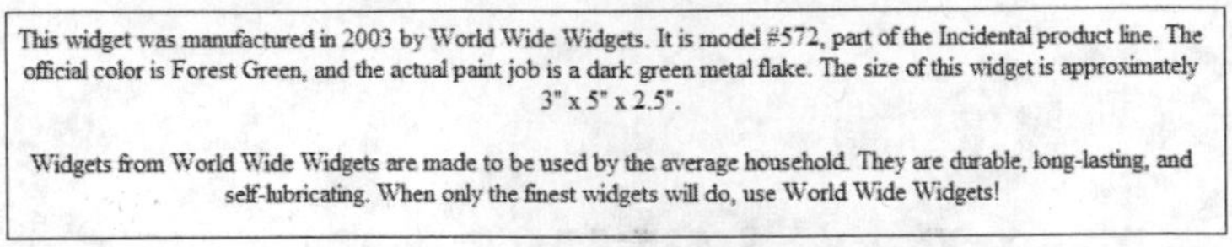

> This widget was manufactured in 2003 by World Wide Widgets. It is model #572, part of the Incidental product line. The official color is Forest Green, and the actual paint job is a dark green metal flake. The size of this widget is approximately 3" x 5" x 2.5".
>
> Widgets from World Wide Widgets are made to be used by the average household. They are durable, long-lasting, and self-lubricating. When only the finest widgets will do, use World Wide Widgets!

FIGURE 6.1

Centered text.

Now, there are two ways to code this template. The first uses simple HTML and the <center> tag, like this:

```
<center>
<p>
This is the first paragraph of the description
</p>

<p>
This is the second paragraph of the description
</P
</center>
```

The second approach uses Cascading Style Sheet (CSS) rules to define each paragraph with centered text, using the **style** attribute and the **text-align: left** declaration. Here's how this code looks:

```
<p style="text-align: center">
This is the first paragraph of the description
</p>

<p style="text-align: center">
This is the second paragraph of the description
</p>
```

You get the same results with either approach—and, in this instance, the simplicity of plain HTML may be preferable to the relative complexity of CSS. But in other instances, you'll find that CSS is a little more efficient, and a lot more accurate in how it defines various attributes—which is why I present this template with both approaches.

> CAUTION Too much centered text becomes difficult to read. For that reason, try to avoid using too many long text paragraphs with this particular template.

Template 6.2: Left-Aligned Text with Bulleted List

CD-ROM When you're selling an item with a long list of dimensions, accessories, features, or benefits—or, in the case of music CDs, an extensive track list—one neat way to present this type of information is in a bulleted list. Template 6.2, shown in Figure 6.2, contains such a list.

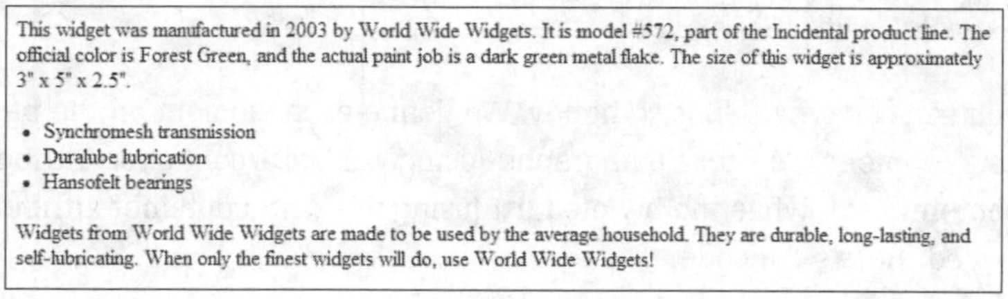

> This widget was manufactured in 2003 by World Wide Widgets. It is model #572, part of the Incidental product line. The official color is Forest Green, and the actual paint job is a dark green metal flake. The size of this widget is approximately 3" x 5" x 2.5".
>
> • Synchromesh transmission
> • Duralube lubrication
> • Hansofelt bearings
>
> Widgets from World Wide Widgets are made to be used by the average household. They are durable, long-lasting, and self-lubricating. When only the finest widgets will do, use World Wide Widgets!

FIGURE 6.2

Left-aligned text with a bulleted list.

If you remember your HTML, you know that creating a bulleted list is relatively easy, thanks to the **<ul>** list container tag and individual **<li>** line item tags. Here's how to code it:

```
<p>
This is the first paragraph of the description
</p>


<ul>
<li>This is the first bullet</li>
<li>This is the second bullet</li>
<li>This is the third bullet</li>
</ul>


<p>
This is the final paragraph of the description
</p>
```

Template 6.3: Centered Text with Left-Aligned Bulleted List

CD-ROM What if you want to include a bulleted list within a description that uses centered text? Well, you probably don't want to center your bulleted list, as unaligned bullets look really strange. Instead, you want to left-align the bulleted list within the centered description text, as we do with Template 6.3 (shown in Figure 6.3).

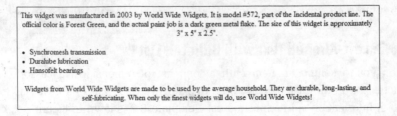

FIGURE 6.3

Centered text with a left-aligned bulleted list.

Here you can see why CSS is so handy. We define each element on the page with its own distinct alignment. The text paragraphs (using the **<p>** container attribute) are defined with centered text, while the bulleted list (using the **<ul>** container attribute) is defined as left-aligned. Here's the code:

```
<p style="text-align: center">
This is the first paragraph of the description
</p>

<ul style="text-align: left">
<li>This is the first bullet</li>
<li>This is the second bullet</li>
<li>This is the third bullet</li>
</ul>

<p style="text-align: center">
This is the final paragraph of the description
</p>
```

Template 6.4: Centered Text with Centered, Non-Bulleted List

CD-ROM Okay, so maybe you don't like the look of centered text with a left-aligned list. Just for you, Template 6.4 (shown in Figure 6.4) presents a non-bulleted list that's centered on the page, just like the rest of the text.

> This widget was manufactured in 2003 by World Wide Widgets. It is model #572, part of the Incidental product line. The official color is Forest Green, and the actual paint job is a dark green metal flake. The size of this widget is approximately 3" x 5" x 2.5".
>
> Synchromesh transmission
> Duralube lubrication
> Hansofelt bearings
>
> Widgets from World Wide Widgets are made to be used by the average household. They are durable, long-lasting, and self-lubricating. When only the finest widgets will do, use World Wide Widgets!

FIGURE 6.4

Centered text with a centered, non-bulleted list.

Creating a non-bulleted list involves a bit of a workaround, as the HTML standard doesn't include a code for non-bulleted lists. Instead, we use a single paragraph for the entire list, but put each list item on a separate line within the paragraph, using the **
** tag to force line breaks after each item. Here's how the code works:

```
<p style="text-align: center">
This is the first paragraph of the description
</p>

<p style="text-align: center">
This is the first list item<br>
This is the second list item<br>
This is the third list item
</p>

<p style="text-align: center">
This is the final paragraph of the description
</p>
```

Template 6.5: Left-Aligned Text with a Section Divider

CD-ROM If you have two or more discrete sections within your description, you might want to visually separate the sections with horizontal rules or lines. That's what we do in this template, shown in Figure 6.5.

You add horizontal rules to your listings by using the **<hr>** code. Just insert the code between the two paragraphs you want to separate, as done in the following code:

```
<p>
This is the first paragraph of the description
</p>
```

> CAUTION A horizontal line can serve as a kind of speed bump for anyone reading your listing. Make sure you really want the reader to pause as he moves from section to section, otherwise forgo the horizontal rule approach.

```
<hr>

<p>
This is the second paragraph of the description
</p>
```

> This widget was manufactured in 2003 by World Wide Widgets. It is model #572, part of the Incidental product line. The official color is Forest Green, and the actual paint job is a dark green metal flake. The size of this widget is approximately 3" x 5" x 2.5".
>
> Widgets from World Wide Widgets are made to be used by the average household. They are durable, long-lasting, and self-lubricating. When only the finest widgets will do, use World Wide Widgets!

FIGURE 6.5

Left-aligned text with a section divider.

Note that in this template, the section divider rule extends across the entire page. To limit the width of the divider, you need to add a **width** attribute to the **<hr>** tag, as we'll do in Template 6.6.

Template 6.6: Centered Text with a Narrow Section Divider

CD-ROM Template 6.5 presented left-aligned text with a horizontal rule. In Template 6.6, shown in Figure 6.6, we apply the horizontal rule to centered text.

> This widget was manufactured in 2003 by World Wide Widgets. It is model #572, part of the Incidental product line. The official color is Forest Green, and the actual paint job is a dark green metal flake. The size of this widget is approximately 3" x 5" x 2.5".
>
> Widgets from World Wide Widgets are made to be used by the average household. They are durable, long-lasting, and self-lubricating. When only the finest widgets will do, use World Wide Widgets!

FIGURE 6.6

Centered text with a narrow section divider.

What's slightly different about this template is that we don't want the horizontal line to spread across the entire page. Sometimes you can improve readability by using a rule that is less wide than the rest of the listing, thus adding some white space on either side of the line. That's what we do here, by adding the **width** attribute to the **<hr>** tag, and defining the width at 50% of the available page width. Here's the code:

```
<center>

<p>
This is the first paragraph of the description
</p>
```

```
<hr width="50%">

<p>
This is the second paragraph of the description
</p>
</center>
```

Working with Titles and Subtitles

A detailed auction template contains more than just the text description, of course. You want to preface the descriptive text with a title—and, perhaps, a subtitle as well. The easiest way to add titles and subtitles is to use HTML **<h1>** and **<h2>** heading tags, as you'll see with the next batch of templates.

Template 6.7: Left-Aligned Title with Left-Aligned Text

CD-ROM Our first title template is as simple as you can get. We take the standard eBay left-aligned Times Roman text description, and add a left-aligned Times Roman title, as shown in Figure 6.7.

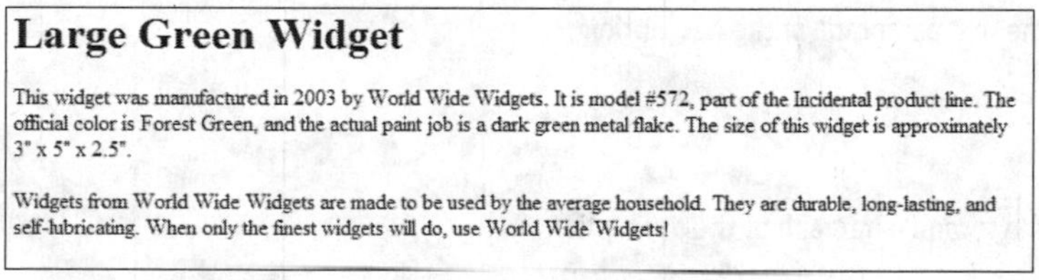

Large Green Widget

This widget was manufactured in 2003 by World Wide Widgets. It is model #572, part of the Incidental product line. The official color is Forest Green, and the actual paint job is a dark green metal flake. The size of this widget is approximately 3" x 5" x 2.5".

Widgets from World Wide Widgets are made to be used by the average household. They are durable, long-lasting, and self-lubricating. When only the finest widgets will do, use World Wide Widgets!

FIGURE 6.7

Left-aligned title with left-aligned text.

The code for this simple title template is equally simple. All you have to do is add the text for your title within the **<h1>** and **</h1>** heading container tags, like this:

```
<h1>This is the title</h1>

<p>
This is the first paragraph of the description
</p>

<p>
This is the second paragraph of the description
</p>
```

Template 6.8: Centered Title with Centered Text

CD-ROM If you prefer both your title and description centered, this is the template for you. As you can see in Figure 6.8, there's nothing fancy here, just centered text and title elements.

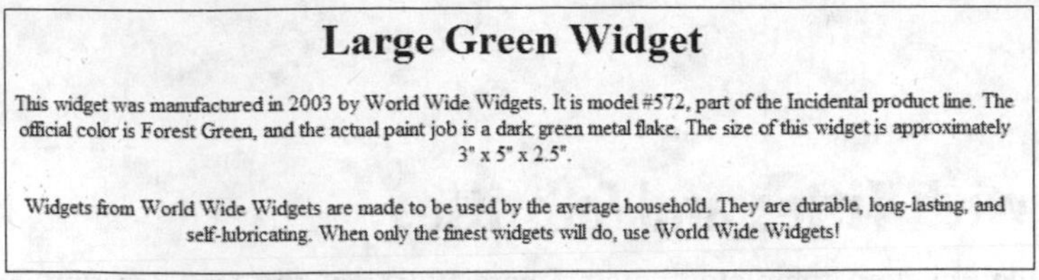

Large Green Widget

This widget was manufactured in 2003 by World Wide Widgets. It is model #572, part of the Incidental product line. The official color is Forest Green, and the actual paint job is a dark green metal flake. The size of this widget is approximately 3" x 5" x 2.5".

Widgets from World Wide Widgets are made to be used by the average household. They are durable, long-lasting, and self-lubricating. When only the finest widgets will do, use World Wide Widgets!

FIGURE 6.8

Centered title with centered text.

There are two ways to code this particular template. The first approach uses simple HTML and the **<center>** tag, like this:

```
<center>
<h1>This is the title</h1>

<p>
This is the first paragraph of the description
</p>

<p>
This is the second paragraph of the description
</p>
</center>
```

The second approach uses CSS code to define each element as centered:

```
<h1 style="text-align: center">This is the title</h1>

<p style="text-align: center">
This is the first paragraph of the description
</p>

<p style="text-align: center">
This is the second paragraph of the description
</p>
```

Template 6.9: Centered Title with Left-Aligned Text

CD-ROM The previous template is all well and good, but remember my admonition about including too much centered body text. Still, having a centered title is a nice effect—so let's combine the best of both worlds by centering the title while left-aligning the descriptive text, as shown in Figure 6.9.

Large Green Widget

This widget was manufactured in 2003 by World Wide Widgets. It is model #572, part of the Incidental product line. The official color is Forest Green, and the actual paint job is a dark green metal flake. The size of this widget is approximately 3" x 5" x 2.5".

Widgets from World Wide Widgets are made to be used by the average household. They are durable, long-lasting, and self-lubricating. When only the finest widgets will do, use World Wide Widgets!

FIGURE 6.9

Centered title with left-aligned text.

This is another example of how CSS makes things easy. Just add a CSS **style** attribute to each page element, and specify the appropriate **text-align** property, like this:

```
<h1 style="text-align: center">This is the title</h1>

<p style="text-align: left">
This is the first paragraph of the description
</p>

<p style="text-align: left">
This is the second paragraph of the description
</p>
```

Template 6.10: Left-Aligned Title and Subtitle with Left-Aligned Text

CD-ROM Sometimes a one-line title isn't enough of a lead-in for your auction listing. If you find yourself wanting to tell potential buyers just a little bit more before they get to the detailed description, add a subtitle below your title, like the one in Figure 6.10.

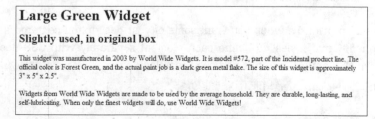

FIGURE 6.10

Left-aligned title and subtitle with left-aligned text.

This template goes with left-aligned title, subtitle, and description. As such, we don't need to specify any alignment, as all elements are left-aligned by default. We do, however, code the subtitle as a level-two heading with the **<h2>** code; a level-two heading is a little smaller than the level-one title.

Here's the code:

```
<h1>This is the title</h1>

<h2>This is the subtitle</h2>

<p>
This is the first paragraph of the description
</p>

<p>
This is the second paragraph of the description
</p>
```

Template 6.11: Centered Title and Subtitle with Left-Aligned Text

CD-ROM This template is for sellers who like centered titles (and subtitles), with left-aligned descriptive text, as shown in Figure 6.11. As in the previous example, we'll use the **<h2>** tag for the subtitle.

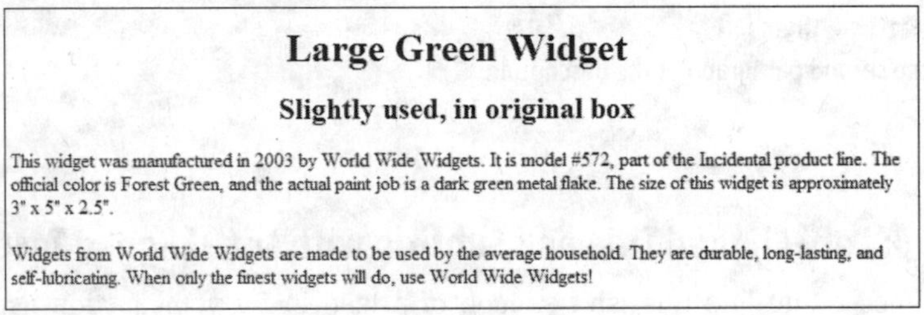

FIGURE 6.11

Centered title and subtitle with left-aligned text.

As I've said previously, when you want some of your description centered and some of it left-aligned, I find it best to define each element separately with CSS declarations. So here's the CSS approach to this particular template:

```
<h1 style="text-align: center">This is the title</h1>

<h2 style="text-align: center">This is the subtitle</h2>
```

```
<p style="text-align: left">
This is the first paragraph of the description
</p>

<p style="text-align: left">
This is the second paragraph of the description
</p>
```

Working with Different Type Faces and Sizes

By default, eBay displays all the text in your item description using Times Roman font. Times Roman is a nice font, but it isn't the only font you can use—and it may not be the most effective for your purposes. You can elect to display your text in any font face you like; you can even use different type faces for different elements in your listing.

You should, however, use a little self-control when using fonts for your item listing. While changing fonts from here to there might be fun (and relatively easy, as you'll see), combining too many different fonts within an item listing looks garish. To that end, you may want to make an initial font choice at the beginning of your description and leave it the same throughout the entire listing.

CAUTION Just because you have a specific font installed on your computer doesn't necessarily mean that all potential buyers who'll be viewing your listing have the same font installed on their PCs. If you change fonts in your listing, change to a common font that is likely to be preinstalled on all personal computers. Arial, Times Roman, and Verdana are always safe bets; choosing something more obscure might mean that your listing displays unpredictably on other computers.

Template 6.12: Arial Title and Description

CD-ROM eBay's default Times Roman font is a serif font, meaning that most letters have a short cross stroke at the ends. Serif type is easy to read in long passages, which is why it is used for most books (like this one) and magazine articles. However, it is not the most dynamic type face for headings and titles; for those elements, many page designers prefer a sans-serif font (without the cross strokes), such as Arial or Helvetica. To that end, this template changes the entire text of your item listing—both the title and description—to Arial, as shown in Figure 6.12.

Large Green Widget

This widget was manufactured in 2003 by World Wide Widgets. It is model #572, part of the Incidental product line. The official color is Forest Green, and the actual paint job is a dark green metal flake. The size of this widget is approximately 3" x 5" x 2.5".

Widgets from World Wide Widgets are made to be used by the average household. They are durable, long-lasting, and self-lubricating. When only the finest widgets will do, use World Wide Widgets!

FIGURE 6.12

Arial title and description.

The simple way to do this is to enclose all the title and description text within **<font>** and **</font>** container tags, with the **face="arial"** attribute, like this:

```
<font face="arial">
<h1 style="text-align: center">This is the title</h1>

<p style="text-align: left">
This is the first paragraph of the description
</p>

<p style="text-align: left">
This is the second paragraph of the description
</p>
</font="arial">
```

That said, a cleaner way of achieving the same effect is to add a second rule to all the **style** attributes, defining **font-family: Arial**. This CSS-based code looks like this:

```
<h1 style="text-align: center; font-family: Arial">
This is the title</h1>

<p style="text-align: left; font-family: Arial">
This is the first paragraph of the description
</p>

<p style="text-align: left; font-family: Arial">
This is the second paragraph of the description
</p>
```

Template 6.13: Arial Title and Times Roman Description

 CD-ROM Given that a serif font is easier to read for body text and a sans-serif font is more dynamic for titles and headings, let's try mixing the two by using Arial text for the title and Times Roman for the description. The resulting template is shown in Figure 6.13.

Large Green Widget

This widget was manufactured in 2003 by World Wide Widgets. It is model #572, part of the Incidental product line. The official color is Forest Green, and the actual paint job is a dark green metal flake. The size of this widget is approximately 3" x 5" x 2.5".

Widgets from World Wide Widgets are made to be used by the average household. They are durable, long-lasting, and self-lubricating. When only the finest widgets will do, use World Wide Widgets!

FIGURE 6.13

Arial title and Times Roman description.

This is another instance where the slightly complicated layout instructions are easier to implement with CSS code, such as the following:

```
<h1 style="text-align: center; font-family: Arial">
This is the title</h1>

<p style="text-align: left; font-family: Times Roman">
This is the first paragraph of the description
</p>

<p style="text-align: left; font-family: Times Roman">
This is the second paragraph of the description
</p>
```

Template 6.14: Verdana Title and Description

CD-ROM Verdana is a common sans-serif font that isn't as widely used as it might be. Because it's a little weightier than Arial, I find Verdana a perfect choice for both titles and body text, as you can see in Figure 6.14.

Large Green Widget

This widget was manufactured in 2003 by World Wide Widgets. It is model #572, part of the Incidental product line. The official color is Forest Green, and the actual paint job is a dark green metal flake. The size of this widget is approximately 3" x 5" x 2.5".

Widgets from World Wide Widgets are made to be used by the average household. They are durable, long-lasting, and self-lubricating. When only the finest widgets will do, use World Wide Widgets!

FIGURE 6.14

Verdana title and description.

While we could code this one with a master **<font face="verdana">** code, I find it cleaner to use CSS declarations instead. Here's how this code looks:

```
<h1 style="text-align: center; font-family: Verdana">
This is the title</h1>

<p style="text-align: left; font-family: Verdana">
This is the first paragraph of the description
</p>

<p style="text-align: left; font-family: Verdana">
This is the second paragraph of the description
</p>
```

Template 6.15: Extra-Large Bold Title

CD-ROM The **<h1>** HTML tag creates large, bold text. But what if you want your title to be even larger and bolder—as shown in Figure 6.15?

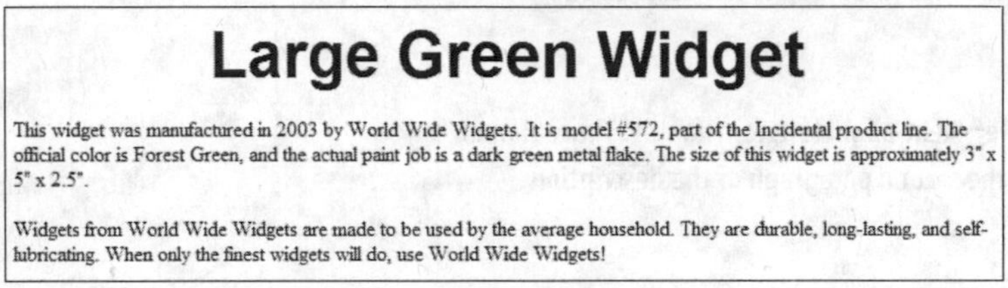

FIGURE 6.15

Extra-large bold title.

There are two solutions to this challenge. The first approach takes the standard **<h1>** tag and enhances it, by using the **<strong>** tag and the **size="6"** attribute within the **<font>** tag, like this:

```
<font size="6"><strong>
<h1 style="text-align: center; font-family: Arial">
This is the title</h1></strong></font>

<p style="text-align: left; font-family: Times Roman">
This is the first paragraph of the description
</p>

<p style="text-align: left; font-family: Times Roman">
This is the second paragraph of the description
</p>
```

The only problem with this approach is that it only pumps the title text up to about 24 points. The key to making the title even larger is to use CSS declarations within the <h1> attribute tag. Using CSS, we can define a precise type size (36 points) and bold weight.

```
<h1 style="text-align: center; font-family: Arial;
font-size: 36pt; font-weight: bold">This is the title</h1>
```

```
<p style="text-align: left; font-family: Times Roman">
This is the first paragraph of the description
</p>
```

```
<p style="text-align: left; font-family: Times Roman">
This is the second paragraph of the description
</p>
```

Template 6.16: Large Times Roman Description Text

CD-ROM This template is for those potential buyers who may have poor eyesight—which, as the eBay population ages, includes more and more people. What we want to do is bump the standard body text up a few points, to make it larger and more legible, as shown in Figure 6.16.

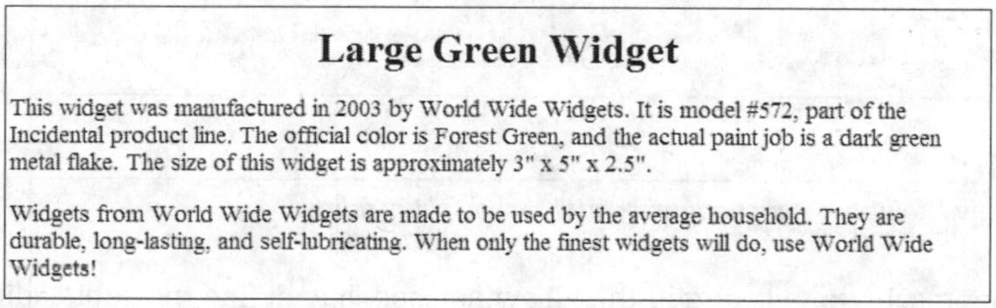

Large Green Widget

This widget was manufactured in 2003 by World Wide Widgets. It is model #572, part of the Incidental product line. The official color is Forest Green, and the actual paint job is a dark green metal flake. The size of this widget is approximately 3" x 5" x 2.5".

Widgets from World Wide Widgets are made to be used by the average household. They are durable, long-lasting, and self-lubricating. When only the finest widgets will do, use World Wide Widgets!

FIGURE 6.16

Large Times Roman description text.

This code uses CSS declarations to increase the font size in the body of the description to 14 points—which should be large enough to see for most people with vision problems or aging eyesight.

```
<h1 style="text-align: center">This is the title</h1>
```

```
<p style="font-size: 14pt">
This is the first paragraph of the description
</p>
```

```
<p style="font-size: 14pt">
This is the second paragraph of the description
</p>
```

Of course, when you use this CSS-based approach, you can specify any type size you want. If 14 points isn't big enough, bump it up to 16 points. Or if 14 points is too large, go with a slightly smaller 12 points instead.

> **NOTE** You can get a similar effect by using the standard HTML `<font>` tag and specifying a font size of "4" or larger. The only drawback to the straight HTML approach is that you're only defining relative type size; you can't specify a precise type size, as you can with CSS.

Template 6.17: Arial Title and Times Roman Description with Arial Section Subheadings

CD-ROM If you have a really long text description (more than two paragraphs), it can be a little difficult to hold readers' attention. To that end, "chunking" your text into two or more discrete sections, each with its own subhead, helps improve readability—which ultimately improves the salability of your item. Figure 6.17 shows what I mean.

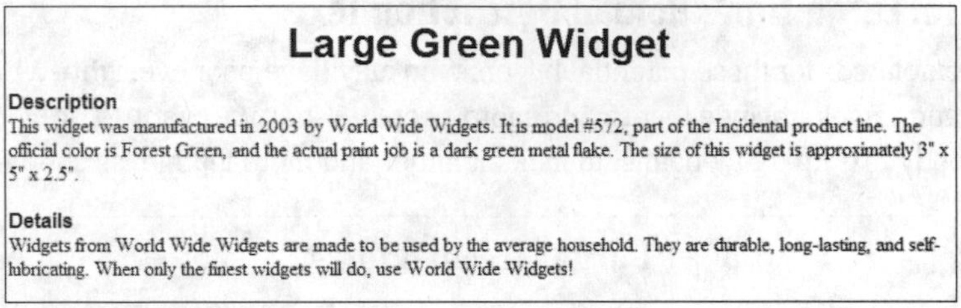

Large Green Widget

Description
This widget was manufactured in 2003 by World Wide Widgets. It is model #572, part of the Incidental product line. The official color is Forest Green, and the actual paint job is a dark green metal flake. The size of this widget is approximately 3" x 5" x 2.5".

Details
Widgets from World Wide Widgets are made to be used by the average household. They are durable, long-lasting, and self-lubricating. When only the finest widgets will do, use World Wide Widgets!

FIGURE 6.17

Arial title and Times Roman description, with Arial section subheadings.

The approach we're taking in the following code is to define the subheadings as 12 point bold Arial text. We also want the subheads to be visually connected to the following section text, which we do by using the **margin-bottom** and **margin-top** CSS rules, applied to the section headers and section text, respectively. Setting each of these properties 0" positions the section header directly on top of the following section text, which helps the reader register the discrete sections in the description.

```
<h1 style="text-align: center; font-family: Arial">
This is the title</h1>

<p style="text-align: left; font-family: Arial;
font-size: 12pt; font-weight: bold; margin-bottom:0">
Subheading 1
</p>
```

```
<p style="text-align: left; font-family: Times Roman;
margin-top:0">
This is the first paragraph of the description
</p>


<p style="text-align: left; font-family: Arial;
font-size: 12pt; font-weight: bold; margin-bottom:0">
Subheading 2
</p>


<p style="text-align: left; font-family: Times Roman;
margin-top:0">
This is the second paragraph of the description
</p>
```

Template 6.18: Times Roman Title and Description with Larger Overview Section

CD-ROM Back in Chapter 1, "The Good, the Bad, and the Ugly: Do's and Don'ts for Effective Auction Listings," I discussed the value of including a brief overview section before the main descriptive text in your listing. This overview section is even more effective when it's formatted slightly differently from the following text—for example, with slightly larger type, as shown in Figure 6.18.

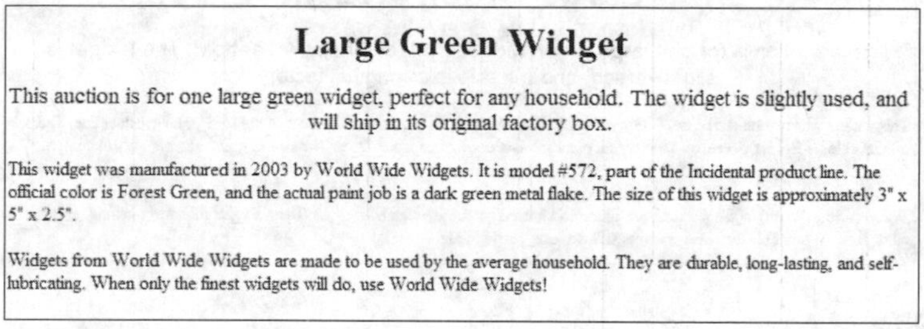

Large Green Widget

This auction is for one large green widget, perfect for any household. The widget is slightly used, and will ship in its original factory box.

This widget was manufactured in 2003 by World Wide Widgets. It is model #572, part of the Incidental product line. The official color is Forest Green, and the actual paint job is a dark green metal flake. The size of this widget is approximately 3" x 5" x 2.5".

Widgets from World Wide Widgets are made to be used by the average household. They are durable, long-lasting, and self-lubricating. When only the finest widgets will do, use World Wide Widgets!

FIGURE 6.18

Times Roman title and description with larger overview section.

The coding approach for this template is deceptively simple. All you have to do is define the overview paragraph with a slightly larger type size than the descriptive text—in this instance 14 points versus 12 points.

```
<h1 style="text-align: center">This is the title</h1>

<p style="text-align: center; font-size: 14pt">
This is the overview paragraph.
</p>

<p style="text-align: left; font-size: 12pt">
This is the first paragraph of the description
</p>

<p style="text-align: left; font-size: 12pt">
This is the second paragraph of the description
</p>
```

Template 6.19: Arial Title with Times Roman Description and Larger Arial Overview Section

CD-ROM Building on the previous template, you can even more effectively set off the overview paragraph by using a different type face than used in the main description. In the template shown in Figure 6.19, we use Arial type for the overview (and title), and Times Roman for the main description.

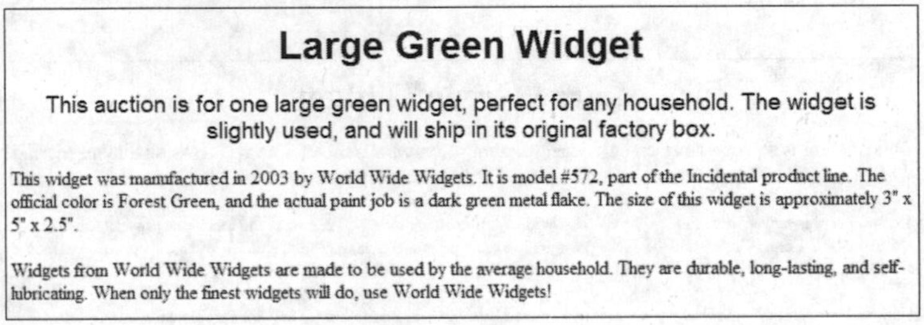

> ### Large Green Widget
>
> This auction is for one large green widget, perfect for any household. The widget is slightly used, and will ship in its original factory box.
>
> This widget was manufactured in 2003 by World Wide Widgets. It is model #572, part of the Incidental product line. The official color is Forest Green, and the actual paint job is a dark green metal flake. The size of this widget is approximately 3" x 5" x 2.5".
>
> Widgets from World Wide Widgets are made to be used by the average household. They are durable, long-lasting, and self-lubricating. When only the finest widgets will do, use World Wide Widgets!

FIGURE 6.19

Arial title, Times Roman description, and larger Arial overview section.

Again, the font size shift is effected by using CSS declarations for each element on the page, as shown here:

```
<h1 style="text-align: center; font-family: Arial">
This is the title</h1>

<p style="text-align: center; font-size: 14pt;
font-family: Arial">
```

```
This is the overview paragraph.
</p>

<p style="text-align: left; font-size: 12pt;
font-family: Times Roman">
This is the first paragraph of the description
</p>

<p style="text-align: left; font-size: 12pt;
font-family: Times Roman">
This is the second paragraph of the description
</p>
```

Template 6.20: Times Roman Title and Description with Smaller Terms of Service

 CD-ROM The overview paragraph isn't the only text element that you might want to put in a different type size. Some people call the terms of service (TOS) at the bottom of a listing the "fine print," which leads us to this template—with the TOS in smaller type than used for the main description, as shown in Figure 6.20.

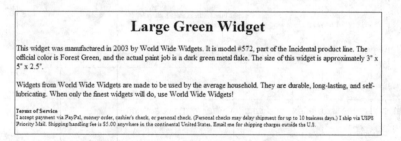

FIGURE 6.20

Times Roman title and description, with smaller terms of service.

This code uses CSS declarations to define the font size for each page element. We've also added a bold subhead for the TOS, which is accomplished by use of the **<strong>** tag for the first line of the TOS paragraph, which then leads (after a line break) for regular-strength text for the body of the TOS.

```
<h1 style="text-align: center">This is the title</h1>

<p style="text-align: left">
This is the first paragraph of the description
</p>
```

```
<p style="text-align: left">
This is the second paragraph of the description
</p>


<p style="text-align: left; font-size: 8pt">
<strong>Terms of Service</strong><br>
This is the terms of service.
</p>
```

Template 6.21: Arial Title with Times Roman Description and Smaller Arial Terms of Service

CD-ROM Another way to set off the TOS is to put it in a different type face. In this template, shown in Figure 6.21, we use Time Roman for the main description and a smaller Arial font for the TOS.

Large Green Widget

This widget was manufactured in 2003 by World Wide Widgets. It is model #572, part of the Incidental product line. The official color is Forest Green, and the actual paint job is a dark green metal flake. The size of this widget is approximately 3" x 5" x 2.5".

Widgets from World Wide Widgets are made to be used by the average household. They are durable, long-lasting, and self-lubricating. When only the finest widgets will do, use World Wide Widgets!

Terms of Service
I accept payment via PayPal, money order, cashier's check, or personal check. (Personal checks may delay shipment for up to 10 business days.) I ship via USPS Priority Mail. Shipping/handling fee is $5.00 anywhere in the continental United States. Email me for shipping charges outside the U.S.

FIGURE 6.21

Arial title, Times Roman description, and smaller Arial terms of service.

As you can see, the code for this template is similar to that for Template 6.20, with the addition of **font-family** properties for each page element.

```
<h1 style="text-align: center; font-family: Arial">
This is the title</h1>


<p style="text-align: left; font-family: Times Roman">
This is the first paragraph of the description
</p>


<p style="text-align: left; font-family: Times Roman">
This is the second paragraph of the description
</p>
```

```
<p style="text-align: left; font-size: 8pt;
font-family: Arial">
<strong>Terms of Service</strong><br>
This is the terms of service.
</p>
```

Working with Different Text Colors

Color is a good way to highlight important parts of your listing. You can put headings or subheadings in a different color or highlight selected words or phrases in the same manner. Don't use too many colors, however; if your ad looks like a rainbow, the color loses its ability to impact.

Template 6.22: Title in Different Color

CD-ROM Our first colorful template keeps the descriptive text in basic black (always a good idea; black is the most readable color when you have a white page background) but uses a different color for the listing title. The template as presented in Figure 6.22 displays the title in blue, but you can edit the code to use any color you like.

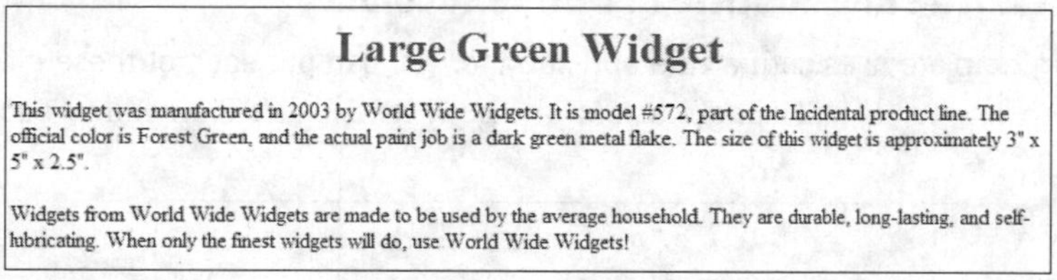

Large Green Widget

This widget was manufactured in 2003 by World Wide Widgets. It is model #572, part of the Incidental product line. The official color is Forest Green, and the actual paint job is a dark green metal flake. The size of this widget is approximately 3" x 5" x 2.5".

Widgets from World Wide Widgets are made to be used by the average household. They are durable, long-lasting, and self-lubricating. When only the finest widgets will do, use World Wide Widgets!

FIGURE 6.22

Title in a different color from the body text.

As with many of these effects, there are two ways to code this template. The first approach is to use the **<font>** tag for the heading accompanied by the **color** attribute, like this:

```
<font color="blue">
<h1 style="text-align: center">This is the title</h1>
</font>

<p style="text-align: left">
This is the first paragraph of the description
</p>
```

```
<p style="text-align: left">
This is the second paragraph of the description
</p>
```

The second way to do this is the all-CSS approach, using the **color** property, like this:

```
<h1 style="text-align: center; color: blue">
This is the title</h1>
```

```
<p style="text-align: left">
This is the first paragraph of the description
</p>
```

```
<p style="text-align: left">
This is the second paragraph of the description
</p>
```

Obviously, you can replace the "blue" color in this code with any color name or hexadecimal code.

Template 6.23: Title and Subtitle in Different Colors

CD-ROM If your template uses both a title and subtitle, you can put each of these elements in a different color—while still using black for the body text. Figure 6.23 shows such an approach.

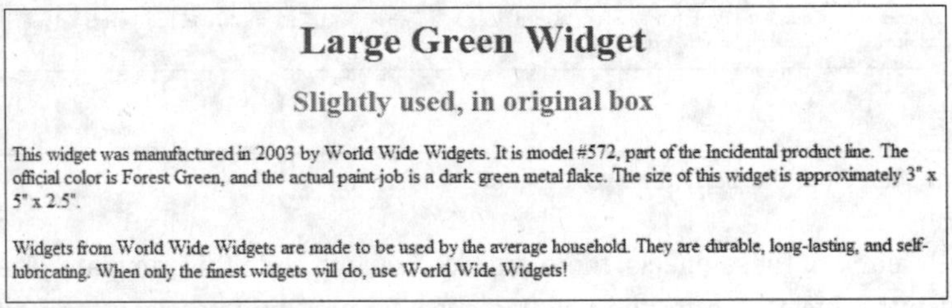

FIGURE 6.23

Title and subtitle in contrasting colors; black body text.

While this template code uses blue for the title and teal for the subtitle, you can choose any color combination you like. Try to avoid overly contrasting colors, however; a red title/ blue subtitle combination might look patriotic, but it's also a bit harsh on the eyes.

```
<h1 style="text-align: center; color: blue">
This is the title</h1>
<h2 style="text-align: center; color: teal">
This is the subtitle</h2>
```

```
<p style="text-align: left">
This is the first paragraph of the description
</p>


<p style="text-align: left">
This is the second paragraph of the description
</p>
```

Template 6.24: Overview Section in Different Color

 CD-ROM If you use an overview paragraph before your main item description, another way to set the overview apart from the main text is to put the overview in a different color. Figure 6.24 shows what this looks like.

Large Green Widget

This auction is for one large green widget, perfect for any household. The widget is slightly used, and will ship in its original factory box.

This widget was manufactured in 2003 by World Wide Widgets. It is model #572, part of the Incidental product line. The official color is Forest Green, and the actual paint job is a dark green metal flake. The size of this widget is approximately 3" x 5" x 2.5".

Widgets from World Wide Widgets are made to be used by the average household. They are durable, long-lasting, and self-lubricating. When only the finest widgets will do, use World Wide Widgets!

FIGURE 6.24

Black body text with the overview section in a different color.

This template uses red for the overview text. This may be a bit bright for some users, so feel free to edit the code with a different overview color. (You can also add the **color** property to the <h1> title code, if you want something other than a black title.)

```
<h1 style="text-align: center">This is the title</h1>


<p style="text-align: center; color: red; font-size: 14pt">
This is the overview section.
</p>


<p style="text-align: left">
This is the first paragraph of the description
</p>


<p style="text-align: left">
This is the second paragraph of the description
</p>
```

Template 6.25: Bulleted List in Different Color

CD-ROM Bulleted lists sometimes look better when displayed in a slightly contrasting color to the body text. That's what we do in Figure 6.25, where the bullet list is in green.

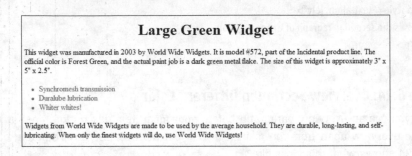

FIGURE 6.25

Black body text with a bulleted list in a different color.

As with all these color examples, feel free to change the color designation to something more pleasing to your eye. Also feel free to add the **color** property to the **<h1>** title tag.

<h1 style="text-align: center">This is the title</h1>

This is the first paragraph of the description

<ul style="text-align: left; color: green">
<li>This is the first bullet</li>
<li>This is the second bullet</li>
<li>This is the third bullet</li>
</ul>

This is the second paragraph of the description

Template 6.26: Terms of Service in Different Color

CD-ROM The terms of service is another page element that sometimes works better when it's in a different color than the description text. In this instance, you want the TOS to be less noticeable than the description, so you want to use a color that's not quite as vivid, as shown in Figure 6.26.

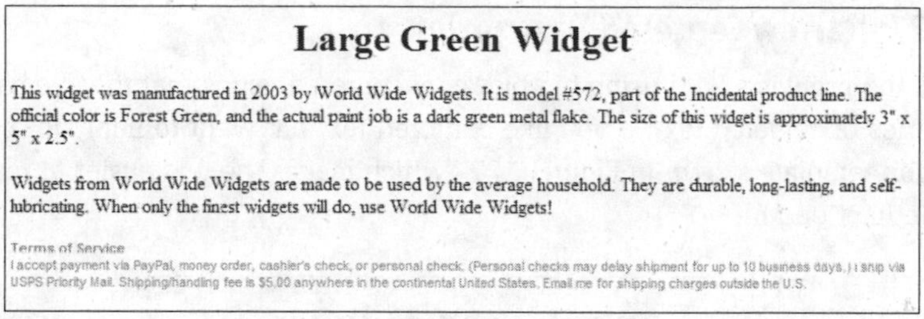

Large Green Widget

This widget was manufactured in 2003 by World Wide Widgets. It is model #572, part of the Incidental product line. The official color is Forest Green, and the actual paint job is a dark green metal flake. The size of this widget is approximately 3" x 5" x 2.5".

Widgets from World Wide Widgets are made to be used by the average household. They are durable, long-lasting, and self-lubricating. When only the finest widgets will do, use World Wide Widgets!

Terms of Service
I accept payment via PayPal, money order, cashier's check, or personal check. (Personal checks may delay shipment for up to 10 business days.) I ship via USPS Priority Mail. Shipping/handling fee is $5.00 anywhere in the continental United States. Email me for shipping charges outside the U.S.

FIGURE 6.26

Black body text with the terms of service in a different color.

For this template, I specified a medium gray color for the terms of service, which makes the TOS look subsidiary to the main text. Obviously, you can specify any color you like for the TOS; just replace *gray* with your color name or hexadecimal color of choice.

```
<h1 style="text-align: center">This is the title</h1>

<p style="text-align: left">
This is the first paragraph of the description
</p>

<p style="text-align: left">
This is the second paragraph of the description
</p>

<p style="text-align: left; font-size: 8pt;
font-family: Arial; color: gray">
<strong>Terms of Service</strong><br>
This is the terms of service.
</p>
```

Working with Widths and Margins

We'll end this chapter with a handful of templates that play around with text widths and margins. Why tinker with margins, you ask? Because putting a little white space here and there or using an inset for selected page elements helps both to divide your listing into separate sections and to subtly move the eye toward the most important elements on the page.

When it comes to making a text element wider or narrower, or insetting it from the left or right margin, we have to turn to cascading style sheet code. CSS lets us use **margin-left** and **margin-right** properties, which set the left and right margins for an element—something you can't easily do with traditional HTML.

Template 6.27: Narrow Centered Description

CD-ROM One of the problems with using big blocks of centered text is that the eye can't easily read long lines of centered text. If you like centered text but want to improve readability, consider the template shown in Figure 6.27—which makes the text easier to read by shortening the line length.

Large Green Widget

This widget was manufactured in 2003 by World Wide Widgets. It is model #572, part of the Incidental product line. The official color is Forest Green, and the actual paint job is a dark green metal flake. The size of this widget is approximately 3" x 5" x 2.5".

Widgets from World Wide Widgets are made to be used by the average household. They are durable, long-lasting, and self-lubricating. When only the finest widgets will do, use World Wide Widgets!

FIGURE 6.27

Wide title with narrow centered description.

This code makes liberal use of the **margin-left** and **margin-right** properties to set the left and right margins. We've specified a 250-pixel margin for both the left and right sides of the main text paragraphs, which creates a very narrow—and easily readable—centered description.

```
<h1 style="text-align: center">This is the title</h1>

<p style="text-align: center; margin-left: 250px;
margin-right: 250px">
This is the first paragraph of the description
</p>

<p style="text-align: center; margin-left:250px;
margin-right:250px">
This is the second paragraph of the description
</p>
```

Template 6.28: Wide Centered Description with Narrower Terms of Service

CD-ROM Another approach is to keep the text description at normal width and use a narrower text block for the terms of service, as shown in Figure 6.28. This helps to set off the TOS from the more important description text.

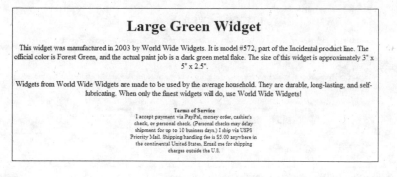

FIGURE 6.28

Centered description with narrower terms of service.

This code uses the **margin-left** and **margin-right** properties to set 250-pixel left and right margins for the TOS paragraph. Naturally, you can choose different margins as your tastes dictate.

```
<h1 style="text-align: center">This is the title</h1>

<p style="text-align: center">
This is the first paragraph of the description
</p>

<p style="text-align: center">
This is the second paragraph of the description
</p>

<p style="text-align: center; font-size: 8pt;
margin-left: 250px; margin-right: 250px">
<strong>Terms of Service</strong><br>
This is the terms of service
</p>
```

Template 6.29: Left-Aligned Description with Offset Terms of Service

CD-ROM Here's a template that uses left-aligned text but still manages to set the TOS apart from the description text. This is done by offsetting the TOS by 100 pixels; the TOS is still left-aligned, but now looks much more like a separate text element, as you can see in Figure 6.29.

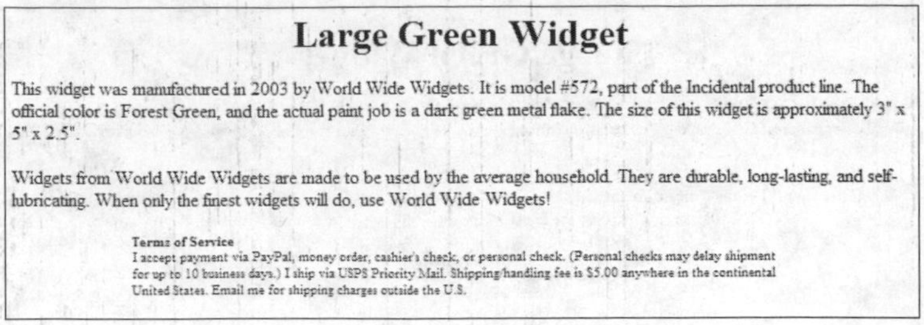

Large Green Widget

This widget was manufactured in 2003 by World Wide Widgets. It is model #572, part of the Incidental product line. The official color is Forest Green, and the actual paint job is a dark green metal flake. The size of this widget is approximately 3" x 5" x 2.5".

Widgets from World Wide Widgets are made to be used by the average household. They are durable, long-lasting, and self-lubricating. When only the finest widgets will do, use World Wide Widgets!

Terms of Service
I accept payment via PayPal, money order, cashier's check, or personal check. (Personal checks may delay shipment for up to 10 business days.) I ship via USPS Priority Mail. Shipping/handling fee is $5.00 anywhere in the continental United States. Email me for shipping charges outside the U.S.

FIGURE 6.29

Left-aligned description with an offset terms of service section.

The code for this template left-aligns all the text elements in the listing, save for the title. The TOS paragraph is defined by **margin-left** and **margin-right** properties to display more toward the middle of the page.

```
<h1 style="text-align: center">This is the title</h1>


<p style="text-align: left">
This is the first paragraph of the description
</p>


<p style="text-align: left">
This is the second paragraph of the description
</p>


<p style="text-align: left; font-size: 8pt;
margin-left: 100px; margin-right: 100px">
<strong>Terms of Service</strong><br>
This is the terms of service
</p>
```

Template 6.30: Wide Centered Overview with Narrower Left-Aligned Offset Description

CD-ROM This template uses different margins to give the overview paragraph a different look from the main text description. The key here is to use wider margins and larger type for the overview paragraph, and narrower margins (and regular-sized type) for the regular paragraphs. As you can see in Figure 6.30, this combination of large type and wider margins makes the overview look *much* bigger than the description—a very neat effect.

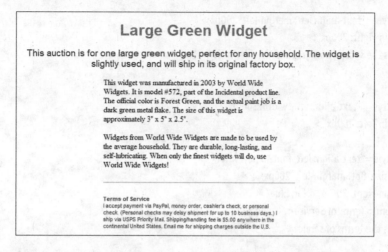

FIGURE 6.30

Wide centered overview paragraph with a narrower left-aligned offset description and terms of service.

Note that the code for this template incorporates a lot of different formatting effects from throughout this chapter. The title is formatted with centered, red, Arial text; the overview is formatted with centered, blue, 14 point Arial text; the description paragraphs are formatted with default size and font (Times Roman) but with 200-pixel left and right margins; there's a 300 point horizontal rule before the terms of service; and the TOS itself is formatted as 8 point blue Arial text with 200-pixel left and right margins (same as the description). It's a good example of how all these various codes can be grouped together to create complex effects.

```
<h1 style="text-align: center; font-family: Arial;
color: red">This is the title</h1>

<p style="text-align: center; font-size: 14pt; color: blue;
font-family: Arial">
This is the overview paragraph.
</p>

<p style="text-align: left; margin-left: 200px;
margin-right: 200px">
This is the first paragraph of the description
</p>
```

```
<p style="text-align: left; margin-left: 200px;
margin-right: 200px">
This is the second paragraph of the description
</p>

<hr style="text-align: left; width: 300pt;
margin-left: 200px">

<p style="text-align: left; font-family: Arial;
font-size: 8pt; margin-left: 200px;
margin-right: 200px; color: blue">
<strong>Terms of Service</strong><br>
This is the terms of service
</p>
```

Adding Pictures to Your Auction Templates

I don't have to remind you that you need to include at least one high-quality photo in all your auction listings. It's imperative that potential buyers see what you're selling before they decide to place their bids; for many products, this means that multiple photos are necessary.

While you could use eBay's standard picture services to add photos to your listings, it's a less-than-ideal solution—particularly if you're going to the effort to create a great-looking template for the rest of your listing. That's why it's important that you learn how to include photos within the body of your item description, via the use of HTML.

Using Pictures in Your Auction Listings

This isn't the place to go into the details on how to take great product photos; there are whole books devoted to that subject. Instead I'm going to focus on the mechanics of placing your photos within your item listings, and then present 20 templates that incorporate various types of photo displays.

Editing Your Photos

I'm going to assume that you've taken at least one really good photo of the item you're selling. The photo should be properly focused, composed so that the item is up front and center, big enough so you can see the necessary details, and properly lit so that it's neither too bright or too dark.

If your photo isn't quite perfect, you need to use a photo-editing program to do some touch-up work. There are lots of good photo editors out there, the most popular of which include:

- Adobe Photoshop (www.adobe.com)
- Adobe Photoshop Elements (www.adobe.com)
- IrfanView (www.irfanview.com)
- Paint Shop Pro (www.corel.com)
- Microsoft Digital Image (www.microsoft.com/products/imaging/)
- Roxio PhotoSuite (www.roxio.com)

NOTE To learn more about taking great eBay product photos, check out *Shooting for Dollars: Simple Photo Techniques for Greater eBay Profits* by Sally Wiener Grotta and Daniel Grotta (Peachpit Press, 2005).

CD-ROM To make your life a little easier, we've included a free copy of IrfanView on the CD that accompanies this book. This is a great program, very versatile, and very popular among experienced eBay sellers. You can use this program to do all manner of basic editing, including cropping, adjusting brightness and contrast, sharpening fuzzy edges, and so on. Use it to do both major and minor touchups before you insert your photos into your auction listings.

Sizing Your Photos

You can also use IrfanView to resize your photos for use in your auction listings. It's important that your photos aren't too small or too big—they need to be just right to display efficiently in your listings. Most pictures you take in a digital camera will come out too big to display in a web browser without scrolling, which is why you typically have to resize the photo to fit within the confines of a normal web page.

eBay recommends that you size your image to no more than 400 pixels wide by 300 pixels high. I think that's unnecessarily small, especially if you need to show fine detail, but you still need to keep in mind the resolution of a typical computer display.

CAUTION Resizing your photos is particularly important if you use eBay Picture Services, which will compress any larger pictures to fit within the 300 x 400 restriction. The results of this compression can be rather yucky-looking, which is one more reason *not* to use eBay Picture Services.

A good number of eBay users have their monitors set for 800 x 600 resolution, which means you need your photos to fit within these dimensions—no more than 800 pixels wide by 600 pixels high. And that's the max; you should probably try not to exceed 600 x 400, if you can.

You also need to optimize the file size of your images so that they don't take forever for people to download. This is especially important for your potential buyers who are using older computers, or are on a slower dial-up Internet connection. My recommendation is to keep your file size below 50KB, which results in reasonable downloads for most users. To reduce the file size, you can either resize the width and height or reduce the resolution (in pixels per inch). Most image editing software lets you perform either of these operations.

Embedding Images vs. Standard eBay Images

Now we come to the challenge of how to include your photos in your eBay item listings. I mentioned earlier that you could use eBay Picture Services, although this is less than an ideal solution. For one, eBay will charge you 15 cents for each picture you use, after the first. Second, when you use eBay Picture Services with your own customized auction template, the photos get inserted *after* your fancy item listing.

So if you want to use auction templates that incorporate photos within the description itself, you need to embed those images in the HTML code for the description. This requires you to host your photos on a separate website, and then point to the URLs of those photos within the HTML code.

In other words, you can't use the templates offered in this chapter if you use eBay's standard Picture Services hosting. You have to find another website to host your photos.

Finding a Picture Host

When it comes to picture hosting, you have a lot of options. First, if you have your own personal page on the web, you can probably upload your pictures to that web server. For example, if you have a personal page on Yahoo! GeoCities or Tripod, you should be able to upload your images to that site.

If you don't have a personal page but *could* have a personal page (via America Online or your Internet service provider), that's another potential place for you to upload picture files. If the company you work for has a web server, there's a chance it will let you use a little space there.

Then there are the dedicated picture hosting websites that offer a variety of picture hosting services, typically for a small fee—along the lines of $5 or so

> **TIP** eBay also offers a subscription-based picture hosting service, dubbed eBay Picture Manager. Picture Manager works a lot like a third-party picture host; you can store up to 50MB of image files for $9.99 per month, 125MB for $19.99 per month, or 300MB for $39.99 per month. (Prices are slightly less if you have an eBay Store.)

per month for 10MB or more of storage. This would let you store 200 images at a time, for less than half of what eBay would charge. Here are some of the most popular of these sites:

- Ándale Images (www.andale.com)
- Auction Pix Image Hosting (www.auctionpix.com)
- Photobucket (www.photobucket.com)
- PictureTrail (www.picturetrail.com)
- Vendio Image Hosting (www.vendio.com)

When you use a picture hosting service, you need to upload your picture files to the service before you create your eBay auction listings. The picture host will provide a URL for each photo you upload; you use that URL within the HTML code for your auction template, to point to the photos you want to use.

Adding Images Within Your Item Description

Now let's get down to business. We'll start with five basic eBay templates that include one or more photos in various places within your listing. All of these templates incorporate the HTML **<img>** tag, which is used to reference the location of a picture file stored elsewhere on the web.

> NOTE In most of these templates, you can include more or fewer photos simply by editing the HTML code to add or delete **<img>** tags.

Template 7.1: Pictures on Top

CD-ROM Our first template places one or more photos centered at the top of your auction listing, below the title but above the first paragraph, as shown in Figure 7.1. Naturally, you can edit this code to incorporate different font styles and alignment, as discussed in Chapter 6, "Creating Text–Based HTML Auction Templates."

For our example code, we'll include tags for two side-by-side photos. To use just a single photo, delete one of the **<img>** tags; to use more photos, insert one or more additional **<img>** tags.

Here's the code:

```
<h1 style="text-align: center">This is the title</h1>

<center>
<img src="URL1">
<img src="URL2">
</center>
```

```
<p style="text-align: left">
This is the first paragraph of the description
</p>


<p style="text-align: left">
This is the second paragraph of the description
</p>
```

FIGURE 7.1

One or more photos displayed between the title and the first paragraph of the description.

Obviously, you should replace *URL1* and *URL2* with the full URL and filename of each photo file. Also, know that if your photos are too large, the centered photos will wrap over to a second line. Using this basic code, it's your responsibility to size your photos appropriately beforehand; with two photos in a row, I'd recommend keeping the width of each to a maximum of 300 pixels. (You can force the 300-pixel width by adding the **width="300"** attribute to each of the **<img>** tags, like this: **<img src="URL" width="300">**.)

Template 7.2: Pictures on the Bottom

CD-ROM This next template is a variation of Template 7.1, with the photos centered below the description text. The result is shown in Figure 7.2.

As you can see, the code is very similar, with the **<img>** tags placed below the final paragraph. Replace *URL1* and *URL2* with the full URL and filename for each photo, of course. And, again, you can force a standard 300-pixel width by rewriting the **<img>** tags like this:

```
<img src="URL" width="300">.
<h1 style="text-align: center">This is the title</h1>

<p style="text-align: left">
This is the first paragraph of the description
</p>

<p style="text-align: left">
This is the second paragraph of the description
</p>

<center>
<img src="URL1">
<img src="URL2">
</center>
```

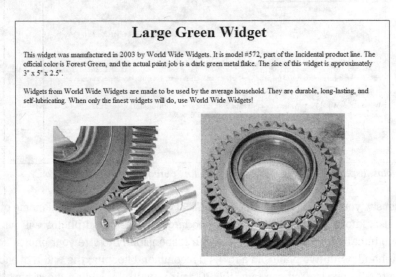

FIGURE 7.2

One or more photos displayed after the text description.

Template 7.3: Picture on the Left

CD-ROM This next template changes things up a bit, by inserting a picture in-line with the description text, as shown in Figure 7.3. In this instance, the photo is left-aligned, with the text wrapping around the picture.

For this template to work, the **<img>** tag must be inserted just after the **<p>** tag for the first paragraph, and before the start of the text itself. To wrap the text around the photo, the

`<img>` tag includes the **align="left"** attribute. We've also added just a little white space around the picture with the **hspace="5"** and **vspace="5"** attributes.

```
<h1 style="text-align: center">This is the title</h1>

<p style="text-align: left">
<img src="URL" align="left" hspace="5" vspace="5">
This is the first paragraph of the description
</p>

<p style="text-align: left">
This is the second paragraph of the description
</p>
```

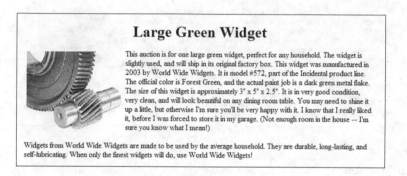

FIGURE 7.3

A single photo displayed to the left of the description text.

You can customize this template to add a second photo to the left of the second paragraph; just add a similar `<img>` tag inside the second paragraph's `<p>` tag. If you do this, make sure that the text for the first paragraph is long enough to extend past the bottom of the first picture; if not, the second photo will be displayed *to the right* of the first photo!

Template 7.4: Pictures on the Right

CD-ROM Now we'll create a flipped version of Template 7.3, with a single photo inserted to the right of the text description. As with the previous template, the text wraps around the photo. The result is shown in Figure 7.4.

The code for this template is identical to that of Template 7.3, except that the **align** attribute for the `<img>` tag is set to **"right"** instead of **"left"**. Amazing what changing one little attribute can do!

```
<h1 style="text-align: center">This is the title</h1>

<p style="text-align: left">
<img src="URL" align="right" hspace="5" vspace="5">
This is the first paragraph of the description
</p>

<p style="text-align: left">
This is the second paragraph of the description
</p>
```

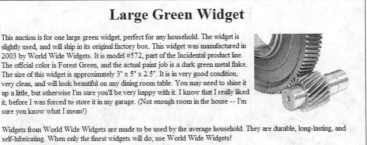

FIGURE 7.4

A single photo displayed to the right of the description text.

As with Template 7.3, you can insert a second photo by adding a similar **<img>** tag after the **<p>** tag for the second paragraph.

Adding Borders to Your Photos

When you apply cascading style sheet rules to the **<img>** tag, you can specify different types of borders to be displayed around your pictures. CSS allows a variety of different border attributes, as we'll discover in the next batch of templates. (You can, of course, add these CSS border attributes to any **<img>** tag used in any template in this chapter.)

Template 7.5: Picture with Thin Border

CD-ROM The first CSS border attribute we'll apply is that for a thin border, like the one shown in Figure 7.5. In this template, we apply the thin border to a single picture centered at the top of the item listing.

We actually have to apply two properties to the **style** attribute in the **<img>** tag. The first attribute, **border-style: solid**, specifies a solid border around the picture; the second attribute, **border-width: thin**, specifies that the solid border is a thin one.

```
<h1 style="text-align: center">This is the title</h1>

<center>
<img src="URL" style="border-style: solid;
border-width: thin">
</center>

<p style="text-align: left">
This is the first paragraph of the description
</p>

<p style="text-align: left">
This is the second paragraph of the description
</p>
```

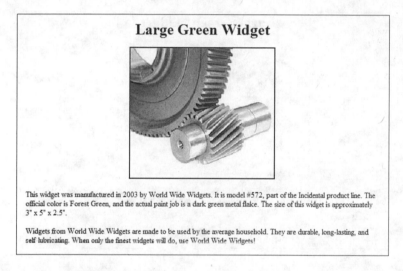

FIGURE 7.5

A single picture with a thin border.

Template 7.6: Picture with Thick Colored Border

CD-ROM This next template places a thicker, colored border around the photo, as shown in Figure 7.6.

The code for this template is similar to that of Template 7.5, except the **border-width: thin** code is replaced with **border-width: thick**. In addition, we define the color of the border by adding a third property to the **style** attribute in the **<img>** tag. This property is **border-color**, which you can define with any HTML color name or hexadecimal value.

```
<h1 style="text-align: center">This is the title</h1>

<center>
<img src="URL" style="border-style: solid;
border-width: thick; border-color: red">
</center>

<p style="text-align: left">
This is the first paragraph of the description
</p>

<p style="text-align: left">
This is the second paragraph of the description
</p>
```

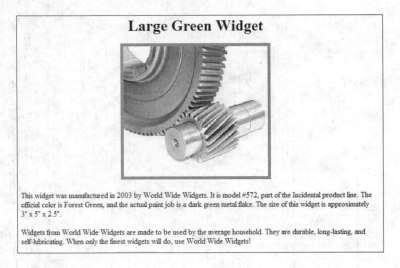

FIGURE 7.6

A single photo with a thick border

Template 7.7: Picture with Ridge Border

CD-ROM Thin and thick aren't the only border styles available. For this template, shown in Figure 7.7, we'll surround the photo with a ridge border, which adds a classy look to your listing.

The ridge border effect is accomplished by defining the **border-style** as **ridge** and the **border-width** as **thick**. You can, of course, make the ridge a different color, by adding the **border-color** property to the **style** attribute.

```
<h1 style="text-align: center">This is the title</h1>

<center>
<img src="URL" style="border-style: ridge;
border-width: thick">
</center>

<p style="text-align: left">
This is the first paragraph of the description
</p>

<p style="text-align: left">
This is the second paragraph of the description
</p>
```

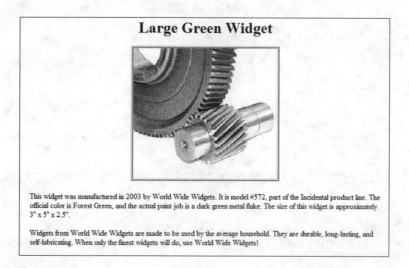

Large Green Widget

This widget was manufactured in 2003 by World Wide Widgets. It is model #572, part of the Incidental product line. The official color is Forest Green, and the actual paint job is a dark green metal flake. The size of this widget is approximately 3" x 5" x 2.5".

Widgets from World Wide Widgets are made to be used by the average household. They are durable, long-lasting, and self-lubricating. When only the finest widgets will do, use World Wide Widgets!

FIGURE 7.7

A single photo with a ridge border.

Applying Special Picture Effects

The previous seven templates use relatively simple picture effects—that is, all you have to do is dictate where on the page the photo will display, and that's what you get. That's well and good, but there are some fancier photo effects you can employ in your listings, which we'll examine next.

Template 7.8: Link to a Larger Picture

CD-ROM Some potential buyers are on high-speed broadband connections, and have no problems downloading large, high-resolution images. Other potential buyers are on slow dial-up connections that take forever to download large images. This is why, in general, you want to include only smaller images in your listings, so that your page loads acceptably for all potential buyers.

That doesn't mean, however, that having larger, higher-resolution photos available isn't a good idea. You just don't want to burden all potential buyers with those slow-to-download image files that require a higher-resolution desktop to display properly. To that end, you can choose to display a standard low-resolution photo in the listing itself, as shown in Figure 7.8, but then link to a higher-resolution photo, hosted on another website. When potential bidders click on the low-res photo, the high-res photo is displayed.

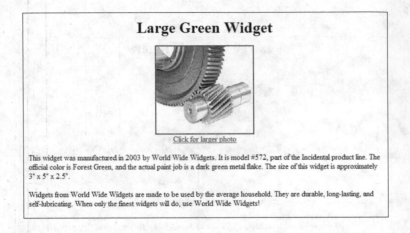

FIGURE 7.8

A small, low-resolution photo displayed in the body of the listing; click on the photo and a larger, higher-resolution photo is displayed.

This technique requires you to upload two different photos to your picture hosting service. In the following code, *URL-BIG* is the larger, higher-resolution photo, while *URL-SMALL* is the smaller, lower-resolution photo. The code is simple; all you do is add a link around the low-res photo to the high-res one.

```
<h1 style="text-align: center">This is the title</h1>

<center>
<a href="URL1"><img src="URL2"><BR>
Click for larger photo</a>
</center>
```

```
<p style="text-align: left">
This is the first paragraph of the description
</p>

<p style="text-align: left">
This is the second paragraph of the description
</p>
```

Note that we also added a "click for larger photo" text instruction under the photo. Clicking either the photo or the text will display the larger photo.

Template 7.9: Big Picture with Multiple Click-to-Display Buttons

CD-ROM Now we'll get really fancy. The template shown in Figure 7.9 displays a single large picture, with a row of buttons underneath. When a visitor clicks a button, the picture changes. It's a great way to display multiple photos in the limited space of an eBay item listing.

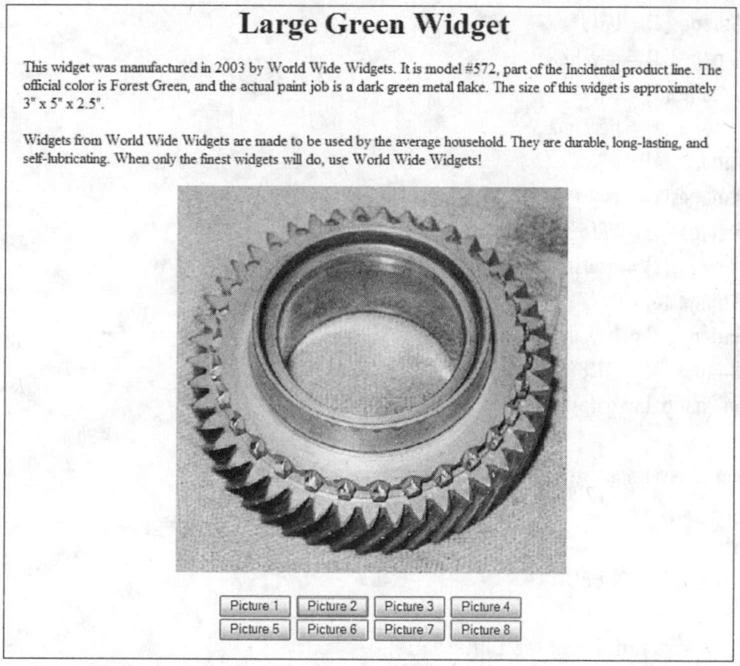

FIGURE 7.9

Displaying a single large picture with multiple click-to-display buttons.

The code for this trick is a trifle complex, so pay close attention. As written, the code creates eight buttons (for eight photos), but if you don't have that many you can cut the excess lines of code.

Start by putting the following code at the very beginning of your listing:

```
<!--BEGINNING OF FIRST CODE BLOCK-->
<!--INSERT AT THE VERY BEGINNING OF THE BODY SECTION-->
<script language="JavaScript">
var CachedImages
CachedImages = new Array(8)
CachedImages[0] = new Image
CachedImages[0]="URL1"
CachedImages[1] = new Image
CachedImages[1]="URL2"
CachedImages[2] = new Image
CachedImages[2]="URL3"
CachedImages[3] = new Image
CachedImages[3]="URL4"
CachedImages[4] = new Image
CachedImages[4]="URL5"
CachedImages[5] = new Image
CachedImages[5]="URL6"
CachedImages[6] = new Image
CachedImages[6]="URL7"
CachedImages[7] = new Image
CachedImages[7]="URL8"
function ChangeImage(n)
{
document.SpaceImage.src=CachedImages[n]
}
</script>
<!--END OF FIRST CODE BLOCK-->
```

Then use the following template code:

```
<!--REGULAR TEMPLATE CODE-->
<h1 style="text-align: center">This is the title</h1>

<p style="text-align: left">
This is the first paragraph of the description
</p>
```

NOTE In several of the following examples, you'll note lines of code that begin with an exclamation point following a left-bracket, like this: <!. This exclamation point code indicates a comment line—that is, a line that is not read as code, but is instead used to insert comments to anyone reading or editing the code.

```
<p style="text-align: left">
This is the second paragraph of the description
</p>
<!--END OF REGULAR TEMPLATE CODE-->

<!--BEGINNING OF SECOND CODE BLOCK-->
<!--INSERT WHERE YOU WANT THE PHOTOS TO APPEAR-->
<center>
<img src="URL1" name="SpaceImage" height="400">
</center>
<p>
<form name="ImageSelector">
<center>
<input type="button" value="Picture 1"
➥onClick="ChangeImage(0)">
<input type="button" value="Picture 2"
➥onClick="ChangeImage(1)">
<input type="button" value="Picture 3"
➥onClick="ChangeImage(2)">
<input type="button" value="Picture 4"
➥onClick="ChangeImage(3)"><br>
<input type="button" value="Picture 5"
➥onClick="ChangeImage(4)">
<input type="button" value="Picture 6"
➥onClick="ChangeImage(5)">
<input type="button" value="Picture 7"
➥onClick="ChangeImage(6)">
<input type="button" value="Picture 8"
➥onClick="ChangeImage(7)">
</center>
</form>
</p>
<!--END OF SECOND CODE BLOCK-->
```

NOTE If you try to test this code with pictures stored locally on your hard disk, it won't work. This code works only with pictures actually uploaded to a web server.

Whew—that's a lot of code! If you choose to adapt this code for use in other templates, know that there are two separate code blocks you have to deal with. The first code block should go at the very beginning of the **<body>** section—that is, it should be the initial code in your template. The second code block should be placed wherever you want the photos to display in your listing.

Template 7.10: Big Picture with Click-to-Enlarge Thumbnails

CD-ROM This next trick creates a similar picture effect, this time with thumbnails of the additional pictures below the main picture. As you can see in Figure 7.10, when the potential buyer clicks a thumbnail, the big picture changes to display the new picture.

FIGURE 7.10

A large master picture with multiple click-to-enlarge thumbnails.

This code requires you to create both large and small (thumbnail) versions of each of your photos. (The small versions of your pictures should be no more than 100 pixels wide.) The thumbnails are displayed in the picture grid; the large versions are displayed when you click the thumbnails.

```
<!--REGULAR TEMPLATE CODE-->
<h1 style="text-align: center">This is the title</h1>

<p style="text-align: left">
This is the first paragraph of the description
</p>
```

```html
<p style="text-align: left">
This is the second paragraph of the description
</p>
<!--END OF REGULAR TEMPLATE CODE-->

<!--BEGINNING OF PICTURE CODE-->
<table align="center" cellspacing="20" height="500">
<tr>
<td>
<center>
<img src="URL1-BIG" height="400" border="0"
alt name="the_pic"><br><br>
<a href="#"; onClick="document.the_pic.src='URL1-BIG';
➥return false;">
  <img src="URL1-SMALL" border="0"></a>
<a href="#"; onClick="document.the_pic.src='URL2-BIG';
➥return false;">
  <img src="URL2-SMALL" border="0"></a>
<a href="#"; onClick="document.the_pic.src='URL3-BIG';
➥return false;">
  <img src="URL3-SMALL" border="0"></a>
<a href="#"; onClick="document.the_pic.src='URL4-BIG';
➥return false;">
  <img src="URL4-SMALL" border="0"></a>
<a href="#"; onClick="document.the_pic.src='URL5-BIG';
➥return false;">
  <img src="URL5-SMALL" border="0"></a>
<a href="#"; onClick="document.the_pic.src='URL6-BIG';
➥return false;">
  <img src="URL6-SMALL" border="0"></a>
</center>
<p style="text-align: center; font-family: Arial;
font-weight: bold; font-size: 12pt">
Click on thumbnails to enlarge</p>
</td>
</tr>
</table>
<!--END OF PICTURE CODE-->
```

The picture code should be inserted wherever in your template you want to display the picture grid. Replace *URL1-BIG, URL2-BIG,* and so on with the URLs for your large pictures; replace *URL1-SMALL, URL2-SMALL,* and so on with the URLs for your thumbnail pictures.

Template 7.11: Scrolling Picture Slideshow

 CD-ROM This template features a scrolling slideshow of pictures, as shown in Figure 7.11. All the pictures for your listing will scroll by in a repeating loop—another good way to display multiple photos in a limited space.

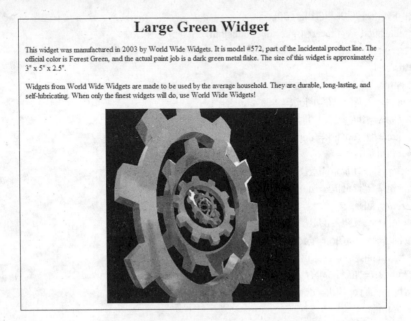

FIGURE 7.11

A scrolling picture slideshow.

To create this complex slideshow, we need to use some complex JavaScript code. This example allows for four photos; you can use more photos by adding extra **slideimages** lines, with consecutive numbering. Replace *URL1*, *URL2*, and so on with the URLs of your picture files. Make sure you place the slideshow code in your template where you want the slideshow to display.

```
<!--REGULAR TEMPLATE CODE-->
<h1 style="text-align: center">This is the title</h1>

<p style="text-align: left">
This is the first paragraph of the description
</p>

<p style="text-align: left">
This is the second paragraph of the description
```

```
</p>
<!--END OF REGULAR TEMPLATE CODE-->

<!--BEGINNING OF SLIDESHOW CODE-->
<script language="JavaScript1.2">

var scrollerwidth='400px'
var scrollerheight='400px'
var scrollerbgcolor='white'
var pausebetweenimages=3000

var slideimages=new Array()
slideimages[0]='<img src="URL1" border=0" height="400"
➥width="400">'
slideimages[1]='<img src="URL2" border=0" height="400"
➥width="400">'
slideimages[2]='<img src="URL3" border=0" height="400"
➥width="400">'
slideimages[3]='<img src="URL4" border=0" height="400"
➥width="400">'

var ie=document.all
var dom=document.getElementById

if (slideimages.length>1)
i=2
else
i=0

function move1(whichlayer){
tlayer=eval(whichlayer)
if (tlayer.left>0&&tlayer.left<=5){
tlayer.left=0
setTimeout("move1(tlayer)",pausebetweenimages)
setTimeout("move2(document.main.document.second)",
➥pausebetweenimages)
return
}
if (tlayer.left>=tlayer.document.width*-1){
tlayer.left-=5
setTimeout("move1(tlayer)",50)
```

```
}
else{
tlayer.left=parseInt(scrollerwidth)+5
tlayer.document.write(slideimages[i])
tlayer.document.close()
if (i==slideimages.length-1)
i=0
else
i++
}
}

function move2(whichlayer){
tlayer2=eval(whichlayer)
if (tlayer2.left>0&&tlayer2.left<=5){
tlayer2.left=0
setTimeout("move2(tlayer2)",pausebetweenimages)
setTimeout("move1(document.main.document.first)",
➡pausebetweenimages)
return
}
if (tlayer2.left>=tlayer2.document.width*-1){
tlayer2.left-=5
setTimeout("move2(tlayer2)",50)
}
else{
tlayer2.left=parseInt(scrollerwidth)+5
tlayer2.document.write(slideimages[i])
tlayer2.document.close()
if (i==slideimages.length-1)
i=0
else
i++
}
}

function move3(whichdiv){
tdiv=eval(whichdiv)
if (parseInt(tdiv.style.left)>0&&parseInt(tdiv.style.left)
➡<=5){
tdiv.style.left=0+"px"
```

```
setTimeout("move3(tdiv)",pausebetweenimages)
setTimeout("move4(scrollerdiv2)",pausebetweenimages)
return
}
if (parseInt(tdiv.style.left)>=tdiv.offsetWidth*-1){
tdiv.style.left=parseInt(tdiv.style.left)-5+"px"
setTimeout("move3(tdiv)",50)
}
else{
tdiv.style.left=scrollerwidth
tdiv.innerHTML=slideimages[i]
if (i==slideimages.length-1)
i=0
else
i++
}
}

function move4(whichdiv){
tdiv2=eval(whichdiv)
if (parseInt(tdiv2.style.left)>0&&parseInt(tdiv2.style.left)
➥<=5){
tdiv2.style.left=0+"px"
setTimeout("move4(tdiv2)",pausebetweenimages)
setTimeout("move3(scrollerdiv1)",pausebetweenimages)
return
}
if (parseInt(tdiv2.style.left)>=tdiv2.offsetWidth*-1){
tdiv2.style.left=parseInt(tdiv2.style.left)-5+"px"
setTimeout("move4(scrollerdiv2)",50)
}
else{
tdiv2.style.left=scrollerwidth
tdiv2.innerHTML=slideimages[i]
if (i==slideimages.length-1)
i=0
else
i++
}
}
```

```
function startscroll(){
if (ie||dom){
scrollerdiv1=ie? first2 : document.getElementById("first2")
scrollerdiv2=ie? second2 : document.getElementById
➡("second2")
move3(scrollerdiv1)
scrollerdiv2.style.left=scrollerwidth
}
else if (document.layers){
document.main.visibility='show'
move1(document.main.document.first)
document.main.document.second.left=parseInt(scrollerwidth)+5
document.main.document.second.visibility='show'
}
}

window.onload=startscroll

</script>

<div align="center">
<script language="JavaScript1.2">
if (ie||dom){
document.writeln('<div id="main2"
➡style="position:relative;width:'+scrollerwidth+';
➡height:'+scrollerheight+';overflow:hidden;
➡background-color:'+scrollerbgcolor+'">')
document.writeln('<div
➡style="position:absolute;width:'+scrollerwidth+';
➡height:'+scrollerheight+';clip:rect
➡ (0 '+scrollerwidth+' '+scrollerheight+' 0);
➡left:0px;top:0px">')
document.writeln('<div id="first2"
➡style="position:absolute;width:'+scrollerwidth+';
➡left:1px;top:0px;">')
document.write(slideimages[0])
document.writeln('</div>')
document.writeln('<div id="second2"
➡style="position:absolute;width:'+scrollerwidth+';
➡left:0px;top:0px">')
```

```
document.write(slideimages[1])
document.writeln('</div>')
document.writeln('</div>')
document.writeln('</div>')
}
</script>
</div>
<!--END OF SLIDESHOW CODE-->
```

Template 7.12: Animated Picture Flipshow

Another approach to the picture slideshow is the animated flipshow, as shown in Figure 7.12. With this type of slideshow, the pictures don't scroll, they flip from one to another.

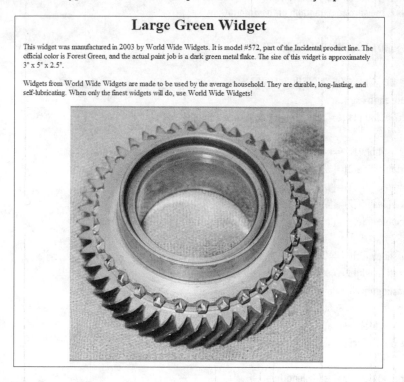

FIGURE 7.12

An animated flip-type picture slideshow.

This is another JavaScript template. This particular code allows for four pictures (**variableslide** 0 through 3). To use more pictures, add additional **variableslide** lines (numbering upward from 4); to use fewer pictures, delete one or more **variableslide** lines starting from the last one backward. Again, you insert the slideshow code in your auction template where you want the slideshow to appear. And make sure that your pictures are sized to the 400 x 400 size specified in the code, or they'll be stretched or squeezed to fit. (Alternately, you can change the 400 x 400 specification to match the size of your particular photos.)

```
<!--REGULAR TEMPLATE CODE-->
<h1 style="text-align: center">This is the title</h1>

<p style="text-align: left">
This is the first paragraph of the description
</p>

<p style="text-align: left">
This is the second paragraph of the description
</p>
<!--END OF REGULAR TEMPLATE CODE-->

<!--BEGINNING OF SLIDESHOW CODE-->
<div align=center>
<script language="JavaScript1.2">

var variableslide=new Array()
variableslide[0]=['URL1','','']
variableslide[1]=['URL2','','']
variableslide[2]=['URL3','','']
variableslide[3]=['URL4','','']

var slidewidth='400px' //set to width of LARGEST image
var slideheight='400px' //set to height of LARGEST image
var slidebgcolor='gray'
var slidedelay=3000
var ie=document.all
var dom=document.getElementById

for (i=0;i<variableslide.length;i++){
var cacheimage=new Image()
cacheimage.src=variableslide[i][0]
}

var currentslide=0
```

```
function rotateimages(){
contentcontainer='<center>'
if (variableslide[currentslide][1]!="")
contentcontainer+='<a href="'+variableslide
➥[currentslide][1]+'">'
contentcontainer+='<img src="'+variableslide
➥[currentslide][0]+'" border="0" vspace="3">'
if (variableslide[currentslide][1]!="")
contentcontainer+='</a>'
contentcontainer+='</center>'
if (variableslide[currentslide][2]!="")
contentcontainer+=variableslide[currentslide][2]

if (document.layers){
crossrotateobj.document.write(contentcontainer)
crossrotateobj.document.close()
}
else if (ie||dom)
crossrotateobj.innerHTML=contentcontainer
if (currentslide==variableslide.length-1) currentslide=0
else currentslide++
setTimeout("rotateimages()",slidedelay)
}

if (ie||dom)
document.write('<div id="slidedom"
➥style="width:'+slidewidth+';height:'+slideheight+';
➥background-color:'+slidebgcolor+'"></div>')

function start_slider(){
crossrotateobj=dom? document.getElementById
➥("slidedom") : ie? document.all.slidedom :
➥ document.slidensmain.document.slidenssub
if (document.layers)
document.slidensmain.visibility="show"
rotateimages()
}

if (ie||dom)
start_slider()
```

```
else if (document.layers)
window.onload=start_slider

</script>
</div>
<!--END OF SLIDESHOW CODE-->
```

Template 7.13: Manual Advance Picture Slideshow

CD-ROM This next template presents yet another type of slideshow. This manual advance slideshow is nifty because it includes both automatic play (via the Start button) and manual advance, via backward/foreword buttons. As you can see in Figure 7.13, visitors can even use the pull-down list to go directly to a particular photo. It's the ultimate in shopper convenience!

FIGURE 7.13

Multiple photos displayed in manual advance slideshow.

Like most of these slideshows, this template uses some complicated JavaScript code. This particular example is coded for four photos, but you can add more by including additional <option> statements, increasing the numbering in order. Or, if you have fewer photos, just delete the last **<option>** line(s). Of course, you should replace *URL1*, *URL2*, and so forth with the URLs for your image files. And, as with the previous template, make sure that your photos don't exceed the 400 x 400 size.

```
<!--REGULAR TEMPLATE CODE-->
<h1 style="text-align: center">This is the title</h1>

<p style="text-align: left">
This is the first paragraph of the description
</p>

<p style="text-align: left">
This is the second paragraph of the description
</p>
<!--END OF REGULAR TEMPLATE CODE-->

<!--BEGINNING OF SLIDESHOW CODE-->
<script language="JavaScript">
<!--start
var x = 0;

function rotate(num){
x=num%document.slideForm.slide.length;
if(x<0){x=document.slideForm.slide.length-1};
document.images.show.src=
➥document.slideForm.slide.options[x].value;
document.slideForm.slide.selectedIndex=x;
}

function apRotate() {
if(document.slideForm.slidebutton.value == "Stop"){
rotate(++x);window.setTimeout("apRotate()", 5000);}
}
//end -->
</script>

<form name="slideForm">
<table cellspacing=1 cellpadding=4
➥style="border:1px black solid;
➥border-collapse:collapse" align="center">
<tr><td align="center">
```

```
<strong><font face="Arial" size="3">
Product Photos</font></strong>
</td></tr>

<tr><td align=center width=400 height=400>
<img src="URL1" name="show">
</td></tr>

<tr><td align=center style="border:1px black solid;">
<select name="slide" onChange="rotate(this.selectedIndex);">
<option value="URL1" selected>Photo 1
<option value="URL2">Photo 2
<option value="URL3">Photo 3
<option value="URL4">Photo 4
</select>
</td></tr>

<tr><td align=center style="border:1px black solid;">
<input type=button onclick="rotate(0);"
➥value="ll&lt;&lt;" title="Jump to beginning"
➥style="border:1px black solid;">
<input type=button onclick="rotate(x-1);"
➥value="&lt;&lt;" title="Last Picture"
➥style="border:1px black solid;">
<input type=button name="slidebutton"
➥onClick="this.value=((this.value=='Stop')
➥?'Start':'Stop');apRotate();" value="Start"
➥title="Autoplay" style="width:75px;
➥border:1px black solid;">
<input type=button onclick="rotate(x+1);"
➥value="&gt;&gt;" title="Next Picture"
➥style="border:1px black solid;">
<input type=button
➥onclick="rotate(this.form.slide.length-1);"
➥value="&gt;&gt;ll" title="Jump to end"
➥style="border:1px black solid;">
</td></tr>
</table>
</form>
<!--END OF SLIDESHOW CODE-->
```

Protecting Your Pictures from Image Theft

While we're on the topic of product photos, it's appropriate to address the issue of image theft. You may have had it happen to you—another eBay seller stealing your photos for use in his auction. This type of image theft is against eBay's rules, of course which means you can always report the offenders to big brother. But wouldn't it be better to keep the problem from occurring in the first place?

Template 7.14: Picture with Watermark

CD-ROM One way to prevent image theft is to place a translucent watermark on top of your product photos. As you can see in Figure 7.14, this is a piece of text or an image that appears on top of your photo, identifying it in a way that discourages theft. You can create a watermark on the photo level, using your picture editing program to add a layer of text on top of the main image, or you can use HTML to add a watermark on the code level.

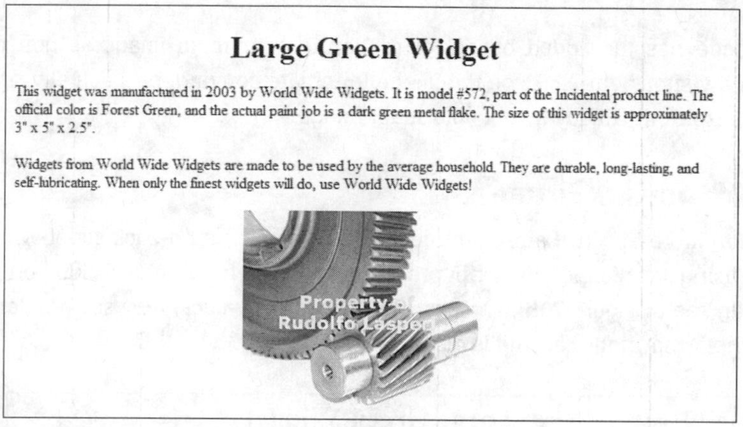

FIGURE 7.14

A picture with a translucent watermark.

The key to using this template is to create two image files. The first file (*URL-MAIN*) is your main product photo. The second file (*URL-WATERMARK*) is a transparent GIF file you have to create separately. The transparent GIF file should include the watermark text you want to display on top of your image. This code stacks the transparent GIF on top of the main image, using HTML tables, for the nifty watermark effect.

```
<!--REGULAR TEMPLATE CODE-->
<h1 style="text-align: center">This is the title</h1>


<p style="text-align: left">
This is the first paragraph of the description
```

```
</p>

<p style="text-align: left">
This is the second paragraph of the description
</p>
<!--END OF REGULAR TEMPLATE CODE-->

<!--BEGINNING OF WATERMARK CODE-->
<table border="0" cellpadding="0"
➥cellspacing="0" align="center">
<tr><td background="URL-MAIN">
<img src="URL-WATERMARK" border="0">
</td></tr>
</table>
<!--END OF WATERMARK CODE-->
```

This code has the added benefit of rendering your main image as non-right-clickable. When a visitor right-clicks on the image to initiate copying, he's actually right-clicking on the transparent GIF layer—not your main image.

Template 7.15: No-Click Picture

CD-ROM An even more effective anti-theft method is to employ a no-click script within your HTML code, using JavaScript. This script prevents any users from right-clicking on your image. As you can see in Figure 7.15, when someone does right-click, they see an alert window that tells them that right-clicking is disabled.

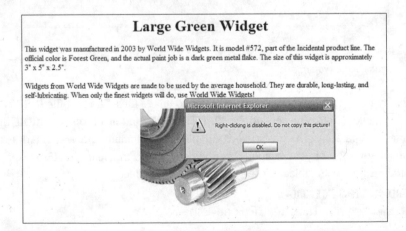

FIGURE 7.15

A photo displayed with a no-click warning.

This no-click code displays a single photograph. You can add more pictures by inserting additional **<img>** tags; make sure you include the **onMouseDown="noclick()"** attribute with each tag you add. (You only have to insert the subsequent JavaScript code a single time.)

```
<!--REGULAR TEMPLATE CODE-->
<h1 style="text-align: center">This is the title</h1>

<p style="text-align: left">
This is the first paragraph of the description
</p>

<p style="text-align: left">
This is the second paragraph of the description
</p>
<!--END OF REGULAR TEMPLATE CODE-->

<!--BEGINNING OF NO-CLICK CODE-->
<center>
<img src="URL" onMouseDown="noclick()">
</center>

<script language="JavaScript">
function noclick (scx)
{
  if (navigator.appName == "Netscape" && scx.which == 3)
   { alert ('Right-clicking is disabled.
➥Do not copy this picture!');
     return false;
   }
  if (navigator.appVersion.indexOf("MSIE") != -1 &&
      event.button == 2)
   { alert ('Right-clicking is disabled.
➥Do not copy this picture!');
     return false;
   }
}
</SCRIPT>
<!--END OF NO-CLICK CODE-->
```

NOTE   This no-click code works only with users with Windows-based computers. Mac users will still be able to right-click and copy the photo.

Working with Tables, Borders, and Backgrounds

Here's the secret to cool-looking eBay listings.

Tables.

That's right, tables. HTML tables let you structure your listing using all manner of grids, and then apply borders and backgrounds to all or part of the listing. Without tables you're limited to a single-column listing with no fancy backgrounds; with tables, the available template designs are virtually limitless.

Creating Listings with Multiple Sections

We'll start by using tables to divide your listing into multiple sections. As you learned in Chapter 1, "The Good, the Bad, and the Ugly: Do's and Don'ts for Effective Auction Listings," your listing can (and should) contain a number of discrete sections, each devoted to a particular type of information—the item title, subtitle, overview paragraph, text description, and terms of sale (TOS). The following templates, then, use table rows and columns to arrange these sections in an orderly fashion.

Template 8.1: Separate Title, Picture, Description, and TOS Sections

CD-ROM Our first template breaks your listing into four discrete sections, one above the other—title, pictures, description, and TOS, as shown in Figure 8.1. This requires the creation of a table with four rows, one column per row.

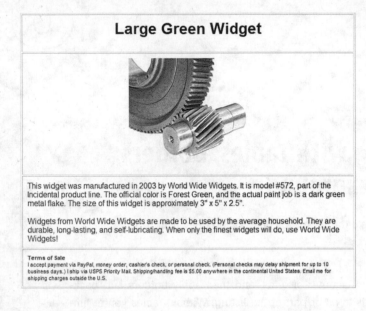

FIGURE 8.1

Four stacked sections defined by four table rows.

The code for this table is relatively simple. We've defined the width of the table to be 80% of the available page width; the height of each row will vary depending on the content you insert. To emphasize the tabular grid of this design, we've specified a thin border for the table, using the default page colors. The border surrounds not only the outside of the table, but also each of the table's cells. You can add additional pictures by including more <img> tags in the second row.

Here's the code:

```
<table width="80%" align="center" border="1"
cellpadding="10">
<tr>
  <td align="center">
  <h1 style="font-family: Arial; font-size: 24pt;
  font-weight: bold">Title</h1>
  </td>
```

```
  </tr>

  <tr>
    <td align="center">
    <img src="url">
    </td>
  </tr>

  <tr>
    <td>
    <p style="text-align: left; font-size: 12pt;
    font-family: Arial">
    Description paragraph one
    </p>
    <p style="text-align: left; font-size: 12pt;
    font-family: Arial">
    Description paragraph two
    </p>
    </td>
  </tr>

  <tr>
    <td>
    <p style="text-align: left; font-size: 8pt;
    font-family: Arial">
    <strong>Terms of Sale</strong>
    <br>Terms of service</p>
    </td>
  </tr>

</table>
```

Template 8.2: Separate Description, Payment, and Shipping Sections

CD-ROM This next template follows the same basic design as Template 8.1, but separates the general terms of service into separate payment and shipping sections. As you can see in Figure 8.2, what's unique about this is that we take that final row and divide it into two equal columns—one each for payment and shipping. So you end up with a table where some rows have just one cell, and the last row has two cells.

Large Green Widget

This widget was manufactured in 2003 by World Wide Widgets. It is model #572, part of the Incidental product line. The official color is Forest Green, and the actual paint job is a dark green metal flake. The size of this widget is approximately 3" x 5" x 2.5".

Widgets from World Wide Widgets are made to be used by the average household. They are durable, long-lasting, and self-lubricating. When only the finest widgets will do, use World Wide Widgets!

Payment Information
I accept payment via PayPal, money order, cashier's check, or personal check. (Personal checks may delay shipment for up to 10 business days.)

Shipping Information
I ship via USPS Priority Mail. Shipping/handling fee is $5.00 anywhere in the continental United States. Email me for shipping charges outside the U.S.

FIGURE 8.2

Dividing the final row of the table into two cells—one for payment information, one for shipping information.

You might think that the code for this template would be identical to that of Template 8.1, save for the final row, but you'd be wrong. If you simply add a second cell to the final row, the cells in all the previous rows end up being assigned to the first column of the table only. To make the single-cell rows span the entire width of the table, you have to add **colspan="2"** attributes to each **<td>** tag. Here's how the new code looks:

```
<table width="80%" align="center" border="1"
cellpadding="10">
<tr>
  <td align="center" colspan="2">
  <h1 style="font-family: Arial; font-size: 24pt;
font-weight: bold">
  Title
  </h1>
  </td>
</tr>

<tr>
  <td align="center" colspan="2">
  <img src="url">
  </td>
</tr>
```

```
<tr>
  <td colspan="2">
  <p style="text-align: left; font-size: 12pt;
  font-family: Arial">
  Description paragraph one
  </p>
  <p style="text-align: left; font-size: 12pt;
  font-family: Arial">
  Description paragraph two
  </p>
  </td>
</tr>

<tr>
  <td width="50%">
  <p style="text-align: left; font-size: 8pt;
  font-family: Arial">
  <strong>Payment Information</strong>
  <br>Payment terms</p>
  </td>
  <td width="50%">
  <p style="text-align: left; font-size: 8pt;
  font-family: Arial">
  <strong>Shipping Information</strong>
  <br>Shipping terms</p>
  </td>
</tr>

</table>
```

Creating Multiple-Column Listings

Now that you've gotten a taste for working with multiple columns in part of the item listing, let's use that same approach to divide the entire listing into multiple columns.

Template 8.3: Two Equal Columns with Centered Title and TOS

 CD-ROM In this template, we've simply split the listing into two vertical halves, as shown in Figure
8.3. Each half has a mix of text and pictures, alternating one and the other. The title and
TOS span both columns, at the top and the bottom of the listing, respectively.

FIGURE 8.3

Using two columns to position text and pictures on a 2 x 2 grid in the middle of the listing.

Technically, what we're dealing with here is a table with four rows and two columns. The first and last row (title and TOS) span across the two columns; the two middle rows are both divided in two. The two middle rows form a 2 x 2 grid, and are set to align the text at the top of each row (via the **valign="top"** attribute). For this example, we've done away with the table borders, for a cleaner look.

```
<table width="80%" align="center" cellpadding="10">
<tr>
  <td align="center" colspan="2">
  <h1 style="font-family: Arial; font-size: 24pt;
  font-weight: bold">
  Title
  </h1>
  </td>
</tr>

<tr valign="top">
  <td width="50%">
  <p style="text-align: left; font-size: 12pt;
  font-family: Arial">
```

```
Description paragraph one
</p>
</td>
<td width="50%">
<img src="url1">
</td>
</tr>

<tr valign="top">
  <td width="50%">
  <img src="url2">
  </td>
  <td width="50%">
  <p style="text-align: left; font-size: 12pt;
  font-family: Arial">
  Description paragraph two
  </p>
  </td>
</tr>

<tr>
  <td align="center" colspan="2">
  <p style="text-align: center; font-size: 8pt;
  font-family: Arial">
  <strong>Terms of Sale</strong><br>
  Terms of service
  </p>
  </td>
</tr>

</table>
```

Template 8.4: Wide Left Column, Narrow Right Column

CD-ROM Now we'll do something a little different. The design shown in Figure 8.4 is similar to Template 8.3, except we've made the left column wider than the right column. This lets us put the main descriptive text and pictures in the big left column, while reserving the narrower right column for bulleted item details.

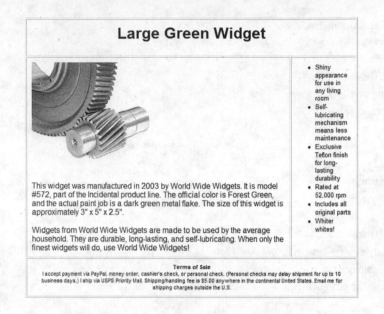

FIGURE 8.4

Descriptive text paragraphs in the wide left column, short text bullets in the narrow right column.

The key to this approach is to define the width of the left column as 75% of the total table width in the **<td>** tag, and then define the width of the right column as 25% of the table width. That's a good ratio; since the right column contains short text bullets, it doesn't have to be any wider than that. (We've also turned back on the table borders; you can turn them off by deleting the **border** attribute in the **<table>** tag.)

```
<table width="80%" align="center" cellpadding="10"
border="1">
<tr>
  <td align="center" colspan="2">
  <h1 style="font-family: Arial; font-size: 24pt;
  font-weight: bold">
  Title
  </h1>
  </td>
</tr>

<tr valign="top">
  <td width="80%">
  <img src="url">
  <p style="text-align: left; font-size: 12pt;
  font-family: Arial">
```

```
First description paragraph
</p>
<p style="text-align: left; font-size: 12pt;
font-family: Arial">
Second description paragraph
</p>
</td>
<td width="20%">
<ul style="font-family: Arial; font-size: 10pt">
<li>Bullet one</li>
<li>Bullet two</li>
<li>Bullet three</li>
<li>Bullet four</li>
</ul>
</td>
</tr>

<tr>
<td align="center" colspan="2">
<p style="text-align: center; font-size: 8pt;
font-family: Arial">
<strong>Terms of Sale</strong><br>
Terms of service
</p>
</td>
</tr>

</table>
```

Template 8.5: Two Columns with Centered Top Picture and Title

 CD-ROM This template is similar to Template 8.4, except that it places the photo(s) in a full-width row above the two-column description. As you can see in Figure 8.5, this approach works especially well if you have two or three pictures that can span the entire width of the listing.

This code inserts a new row between the title row and the description row. This second row is set to span both columns; just insert one **<img>** tag after another to have your pictures line up in a horizontal row. (We've also specified the height for each image as a uniform 150 pixels.) As with the previous template, you can turn off the table borders by deleting the **border** attribute in the **<table>** tag.

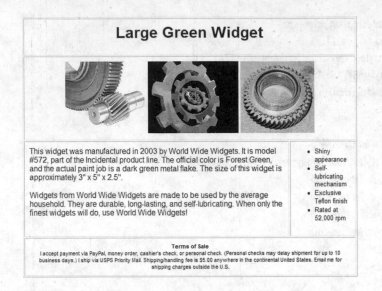

FIGURE 8.5

Centered top pictures above uneven dual columns.

```
<table width="80%" align="center" cellpadding="10"
border="1">
<tr>
  <td align="center" colspan="2">
  <h1 style="font-family: Arial; font-size: 24pt;
  font-weight: bold">
  Title
  </h1>
  </td>
</tr>

<tr>
  <td align="center" colspan="2">
  <img src="url1" height="150">
  <img src="url2" height="150">
  <img src="url3" height="150">
  </td>
</tr>

<tr valign="top">
  <td width="80%">
  <p style="text-align: left; font-size: 12pt;
```

```
      font-family: Arial">
      First description paragraph
      </p>
      <p style="text-align: left; font-size: 12pt;
      font-family: Arial">
      Second description paragraph
      </p>
      </td>
      <td width="20%">
      <ul style="font-family: Arial; font-size: 10pt">
      <li>Bullet one</li>
      <li>Bullet two</li>
      <li>Bullet three</li>
      <li>Bullet four</li>
      </ul>
      </td>
    </tr>

    <tr>
      <td align="center" colspan="2">
      <p style="text-align: center; font-size: 8pt;
      font-family: Arial">
      <strong>Terms of Sale</strong><br>
      Terms of service
      </p>
      </td>
    </tr>

  </table>
```

Arranging Images on the Page

We've already done some image arrangement in a few of the previous templates. Now we'll go a step or two beyond, with some more complex vertical and horizontal grids.

Template 8.6: Multiple Pictures in a Vertical Grid

 CD-ROM If you have a lot of photos to display, you don't want them aligned willy-nilly in your listing. This template (shown in Figure 8.6) takes six separate photos and aligns them in a neat grid of two rows by three columns.

FIGURE 8.6

A 2 x 3 photo grid.

In this template, the photo grid is inserted between the title and the description rows. The grid consists of two rows, each with three cells; one photo is inserted into each of the six total cells. Naturally, the title, description, and TOS rows are set to span all three columns, using the **colspan="3"** attribute in the **<tr>** tags. We've also turned off the table borders, for a cleaner look.

```
<table width="80%" align="center" cellpadding="10">
<tr>
  <td align="center" colspan="3">
  <h1 style="font-family: Arial; font-size: 24pt;
  font-weight: bold">
  Title
  </h1>
  </td>
</tr>

<tr>
  <td>
  <p align="center"><img src="URL1" height="150">
  </td>
  <td>
```

```html
      <p align="center"><img src="URL2" height="150">
      </td>
      <td>
      <p align="center"><img src="URL3" height="150">
      </td>
   </tr>

   <tr>
     <td>
     <p align="center"><img src="URL4" height="150">
     </td>
     <td>
     <p align="center"><img src="URL5" height="150">
     </td>
     <td>
     <p align="center"><img src="URL6" height="150">
     </td>
   </tr>

   <tr>
     <td colspan="3">
     <p style="text-align: left; font-size: 12pt;
     font-family: Arial">
     Description paragraph one
     </p>
     <p style="text-align: left; font-size: 12pt;
     font-family: Arial">
     Description paragraph two
     </p>
     </td>
   </tr>

   <tr>
     <td align="center" colspan="3">
     <p style="text-align: center; font-size: 8pt;
     font-family: Arial">
     <strong>Terms of Sale</strong><br>
     Terms of service
     </p>
     </td>
   </tr>

</table>
```

By the way, to make things look as clean as possible, we force a common height for all the pictures by using **height="150"** attribute in each **<img>** tag. You can play around with the height number to best work with your particular photos.

Template 8.7: Multiple Pictures in a Vertical Column

CD-ROM If we can align photos in horizontal rows, why not flip things around and align them in vertical columns? That's what we do in this template, shown in Figure 8.7; it's actually a good way to display multiple photos.

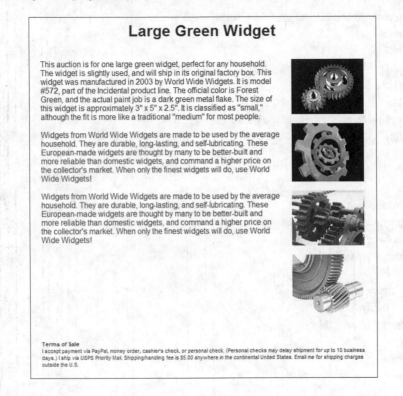

FIGURE 8.7

Multiple pictures aligned in a vertical column to the right of the item description.

To ensure a uniform look to the listing, we've limited the width of each photo (and the right-hand column itself) to 150 pixels. We've also specified that the description text and the photos are vertically aligned to the top of each cell, by specifying the **valign="top"** attribute to the **<td>** tags in that row.

```
<table width="80%" align="center" cellpadding="10">
<tr>
```

```
<td align="center" colspan="2">
<h1 style="font-family: Arial; font-size: 24pt;
font-weight: bold">
Title
</h1>
</td>
</tr>

<tr valign="top">
  <td>
  <p style="text-align: left; font-size: 12pt;
font-family: Arial">
Description paragraph one
  </p>
  <p style="text-align: left; font-size: 12pt;
font-family: Arial">
Description paragraph two
  </p>
  </td>

  <td width="150">
  <img src="URL1" width="150"><br><br>
  <img src="URL2" width="150"><br><br>
  <img src="URL3" width="150"><br><br>
  <img src="URL4" width="150"><br><br>
  </td>
</tr>

<tr>
  <td align="center" colspan="2">
  <p style="text-align: left; font-size: 8pt;
font-family: Arial">
<strong>Terms of Sale</strong><br>
Terms of service</p>
  </td>
</tr>

</table>
```

Adding Color Borders

By now I hope you've realized how incredibly useful tables are for structuring the layout of your auction listings. You've also seen, albeit as a bit of an afterthought, how turning on or off table borders can affect the look of this structure.

Let us now turn our full attention to those table borders, and use them to a more prominent design effect.

Template 8.8: Full-Page Color Border

CD-ROM   One way to unify your auction template is to put a color border around the entire listing. That's exactly what this template does—it turns on the outside table border, while leaving the internal cell borders off, as you can see in Figure 8.8.

FIGURE 8.8

A standard template with a thick external color border.

What we've done here is create a simple single-row, single-column table, and inside it inserted our entire item listing—text and pictures. Then we've turned on the table borders and assigned the attributes **border="10"** and **bordercolor="blue"** to the **\<table\>** tag. (You can substitute any color name or code that you like.) However, we also need to hide the internal cell border, which we do by turning it white with the **bordercolor="white"** attribute in the **\<td\>** tag. The result is a simple color border around the outside of the table.

```
<table width="80%" cellpadding="10" border="10"
bordercolor="blue" align="center">
<tr>
```

```
<td align="center" border="0" bordercolor="white">
<h1 style="font-family: Arial; font-size: 24pt;
font-weight: bold">
Title
</h1>
<p><img src="URL"></p>
<p style="text-align: left; font-size: 12pt;
font-family: Arial">
Description paragraph one
</p>
<p style="text-align: left; font-size: 12pt;
font-family: Arial">
Description paragraph two
</p>
<p style="text-align: center; font-size: 8pt;
font-family: Arial">
<strong>Terms of Sale</strong><br>
Terms of service
</p>
</td>
</tr>

</table>
```

Template 8.9: Full-Page Nested Color Border

CD-ROM If a single-color border is a little too plain for your tastes, consider the border in this template, shown in Figure 8.9. To create a border of many colors, we have to nest one table within another—within another within another. This nested tables approach lets us insert an infinite number of tables—with an infinite number of border colors—one within the next.

This template nests a total of four different tables, each with a single row and column. I've assigned the colors green, yellow, red, and blue to the borders (from the outside in); feel free to change the colors to your own personal palette.

```
<table width="80%" border="10" bordercolor="green"
align="center">
<tr>
<td bordercolor="white">

<table width="100%" border="10" bordercolor="yellow"
align="center">
```

```
<tr>
<td bordercolor="white">


<table width="100%" border="10" bordercolor="red"
align="center">
<tr>
<td bordercolor="white">

<table width="100%" border="10" bordercolor="blue"
cellpadding="10" align="center">
<tr>
  <td align="center" bordercolor="white">
  <h1 style="font-family: Arial; font-size: 24pt;
  font-weight: bold">Title</h1>
  <p><img src="URL" width="150"></p>
  <p style="text-align: left; font-size: 12pt;
  font-family: Arial">
  Description paragraph one
  </p>
  <p style="text-align: left; font-size: 12pt;
  font-family: Arial">
  Description paragraph two
  </p>
  <p style="text-align: center; font-size: 8pt;
  font-family: Arial">
  <strong>Terms of Sale</strong><br>
  Terms of service</p>
  </td>
  </tr>
</table>


</td></tr>
</table>


</td></tr>
</table>


</td></tr>
</table>
```

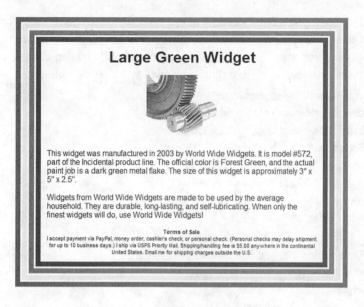

FIGURE 8.9

A border composed of multiple colors—thanks to nested tables.

Template 8.10: Top and Bottom Color Borders Only

CD-ROM Maybe you don't want a border around your entire table. This template places a thick color border at the top and bottom only of the item description—nothing on the sides. It's a nice, airy effect, as you can see in Figure 8.10.

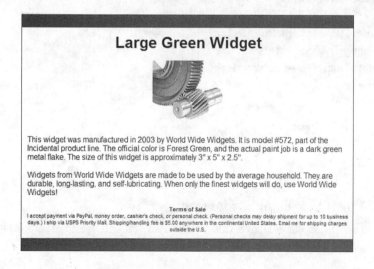

FIGURE 8.10

Thick top and bottom borders

To achieve the top and bottom border effect, we have to introduce the CSS (Cascading Style Sheets) **style** attribute to the **<table>** tag. Attached to this attribute are various **margin-top** and **margin-bottom** properties, for color (blue in this example; you can change to any color you like), width (a thickness of 20 points), and style (solid). Here's the code:

```
<table style="border-top-style: solid;
border-top-color: blue; border-top-width: 20pt;
border-bottom-style: solid; border-bottom-color: blue;
border-bottom-width: 20pt" width="80%"
align="center" cellpadding="10">

<tr>
  <td align="center">

  <h1 style="font-family: Arial; font-size: 24pt;
  font-weight: bold">
  Title
  </h1>
  <p><img src="URL" width="150"></p>
  <p style="text-align: left; font-size: 12pt;
  font-family: Arial">
  Description paragraph one
  </p>
  <p style="text-align: left; font-size: 12pt;
  font-family: Arial">
  Description paragraph two
  </p>
  <p style="text-align: left; font-size: 8pt;
  font-family: Arial">
  <strong>Terms of Sale</strong><br>
  Terms of service</p>

  </td>
  </tr>
  </table>
```

Template 8.11: Left Side Color Border Only

CD-ROM Here's another use of selective side borders. As you can see in Figure 8.11, this template features a very thick color border on the left side of the listing only.

FIGURE 8.11

A thick green border to the left of the item description.

As with the previous template, this one uses the CSS **style** attribute, this time with **margin-left** properties. Feel free to replace the green color with the color name or code of your choice.

```
<table style="border-left-style: solid;
border-left-color: green; border-left-width: 40pt"
width="80%" align="center" cellpadding="10">

<tr>
  <td align="center">

    <h1 style="font-family: Arial; font-size: 24pt;
    font-weight: bold">
    Title
    </h1>
    <p><img src="URL" width="150"></p>
    <p style="text-align: left; font-size: 12pt;
    font-family: Arial">
    Description paragraph one</p>
    <p style="text-align: left; font-size: 12pt;
    font-family: Arial">
    Description paragraph two</p>
    <p style="text-align: left; font-size: 8pt;
    font-family: Arial">
    <strong>Terms of Sale</strong><br>
    Terms of service</p>
```

```
  </td>
 </tr>
</table>
```

Template 8.12: Fancy Listing Border

CD-ROM While we're playing around with CSS **margin** properties, it's worth remembering that CSS lets us specify all manner of border styles, including **dotted, dashed, solid, double, groove, ridge, inset,** and **outset**. This lets us create a template with a fancy border, as shown in Figure 8.12.

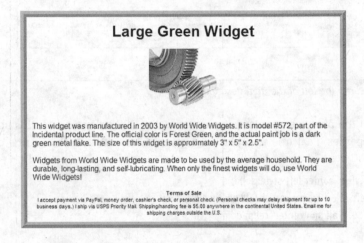

FIGURE 8.12

A yellow ridge border around the entire listing.

This template puts a 10 point yellow ridge border around the entire item listing, using the **border-style, border-color,** and **border-width** properties. Feel free to replace the **ridge** style or color with any other border style and color of your liking.

```
<table style="border-style: ridge; border-color: yellow;
border-width: 10pt" width="80%" align="center"
cellpadding="10">

<tr>
 <td align="center">

 <h1 style="font-family: Arial; font-size: 24pt;
 font-weight: bold">
 Title
 </h1>
 <p><img src="URL" width="150"></p>
 <p style="text-align: left; font-size: 12pt;
```

```
font-family: Arial">
Description paragraph one
</p>
<p style="text-align: left; font-size: 12pt;
font-family: Arial">
Description paragraph two
</p>
<p style="text-align: left; font-size: 8pt;
font-family: Arial">
<strong>Terms of Sale</strong><br>
Terms of service
</p>

</td>
</tr>
</table>
```

Template 8.13: Color Borders Around Each Section

CD-ROM Now let's return to the layout first used in Template 8.2, which has separate sections for title, pictures, description, payment info, and shipping info. What we'll do now is put a different colored border around each section—that is, around each cell in the table, as shown in Figure 8.13.

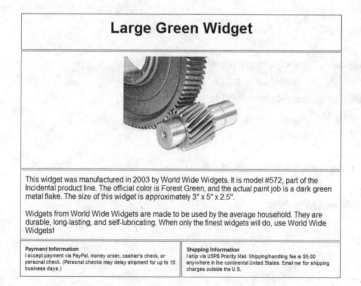

FIGURE 8.13

Color borders around each section of the listing.

We could accomplish this effect by using the **border-color** attribute within each individual <td> tag, but this approach only works with the Internet Explorer browser. To get colored borders with Firefox and Safari (as well as IE), we have to use the CSS approach, with the **border-style**, **border-width**, and **border-color** properties. Naturally, you can change the colors for each cell as you like.

```
<table width="80%" cellpadding="10">
<tr>
  <td align="center" colspan="2"
  style="border-style: solid;
  border-width: thin; border-color: blue">
  <h1 style="font-family: Arial; font-size: 24pt;
  font-weight: bold">
  Title
  </h1>
  </td>
</tr>

<tr>
  <td align="center" colspan="2"
  style="border-style: solid;
  border-width: thin; border-color: green">
  <img src="url">
  </td>
</tr>

<tr>
  <td colspan="2" style="border-style: solid;
  border-width: thin; border-color: red">
  <p style="text-align: left; font-size: 12pt;
  font-family: Arial">
  Description paragraph one
  </p>
  <p style="text-align: left; font-size: 12pt;
  font-family: Arial">
  Description paragraph two
  </p>
  </td>
</tr>

<tr>
  <td width="50%" style="border-style: solid;
  border-width: thin; border-color: blue">
```

```
<p style="text-align: left; font-size: 8pt;
font-family: Arial">
<strong>Payment Information</strong>
<br>Payment terms</p>
</td>
<td width="50%" style="border-style: solid;
border-width: thin; border-color: green">
<p style="text-align: left; font-size: 8pt;
font-family: Arial">
<strong>Shipping Information</strong>
<br>Shipping terms</p>
</td>
</tr>

</table>
```

Template 8.14: Color Borders Around Payment and Shipping Sections

CD-ROM I'll be the first to admit that putting different color borders around each section of your listing, as we did with the previous template, can be a little garish—depending on which colors you choose, of course. To that end, I prefer the approach of this template, shown in Figure 8.14, which uses borders only for the payment and shipping info sections.

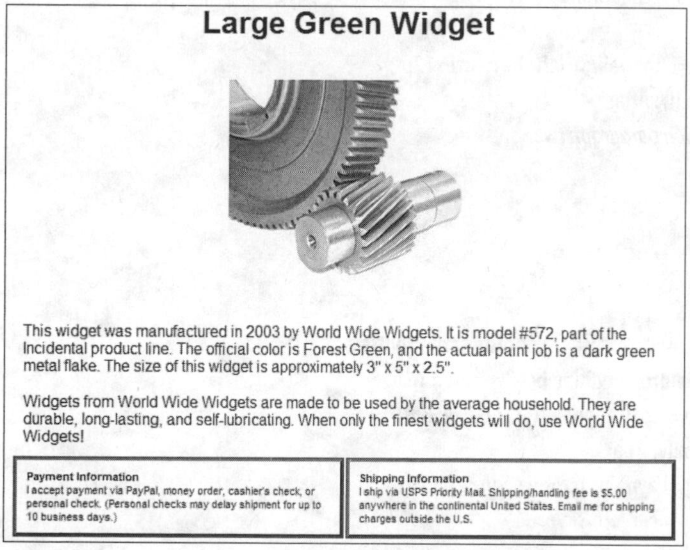

FIGURE 8.14

Separating the payment and shipping info section with color borders.

In this instance, we use CSS code to put medium teal borders around the last two cells in the table. It's pretty simple, as you can see.

```
<table width="80%" align="center" cellpadding="10">
<tr>
  <td align="center" colspan="2">
  <h1 style="font-family: Arial; font-size: 24pt;
  font-weight: bold">
  Title
  </h1>
  </td>
</tr>

<tr>
  <td align="center" colspan="2">
  <img src="url">
  </td>
</tr>

<tr>
  <td colspan="2">
  <p style="text-align: left; font-size: 12pt;
  font-family: Arial">
  Description paragraph one
  </p>
  <p style="text-align: left; font-size: 12pt;
  font-family: Arial">
  Description paragraph two
  </p>
  </td>
</tr>

<tr>
  <td width="50%" style="border-style: outset;
  border-width: medium; border-color: teal">
  <p style="text-align: left; font-size: 8pt;
  font-family: Arial">
  <strong>Payment Information</strong>
  <br>Payment terms</p>
  </td>
  <td width="50%" style="border-style: outset;
  border-width: medium; Border-color: teal">
```

```
<p style="text-align: left; font-size: 8pt;
font-family: Arial">
<strong>Shipping Information</strong>
<br>Shipping terms</p>
</td>
</tr>

</table>
```

Template 8.15: Top-of-Section Color Borders

CD-ROM Let's continue with our CSS code to put thick color ridge borders above the description, payment, and shipping sections of the template, as shown in Figure 8.15.

FIGURE 8.15

Thick color borders above key sections of the item listing.

The operative code for this template involves the **border-top-style**, **border-top-width**, and **border-top-color** attributes. As always, feel free to edit these three properties to fine-tune your own custom template.

```
<table width="80%" align="center" cellpadding="10">
<tr>
  <td align="center" colspan="2">
```

```
    <h1 style="font-family: Arial; font-size: 24pt;
    font-weight: bold">
    Title
    </h1>
    </td>
</tr>

<tr>
    <td align="center" colspan="2">
    <img src="url">
    </td>
</tr>

<tr>
    <td colspan="2" style="border-top-style: solid;
    border-top-width: 10pt; border-top-color: #66CCFF">
    <p style="text-align: left; font-size: 12pt;
    font-family: Arial">
    Description paragraph one
    </p>
    <p style="text-align: left; font-size: 12pt;
    font-family: Arial">
    Description paragraph two
    </p>
    </td>
</tr>

<tr>
    <td width="50%" style="border-top-style: solid;
    border-top-width: 10pt; border-top-color: #66CCFF">
    <p style="text-align: left; font-size: 8pt;
    font-family: Arial">
    <strong>Payment Information</strong>
    <br>Payment terms</p>
    </td>
    <td width="50%" style="border-top-style: solid;
    border-top-width: 10pt; border-top-color: #66CCFF">
    <p style="text-align: left; font-size: 8pt;
    font-family: Arial">
    <strong>Shipping Information</strong>
    <br>Shipping terms</p>
```

```
        </td>
    </tr>

</table>
```

Adding Color Backgrounds

Just as we can add borders around the cells of a table, we can also add color fills to each cell. This enables us to add background color to our item listings—either to the entire listing, or to individual sections (cells) within the whole.

Template 8.16: Full-Page Color Background

CD-ROM This template, shown in Figure 8.16, is a popular one. It takes our standard single-row, single-column layout and adds a light color background. (This example uses a light blue; feel free to change the color name or code to any other color of your choosing.)

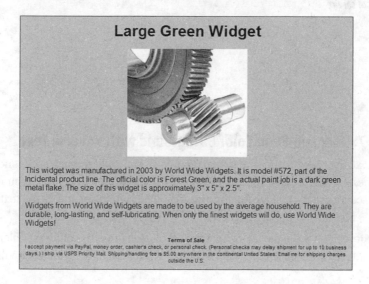

FIGURE 8.16

A light color background behind the entire item listing.

The code for this template is based on the code for Template 8.8. The background color is added via the **bgcolor** attribute in the **<table>** tag. It's a simple addition that adds color behind the entire listing.

```
<table width="80%" cellpadding="10" align="center"
bgcolor="#99CCFF">
<tr>
```

```
<td align="center">
<h1 style="font-family: Arial; font-size: 24pt;
font-weight: bold">
Title
</h1>
<p><img src="URL"></p>
<p style="text-align: left; font-size: 12pt;
font-family: Arial">
Description paragraph one</p>
<p style="text-align: left; font-size: 12pt;
font-family: Arial">
Description paragraph two
</p>
<p style="text-align: center; font-size: 8pt;
font-family: Arial">
<strong>Terms of Sale</strong><br>
Terms of service
</p>
</td>
</tr>

</table>
```

Template 8.17: Dark Full-Page Color Background with Reverse Text

CD-ROM This next template features a similar approach but with a much different effect. In this instance, we use a dark blue background for the table, which necessitates the use of lighter-colored text—yellow for the title and TOS, white for the body text, as shown in Figure 8.17.

The code here is the same as for Template 8.16, except with a different color choice for the **bgcolor** attribute, and **color** properties assigned within the **style** attributes for all the text paragraphs.

```
<table width="80%" cellpadding="10" align="center"
bgcolor="#000099">
<tr>
<td align="center">
<h1 style="font-family: Arial; font-size: 24pt;
font-weight: bold; color: yellow">Title</h1>
<p><img src="URL"></p>
<p style="text-align: left; font-size: 12pt;
```

```
font-family: Arial; color: white">
Description paragraph one
</p>
<p style="text-align: left; font-size: 12pt;
font-family: Arial; color: white">
Description paragraph two
</p>
<p style="text-align: center; font-size: 8pt;
font-family: Arial; color: yellow">
<strong>Terms of Sale</strong><br>
Terms of service
</p>
</td>
</tr>

</table>
```

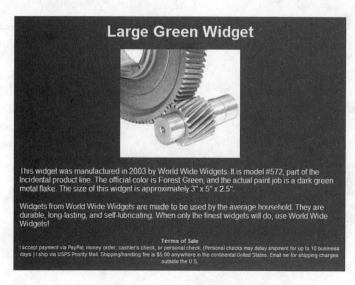

FIGURE 8.17

Dark background with white and yellow text.

Template 8.18: Second Column Different Color Background

 CD-ROM This template builds on the idea behind Template 8.4, but puts a light background behind the wide left column and a darker background behind the narrow right column. As you can see in Figure 8.18, the right-column bulleted text is now displayed in yellow, for better contrast.

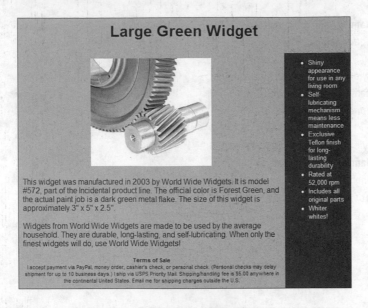

FIGURE 8.18

Second column with dark background and yellow text.

We've made this a relatively simple two-column template, without spanning any rows. The title, picture, description text, and TOS are all in the left column; the bulleted list is in the right column. To accomplish the different shadings for column, we've applied the **bgcolor** attribute to the **<td>** tag for each column. The color for the bulleted list text is specified by a **<font>** container tag around the bulleted list.

```
<table width="80%" align="center" cellpadding="10"
cellspacing="0">
<tr>
  <td align="center" colspan="2" bgcolor="#6699FF">
  <h1 style="font-family: Arial; font-size: 24pt;
  font-weight: bold">
  Title
  </h1>
  </td>
</tr>

<tr valign="top">
  <td width="80%" bgcolor="#6699FF" align="center">
  <img src="url">
  <p style="text-align: left; font-size: 12pt;
```

```
font-family: Arial">
First description paragraph
</p>
<p style="text-align: left; font-size: 12pt;
font-family: Arial">
Second description paragraph
</p>
<p style="text-align: center; font-size: 8pt;
font-family: Arial">
<strong>Terms of Sale</strong><br>
Terms of service
</p>
</td>

<td width="20%" bgcolor="#000099">
<font color="yellow">
<ul style="font-family: Arial; font-size: 10pt">
<li>Bullet one</li>
<li>Bullet two</li>
<li>Bullet three</li>
<li>Bullet four</li>
</ul>
</font>
</td>
</tr>

</table>
```

Template 8.19: TOS Color Background

CD-ROM Now let's take the concept of different colors for different sections of the listing and apply the color background to the TOS section at the bottom of the page. The result is shown in Figure 8.19.

The code for this template builds on the code for Template 8.1. The **bgcolor** attribute is added to the final **<td>** tag; in this instance, the background color is light enough we don't have to change the text from basic black.

```
<table width="80%" align="center" cellpadding="10">
<tr>
  <td align="center">
```

```
<h1 style="font-family: Arial; font-size: 24pt;
font-weight: bold">
Title
</h1>
</td>
</tr>

<tr>
<td align="center">
<img src="url">
</td>
</tr>

<tr>
<td>
<p style="text-align: left; font-size: 12pt;
font-family: Arial">
Description paragraph one
</p>
<p style="text-align: left; font-size: 12pt;
font-family: Arial">
Description paragraph two
</p>
</td>
</tr>

<tr>
<td bgcolor="cyan">
<p style="text-align: left; font-size: 8pt;
font-family: Arial">
<strong>Terms of Sale</strong>
<br>Terms of service</p>
</td>
</tr>

</table>
```

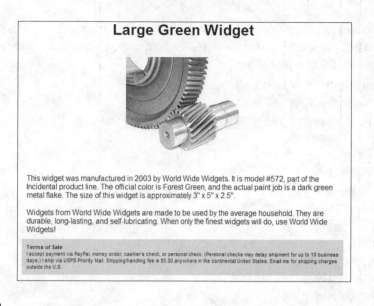

FIGURE 8.19

White background with a light-color TOS.

Template 8.20: Color Background with Different Color Border

CD-ROM Let's finish our exploration of color backgrounds by adding a contrasting color border around a light background color, as shown in Figure 8.20.

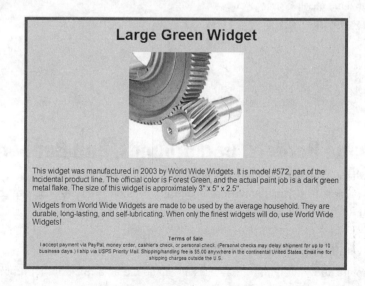

FIGURE 8.20

Light background color with contrasting color border.

This code is based on the code for Template 8.16, with the appropriate CSS **border** properties added. For this template, we've used a light brown background with a maroon (deep red) border. Other combinations, of course, are possible.

```
<table width="80%" cellpadding="10"
align="center" bgcolor="#FFCC66"
style="border-style: solid; border-width: thick;
border-color: maroon">
<tr>
  <td align="center">
  <h1 style="font-family: Arial; font-size: 24pt;
  font-weight: bold">
  Title
  </h1>
  <p><img src="URL"></p>
  <p style="text-align: left; font-size: 12pt;
  font-family: Arial">
  Description paragraph one</p>
  <p style="text-align: left; font-size: 12pt;
  font-family: Arial">
  Description paragraph two
  </p>
  <p style="text-align: center; font-size: 8pt;
  font-family: Arial">
  <strong>Terms of Sale</strong><br>
  Terms of service</p>
  </td>
</tr>

</table>
```

Adding Image Borders, Backgrounds, and Banners

The final templates in this chapter incorporate images for your listings' borders and backgrounds. Unless a particular type of image is specified, you can use any image of your choosing for these templates.

Template 8.21: Full-Page Image Border

CD-ROM The template shown in Figure 8.21 uses an image file as a thick border around your entire item listing. For best effect, the image file you use should use a small pattern, something easily discernable from within the width of the border.

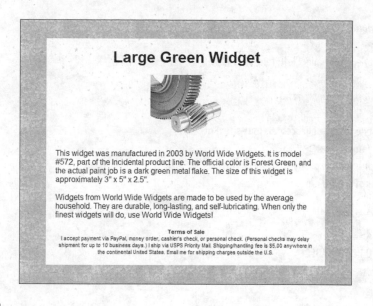

FIGURE 8.21

An image used as a border around the item listing.

This effect is accomplished by means of nested tables. The outside table has a graphic file (*BORDER-URL*) as its background; the inside table has a white background. Thus you see the white background sitting on top of the graphic background. Here's the code:

```
<!--BEGIN OUTSIDE TABLE-->
<table width="80%" border="0" cellpadding="40"
cellspacing="0" align="center"
background="BORDER-URL">
<tr>
<td>

<!--BEGIN INSIDE TABLE-->
<table width="95%" border="0" cellpadding="20"
cellspacing="0" bgcolor="white" align="center">
<tr>
  <td align="center">
  <h1 style="font-family: Arial; font-size: 24pt;
  font-weight: bold">
  Title
  </h1>
  <p><img src="URL" width="150"></p>
  <p style="text-align: left; font-size: 12pt;
  font-family: Arial">
```

```
Description paragraph one
</p>
<p style="text-align: left; font-size: 12pt;
font-family: Arial">
Description paragraph two
</p>
<p style="text-align: center; font-size: 8pt;
font-family: Arial">
<strong>Terms of Sale</strong><br>
Terms of service</p>
</td>
</tr>
</table>
<!--END INSIDE TABLE-->


</td>
</tr>
</table>
<!--END OUTSIDE TABLE-->
```

Template 8.22: Multiple Nested-Table Image Border

CD-ROM

If one image border is cool, then three image borders nested inside each other must be three times as cool. That's the theory behind this template, shown in Figure 8.22, that nests four separate tables to create a three-image border.

The code for this template uses the same approach as the code for Template 8.21, but with two more tables nested around the interior two tables. Make sure you use image files that contrast nicely with each other.

```
<table width="80%" border="0" cellpadding="40"
cellspacing="0" align="center"
background="BORDER-URL1">
<tr>
<td>

<table width="95%" border="0" cellpadding="40"
cellspacing="0"
align="center" background="BORDER-URL2">
<tr>
<td>
```

```
<table width="95%" border="0" cellpadding="40"
cellspacing="0" align="center"
background="BORDER-URL3">
<tr>
<td>

<table width="95%" border="0" cellpadding="20"
cellspacing="0" bgcolor="white" align="center">
<tr>
  <td align="center">
  <h1 style="font-family: Arial; font-size: 24pt;
  font-weight: bold">
  Title
  </h1>
  <p><img src="URL" width="150"></p>
  <p style="text-align: left; font-size: 12pt;
  font-family: Arial">
  Description paragraph one</p>
  <p style="text-align: left; font-size: 12pt;
  font-family: Arial">
  Description paragraph two
  </p>
  <p style="text-align: center; font-size: 8pt;
  font-family: Arial">
  <strong>Terms of Sale</strong><br>
  Terms of service</p>
  </td>
</tr>
</table>

</td>
</tr>
</table>

</td>
</tr>
</table>

</td>
</tr>
</table>
```

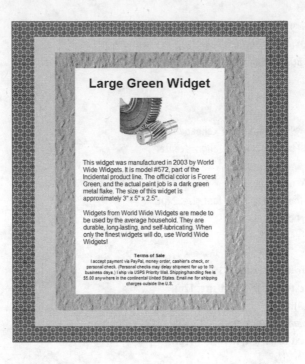

FIGURE 8.22

A nested image border around the item listing.

Template 8.23: Full-Page Image Background

CD-ROM Now let's turn our attention to the background of your listing. Just as you can use a solid color as the background to a table, you can also specify an image file to be used as the background, as shown in Figure 8.23.

The key to adding an image background to your listing is to incorporate the **background** attribute in the **<table>** tag. If the image file you use is small, it will be repeated within the table to form a pattern. If the image file is large enough, you'll see the entire image as the background. This template uses the first approach, with a single small image forming a background pattern.

```
<table width="80%" border="0" cellpadding="40"
cellspacing="0" align="center"
background="BACKGROUND-URL">
```

> **TIP**
> If you use a light background image, you're okay with standard black text. If you use a darker background image, however, you may need to change to white, yellow, or cyan text. In addition, be careful about using background images that are too busy, or that have both dark and light images; a busy background makes your text harder to read.

```
<tr>
<td>

<tr>
  <td align="center">
  <h1 style="font-family: Arial; font-size: 24pt;
  font-weight: bold">Title</h1>
  <p><img src="URL" width="150"></p>
  <p style="text-align: left; font-size: 12pt;
  font-family: Arial">
  Description paragraph one
  </p>
  <p style="text-align: left; font-size: 12pt;
  font-family: Arial">
  Description paragraph two
  </p>
  <p style="text-align: center; font-size: 8pt;
  font-family: Arial">
  <strong>Terms of Sale</strong><br>
  Terms of service</p>
  </td>
</tr>
</table>
```

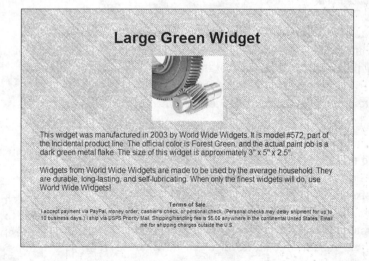

FIGURE 8.23

A small image file forming a repeated background pattern.

Template 8.24: Left-to-Right Gradated Background Image

 CD-ROM The effect you see in this template comes from using a background image that fades (gradates) left to right from dark to light. The left side of the image should be a darker color, and it should fade (quite quickly) to a plain white background. The white part of the background makes it easy to read your description text; the darker part adds necessary, but not intrusive, color to your listing.

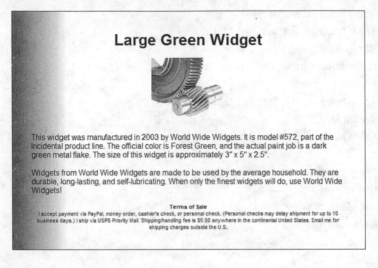

FIGURE 8.24

A gradated color background.

To create this template, we're using the exact same code as in Template 8.23, with one modification. Since we want the gradation to start on the far left side of the page, we're setting the width of the table at 100%, and the width of the interior row to 80%; this is the exact opposite of how we typically set these settings.

The key to this effect is to use a background image that is wide but short. It needs to be wide enough so that the image does not repeat in the middle of your listing; I recommend using an image with a width of 1400 pixels, just to be on the safe side. The height, however, doesn't have to be tall at all—a few pixels high is more than enough. That's because the single image will repeat over and over again down the page, creating a seamless effect.

> **CAUTION** Remember, this code can't add a gradation to a regular solid-color graphic. You have to use an image file that contains a gradated graphic—that is, an image that fades from a dark color on the left to white on the right. It's the choice of graphic that makes this template work, not the HTML code per se.

For the example in Figure 8.24, I've used a blue gradated background file. It's included on the accompanying CD; the filename is **blue-fade.jpg**, and it's sized at 28 x 1800 pixels. Feel free to use this file in your own templates.

```
<table width="100%" border="0" cellpadding="40"
cellspacing="0" align="center" background="BACKGROUND-URL">
<tr>
<td>

<tr>
  <td align="center">
  <h1 style="font-family: Arial; font-size: 24pt;
  font-weight: bold">
  Title
  </h1>
  <p><img src="URL" width="150"></p>
  <p style="text-align: left; font-size: 12pt;
  font-family: Arial">
  Description paragraph one<
  /p>
  <p style="text-align: left; font-size: 12pt;
  font-family: Arial">
  Description paragraph two
  </p>
  <p style="text-align: center; font-size: 8pt;
  font-family: Arial">
  <strong>Terms of Sale</strong><br>
  Terms of service
  </p>
  </td>
</tr>
</table>
```

Template 8.25: Top-of-Page Image Banner

CD-ROM Our final template in this chapter is a popular one. As you can see in Figure 8.25, this template uses an image banner to provide graphic interest at the top of the item listing. There is a plethora of image banners available for download from various sites on the Internet; it's good to choose a banner that ties in with the product you're selling, as well as one that matches the color scheme of the rest of the listing.

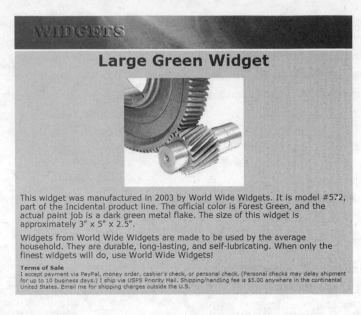

FIGURE 8.25

An image banner at the top of the item listing.

In this template, the image banner is inserted at the top of the listing, in its own table row before the title row. The color of the title and TOS text are specified to tie into the color of the banner graphic. Replace *BANNER-URL* with the URL of the banner image file; replace *PICTURE-URL* with the URL of your normal product image.

```
<table width="80%" align="center" cellpadding="0"
cellspacing="0" border="0"

<tr>
  <td align="center">
  <img src="BANNER-URL">
  </td>
</tr>

<tr bgcolor="lightblue">
  <td align="center">
  <h1 style="font-family: Verdana; font-size: 24pt;
  font-weight: bold; color: darkblue">
  Title
  </h1>
```

```
<img src="PICTURE-URL">

<p style="text-align: left; font-size: 12pt;
font-family: Verdana; margin: 10">
Description paragraph one
</p>

<p style="text-align: left; font-size: 12pt;
font-family: Verdana; margin: 10">
Description paragraph two
</p>

<p style="text-align: left; font-size: 8pt;
font-family: Verdana; color: darkblue;
margin: 10">
<strong>Terms of Sale</strong>
<br
Terms of service
</p>
</td>
</tr>

</table
```

Adding Other Page Elements and Special Effects

This chapter is a little different from the previous chapters in this section, in that it doesn't present complete templates. Instead, it focuses on a variety of specific page elements and special effects that you can add to your auction listings—links to your other auctions, shipping calculators, specification tables, and so on. These elements and effects can be added to any auction template.

To add these elements and effects to your auction template, simply copy the code as written into your existing template code, typically at the place in the template where you want the element or effect to appear. In most cases you'll have some customization to do (such as inserting specific URLs), but it's pretty easy stuff. And, to make it even easier, all of these special effects are included on the accompanying CD. Just cut, paste, and edit, and you're ready to go.

Adding Web Page and Email Links

We'll start by presenting some of the simplest elements you can add to your listing—HTML web page and email links.

Special Effect 9.1: Text Link to More Information in a New Window

 CD-ROM eBay has specific rules as to what you can and can't link to from your auction listings. In general, you can link to other eBay pages, and to non–eBay pages that present additional information pertinent to your specific auction. You *can't* link to pages that encourage non–eBay sales.

To that end, you should be very careful when you choose which pages to link to. This special element adds a text link to an external web page, as shown in Figure 9.1, and opens that web page in a new window—so your eBay auction remains open even while the external page is being read.

Click for more information

FIGURE 9.1

A text link to more information on another web page; when visitors click the link, the new page appears in a separate window.

To force the linked-to page to open in a new window, we use a special attribute within the **<a href>** tag. This attribute is **target="_blank"**; the "_blank" part is what forces a new window to open.

The entire code for this element should be inserted into your template where you want the link to appear. You can change the **text-align** property within the **<p>** tag to change the center alignment; you can also delete the **font-weight** property to make the link appear like the surrounding body text. Obviously, you should replace *URL* with the full URL (including the "http://") of the page you want to link to.

```
<p style="font-weight: bold; text-align: center">
<a href="URL" target="_blank">Click for more information</a>
</p>
```

Special Effect 9.2: Button Link to More Information

 CD-ROM Everybody uses standard text links. How about a link that appears as a button in your listing—like the one in Figure 9.2? When visitors click the button, the linked-to page appears.

FIGURE 9.2

Click the button to link to a page of more information.

This effect creates a very short form with a browser-generated button; you don't need a separate graphics file to create the button. To create this effect, we use a bit of JavaScript code that specifies what happens when the button is clicked—in this instance, a **goToURL** function. Just insert the following code where you want the button to appear in your listing. (You can also change the text on the button itself by editing the "Click for More Info" text.)

```
<script language="JavaScript">
<!-- Begin
function goToURL() { window.location = "URL"; }
// End -->
</script>

<center>
<form>
<input type=button value="Click for More Info"
➥onClick="goToURL()">
</form>
</center>
```

Special Effect 9.3: Click-to-Send Email Link

CD-ROM Another popular use of HTML links is to send email messages. This effect puts a link in your listing that, when it's clicked by a potential buyer, opens a new email message addressed to you. Visitors can use this link, like the one shown in Figure 9.3, to ask questions of you during the auction.

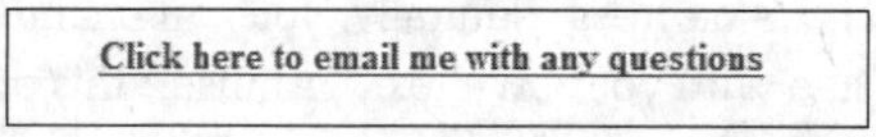

Click here to email me with any questions

FIGURE 9.3

A simple click-to-send email link; clicking the link opens a new blank email message.

This is a simple click-to-send email link, and the code is correspondingly simple. Just insert the code where you want the link to appear—and feel free to format the link text (or the <p> tag, using CSS styles) as you like. Remember to replace *EMAILADDRESS* with your full email address, in the form of *name@domain.com*.

```
<p style="font-weight: bold; text-align: center">
<a href="mailto:EMAILADDRESS">
Click here to email me with any questions
</a>
</p>
```

Special Effect 9.4: Click-to-Send Email Link with Auction Number in the Subject

CD-ROM This effect is a bit more complicated, but also much more useful. The only problem with the standard click-to-send email link is that it doesn't reference any particular auction; it's likely that you'll receive messages from potential buyers where you can't figure out which of your many auctions they're asking about. This effect, shown in Figure 9.4, fixes that problem by adding the number of the auction to the subject line of the email.

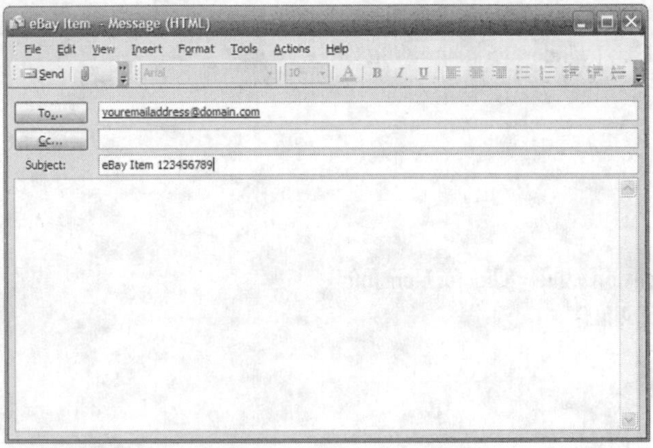

FIGURE 9.4

A click-to-send email link that puts the auction number in the subject line of the email message.

To make this apparently simple change requires quite a bit of extra code—again, using the programming capabilities of JavaScript. In the **document.write** line, you need to replace *EMAILADDRESS* with your own email address as part of the long **mailto:** line, with no spaces before or after the address. Naturally, you can change the "Click here to email me with any questions" line with your own text; just insert this entire block of code where you want the click-to-send link to appear.

```
<script type=text/javascript>
 var itemnumber = '';
 var querystring = document["location"].toString();
 if (querystring) {
  myArray = querystring.split(/&/);
   x = 0;
   while (myArray[x]) {
    values = myArray[x].split(/=/);
    if (values[0] == "item") {
     itemnumber = values[1];
    }
    x = x+1;
   }
```

```
    }
  document.write
  ("<a href='mailto:EMAILADDRESS?subject=
  ➥eBay%20Item%20"+itemnumber+"'>");
  </script>
  <p style="font-weight: bold; text-align: center">
  Click here to email me with any questions
  </p>
  </a>
```

Adding Special Elements

Now we'll examine a variety of special elements you can add to your auction listings. Some of these elements are more style than substance (such as the scrolling marquee); others are much more practical (such as the shipping rate calculators). Have fun with them!

Special Effect 9.5: Scrolling Marquee

CD-ROM This element is a flashy one, but it can help to draw attention to your listing. As you can see in Figure 9.5, it inserts a single-line scrolling marquee into your listing; the message in the marquee scrolls across the page, from right to left.

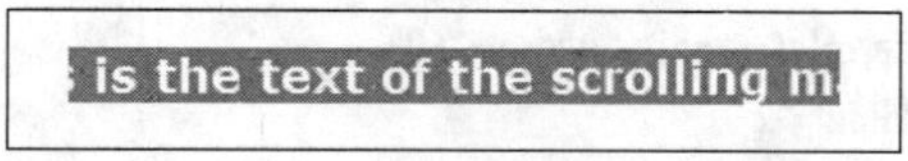

FIGURE 9.5

A scrolling marquee with reverse text.

This element is created via use of the HTML **marquee** tag. This particular marquee is formatted at 50% of the available page width, and features white text against a red background. Feel free to change the width and colors as you like; just insert the code where you want the marquee to appear, and replace *Message text* with your own text message.

```
<center>
<marquee behavior="scroll" width="50%">
<p style="font-family: Verdana; font-weight: bold;
font-size: 14pt; color: white">
<span style="background-color: red">
Message text
</span>
</p>
</marquee>
</center>
```

Special Effect 9.6: Size and Specification Table

CD-ROM Many types of products can benefit from the display of specifications in tabular format. For example, if you're selling an item of clothing you can use a two-column table to present size, color, and fabric information. (Such a table is shown in Figure 9.6.)

Size & Specifications	
Size	Medium
Color	Light blue
Material	100% cotton
Manufacturer	Lasperi Fabrics
Condition	Slightly worn

FIGURE 9.6

A two-column product information table.

This code creates a two-column table. The table header is displayed in a single-column row, using the **colspan** attribute. The cells are all dark blue, with white text and a large white space between the cells. This effect is accomplished by setting the table background color to white, but the row background color to dark blue (with white borders); it's a nice touch. To add more rows to the table, just insert additional **<tr>** blocks. You can even add columns to the table by inserting additional **<td>** column codes under each **<tr>** row code; just remember to adjust the value of the **colspan** attribute accordingly.

```
<table border="2" bordercolor="white" width="60%"
cellspacing="3" cellpadding="2"
bgcolor="white" align="center">
  <tr bordercolor="white" bgcolor="darkblue">
    <td colspan="2" align="center">
    <font color="Yellow" face="Verdana"><strong>
    Table Title</strong></font>
    </td>
  </tr>

  <tr bordercolor="white" bgcolor="darkblue">
    <td align="center" width="50%">
    <font color="white" face="Verdana">
    Specification
    </font>
    </td>
    <td align="center" width="50%">
    <font color="white" face="Verdana">
    Value
    </font>
```

```
      </td>
    </tr>

    <tr bordercolor="white" bgcolor="darkblue">
      <td align="center" width="50%">
      <font color="white" face="Verdana">
Specification
      </font>
      </td>
      <td align="center" width="50%">
      <font color="white" face="Verdana">
Value
      </font>
      </td>
    </tr>

    <tr bordercolor="white" bgcolor="darkblue">
      <td align="center" width="50%">
      <font color="white" face="Verdana">
Specification
      </font>
      </td>
      <td align="center" width="50%">
      <font color="white" face="Verdana">
Value
      </font>
      </td>
    </tr>

    <tr bordercolor="white" bgcolor="darkblue">
      <td align="center" width="50%">
      <font color="white" face="Verdana">
Specification
      </font>
      </td>
      <td align="center" width="50%">
      <font color="white" face="Verdana">
Value
      </font>
      </td>
    </tr>
```

```
<tr bordercolor="white" bgcolor="darkblue">
  <td align="center" width="50%">
  <font color="white" face="Verdana">
  Specification
  </font>
  </td>
  <td align="center" width="50%">
  <font color="white" face="Verdana">
  Value
  </font>
  </td>
</tr>

</table>
```

Special Effect 9.7: eBay Search Box

This next element adds an eBay search box to your item listing, so buyers can search for other auctions items they might like directly from your item listing. The nice thing about this code is that you can use it on other web pages outside of eBay; it's a great way to put an eBay search on a personal web page. (The search box is shown in Figure 9.7.)

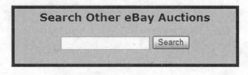

FIGURE 9.7

Let potential buyers search other eBay auctions.

The code for this search box uses HTML form code; users' input is fed into eBay's own search form, as specified in the **<form action>** code. The results are displayed on a standard eBay search results page. (Feel free, by the way, to change the border, background, and text colors in the **<table>** tag.)

```
<table width="50%" style="border-style: ridge;
border-width: 5px; border-color: blue;
background-color: lightblue" align="center">
<tr>
<td>
  <h3 style="font-family: Verdana; text-align: center;
  color: darkblue">
  Search Other eBay Auctions
```

```
</h3>
<center>
<form action="http://search.ebay.com/search/search.dll"
➥ method="get">
<input type="text" maxlength="300" name="satitle"
➥size="20">
<input type="submit" value="Search">
</form>
</center>
</td>
</tr>
</table>
```

Special Effect 9.8: U.S. Postal Service Shipping Rate Calculator

CD-ROM eBay has its own shipping calculator, of course, but it doesn't display within the body of a custom auction template. You can correct this oversight by inserting your own custom shipping calculator into your template's HTML code; this particular calculator, shown in Figure 9.8, is for U.S. Postal Service shipping. When a potential buyer enters his ZIP code and clicks the Calculate button, the Postal Service's official rate page appears, with shipping rates for the various services (Priority Mail, Media Mail, and so on) listed.

FIGURE 9.8

A shipping calculator for the U.S. Postal Service.

Admittedly, this is a lot of code; some of the code creates the shipping calculator form in your listing, some of the code feeds the buyer's input to the Postal Service's shipping calculator page. You'll need to input all the data for your specific auction, including *ZIPCODE* (your ZIP code), *POUNDS* and *OUNCES* (the weight of the item), and the *LENGTH, WIDTH,* and *HEIGHT* of the shipping box (in inches). You can also alter the **Add $1 handling to above** line to reflect your own additional handling charge.

```
<form action='http://postcalc.usps.gov/speed.asp'
➥name=zipform target=_blank>
<input type=hidden name=OZ value=ZIPCODE>
<input type=hidden name=MT value=2>
<input type=hidden name=M value=0>
<input type=hidden name=MC value=1>
<input type=hidden name=P value=POUNDS>
<input type=hidden name=O value=OUNCES>
<input type=hidden name=Length value=LENGTH>
<input type=hidden name=Width value=WIDTH>
<input type=hidden name=Height value=HEIGHT>

<center>
<table style="padding: 0; border-style: ridge;
border-width: 5px;
border-color: blue; background-color: white">
<tr>
<td>

<table style="padding: 4px; background-color: white">
<tr>
<td>
<center>
<img
src="http://www.usps.com/common/images/hdr_uspsLogo.gif"
alt="USPS" border="0">
</center>
<p style="font-family: Verdana; font-size: 12pt;
color: darkblue; font-weight: bold; text-align: center">
Calculate Shipping Costs
</p>
<p style="font-family: Verdana; font-size: 10pt;
color: black; font-weight: bold; text-align: center">
Enter your U.S. ZIP Code:
</p>
<center>
<input type=text size=5 maxlength=5 name=DZ>
<input type=submit value=Calculate name=zipok2>
</center>
<p style="font-family: Verdana; color: darkblue;
font-size: 8pt; font-style: italic; text-align: center">
```

```
Please add $1 handling to above.
</p>
</td>
</tr>
</table>

</td>
</tr>
</table>

<p style="font-family: Verdana; margin-top: 10pt;
color: black; font-size: 10pt">
This is an estimate. Actual shipping costs may vary.
</p>
</center>
</form>
```

Special Effect 9.9: UPS Shipping Rate Calculator

CD-ROM The previous effect created a Postal Service shipping rate calculator—but what if you don't use the Postal Service for shipping? That's where the special effect shown in Figure 9.9 proves useful; it creates a similar shipping rate calculator for UPS shipping.

FIGURE 9.9

A UPS shipping rate calculator.

The code for this rate calculator is similar to the one for the Postal Service rate calculator. You have to enter the data for your specific auction, including *WEIGHT, LENGTH, WIDTH,* and *HEIGHT* (in inches), along with *INSURED VALUE.* You also need to enter your *ZIPCODE* and *CITY*, and edit the **Add $1 handling to above** line to reflect the actual handling charge you add to your auctions.

```
<form action='http://wwwapps.ups.com/ctc/htmlTool'
➥ target=_blank>
<input type=hidden name=accept_UPS_license_agreement
➥ value=yes>
<input type=hidden name=nonUPS_title
➥ value='UPS Shipping Rate Calculator'>
<input type=hidden name=nonUPS_body value='bgcolor=#FFFFFF'>
<input type=hidden name=nonUPS_light_color value=#C0C0B0>
<input type=hidden name=nonUPS_dark_color value=#B8B8A8>
<input type=hidden name=nonUPS_header value="
➥<Font face=san_serif,verdana,arial>
<h1>
<img src="http://www.ups.com/membership/
➥letter/images/logo.gif'
➥ border=0 align=left>
<Font color=#885533>UPS Shipping Estimate</font><br>
<Font size=+1>
This is an estimate. Actual shipping costs may vary.
</font>
</h1>">
<input type=hidden name=14_origCountry value=US>
<input type=hidden name=15_origPostal value=ZIPCODE>
<input type=hidden name=origCity value="CITY">
<input type=hidden name=49_residential value=01>
<input type=hidden
➥name=47_rate_chart value="Customer Counter">
<input type=hidden name=billToUPS value=Yes>
<input type=hidden name=48_container value=00>
<input type=hidden name=weight_std value=lbs.>
<input type=hidden name=23_weight value=WEIGHT>
<input type=hidden name=length_std value=in.>
<input type=hidden name=25_length value=LENGTH>
<input type=hidden name=26_width value=WIDTH>
<input type=hidden name=27_height value=HEIGHT>
<input type=hidden name=10_action value=4>
<input type=hidden name=24_value value=INSURED-VALUE>
<input type=hidden name=customValue value=100>
```

```
<input type=hidden name=22_destCountry value=US>

<center>
<table style="padding: 0; border-style: ridge;
border-width: 5px;
border-color: #996633; background-color: tan">
<tr>
<td>

<table style="padding: 4px; background-color: tan">
<tr>
<td>
<center>
<img src="http://www.ups.com/membership/
➥letter/images/logo.gif"
➥alt="UPS" border="0">
</center>

<p style="font-family: Verdana; font-size: 12pt;
color: #663300; font-weight: bold; text-align: center">
Calculate Shipping Costs
</p>

<p style="font-family: Verdana; font-size: 10pt;
color: black; font-weight: bold; text-align: center">
Enter your U.S. ZIP Code:
</p>

<center>
<input type=text name=19_destPostal size=5 maxlength=5>
<input type=submit value=Calculate>
</center>

<p style="font-family: Verdana; color: #663300;
font-size: 8pt; font-style: italic; text-align: center">
Please add $1 handling to above.
</p>
</td>
</tr>
</table>
```

Cross-Promoting Your Other Auctions

If you're running more than one auction, it's useful to cross-promote your other auctions in each auction listing. There are a number of ways to do this; the following special elements provide various types of cross-promotional links.

Special Effect 9.10: Link to Your About Me Page

 CD-ROM If you've done a good job creating your About Me page, it's helpful to link to that page from each auction listing. (Your About Me page, after all, should include a listing of all your current auctions—as well as your recent feedback.) This special effect creates a simple text link to your About Me page, as shown in Figure 9.10, nothing fancy involved.

> Click here to view my About Me page

FIGURE 9.10

A text link to your About Me page.

This is a very simple HTML link to your About Me page. Replace *USERID* with your eBay user ID, and insert the code in your template where you want the link to appear. (You can also format the **<p>** tag to change the font face or style.)

```
<p style="font-weight: bold; text-align: center">
<a href="http://cgi3.ebay.com/ws/
➥eBayISAPI.dll?ViewUserPage&userid=USERID">
Click here to view my About Me page
</a>
</p>
```

Special Effect 9.11: Link to Your eBay Store

CD-ROM If you also have an eBay Store, you can link to that store from within your auction template. This special effect creates a simple text link to your Store, as shown in Figure 9.11.

> Click here to visit my eBay Store

FIGURE 9.11

A text link to your eBay Store.

This code creates an HTML link to your eBay Store. Replace *STORE-NAME* with the name of your Store, and insert the code where you want the link to appear.

```
<p style="font-weight: bold; text-align: center">
<a href=" http://stores.ebay.com/STORE-NAME">
Click here to visit my eBay Store
</a>
</p>
```

Special Effect 9.12: Link to Your eBay Store with the eBay Stores Logo

CD-ROM Now let's get a little fancier, by inserting the eBay Stores logo and making that logo link to your Store page. This effect is shown in Figure 9.12.

FIGURE 9.12

Buyers can click the eBay Stores logo to visit your Store.

Insert the following code where you want the logo to appear in your listing. Replace *STORE–NAME* with the name of your Store, of course.

```
<p style="font-family: Verdana; font-weight: bold;
font-size: 8pt; font-color: red; text-align: center">
<a href="http://stores.ebay.com/STORE-NAME">
<img src="http://pics.ebaystatic.com/aw/
➥pics/icon/imgStores_55x16.gif"
➥border="0"><br>
Click to visit my eBay Store
</a>
</p>
```

Special Effect 9.13: Link to Your Auction Listings Page

CD-ROM Now let's get down to real cross-selling, with a text link to all your current eBay auctions, as shown in Figure 9.13.

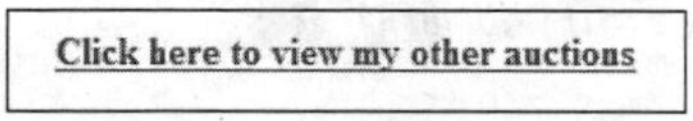

FIGURE 9.13

A text link to your current eBay auctions.

Insert this code snippet into your template where you want the link to appear. Replace *[USERID]* with your eBay user ID, so that your user ID (with no brackets) appears as an unbroken part of the URL.

```
<p style="font-weight: bold; text-align: center">
<a href="http://search.ebay.com/_W0QQsassZ[USERID]QQhtZ-1">
Click here to view my other auctions
</a>
</p>
```

Special Effect 9.14: Individual Text Links to Your Other Auctions

CD-ROM Special Effect 9.13 created a text link to a list of all your auction listings. You can also create individual text links to your current auctions, as presented in Figure 9.14.

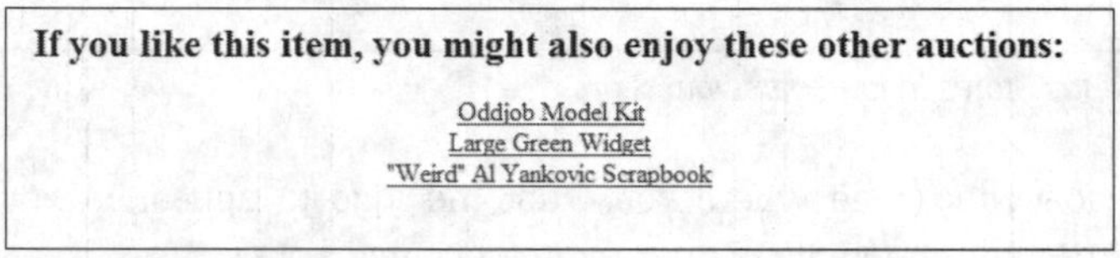

> **If you like this item, you might also enjoy these other auctions:**
>
> Oddjob Model Kit
> Large Green Widget
> "Weird" Al Yankovic Scrapbook

FIGURE 9.14

Text links to individual auction listings.

To use this special element, you need to know the item numbers of the auctions you want to link to. Insert each item number as part of the long URL, replacing the *ITEMNUMBER* text. You should also replace *Auction name* with the title of each auction. This code snippet allows for three auction listings; just insert additional **<a href>** tags to include additional listings.

```
<center>
<h2>
If you like this item, you might also enjoy
these other auctions:
</h2>
<p>
<a href="http://cgi.ebay.com/ws/
➥eBayISAPI.dll?ViewItem&item=ITEMNUMBER1">
Auction name</a><br>
<a href="http://cgi.ebay.com/ws/
➥eBayISAPI.dll?ViewItem&item=ITEMNUMBER2">
Auction name</a><br>
```

```
<a href="http://cgi.ebay.com/ws/
➥eBayISAPI.dll?ViewItem&item=ITEMNUMBER3">
Auction name</a>
</p>
</center>
```

Special Effect 9.15: Drop-Down Menu of Your Other Auctions

CD-ROM   Here's another way to include links to your other auctions. This special effect, shown in Figure 9.15, creates a drop-down menu that includes menu items for each of your other auctions; when a visitor clicks a menu item, that auction is displayed.

FIGURE 9.15

A drop-down menu of your current auction listings.

This code requires a bit of input on your part. First, you need to insert the item numbers for each of your auctions in place of the *ITEMNUMBER* text. Then replace *Auction name* with the title of each auction. Finally, insert this entire code snippet into your template HTML where you want the drop-down menu to appear.

```
<center>
<form>
<select name="URL"
onChange="if(options[selectedIndex].value)
window.location.href=
(options[selectedIndex].value)">
<OPTION value="">My Other Auctions</OPTION>
<OPTION value=http://cgi.ebay.com/ws/
➥eBayISAPI.dll?ViewItem&item=ITEMNUMBER1>
Auction name</OPTION>
<OPTION value= http://cgi.ebay.com/ws/
➥eBayISAPI.dll?ViewItem&item=ITEMNUMBER2>
Auction name</OPTION>
<OPTION value= http://cgi.ebay.com/ws/
➥eBayISAPI.dll?ViewItem&item=ITEMNUMBER3>
Auction name</OPTION>
<OPTION value= http://cgi.ebay.com/ws/
➥eBayISAPI.dll?ViewItem&item=ITEMNUMBER4>
```

```
Auction name</OPTION>
</select>

<noscript>
<input type=submit value="Go">
</noscript>
</input>
</form>
</center>
```

Special Effect 9.16: Picture Gallery Links to Your Other Auctions

CD-ROM Finally, let's examine the most visual way to cross-promote your other auctions—by including a picture gallery of those auctions in your auction listing. Figure 9.16 shows what this type of gallery looks like.

FIGURE 9.16

A picture gallery of all your other auction items.

This code creates a table that houses thumbnail images of all your current auction items. This particular HTML is for a two-row, five-column table that can display 10 auction items. You can add additional rows to display more photos, or delete a row to display fewer items. Each image is set for a standard 75-pixel width, which is an okay compromise for pictures of varying sizes and dimensions. Naturally, you need to replace the *ITEMNUMBER* text (in both the **<a href>** and **<img>** tags) with the item numbers of your particular auctions.

```
<table align="center">
<tr>
td>
<font style="font-family: Verdana; font-size: 14pt;
font-weight: bold; color: darkblue; align: center">
Click the thumbnails to view my other auctions
</p>
```

```
</td>
</tr>
</table>

<table style="border-style: ridge; border-color: blue;
border-width: 4px; padding: 0" align="center">
<tr>
<td width="75" height="96" border="0" cellpadding="0"
cellspacing="0" bordercolor="blue">

<table align="center" width="75" height="96" border="1"
cellpadding="0" cellspacing="0" bordercolor="white">
<tr>
<td>
<a href="http://cgi.ebay.com/ws/
➥eBayISAPI.dll?ViewItem&item=ITEMNUMBER1"
➥target="_self">
<img src="http://thumbs.ebay.com/pict/ITEMNUMBER1.jpg"
➥width="75" border="0">
</a>
</td>

<td>
<a href="http://cgi.ebay.com/ws/
➥eBayISAPI.dll?ViewItem&item=ITEMNUMBER2"
➥target="_self">
<img src="http://thumbs.ebay.com/pict/ITEMNUMBER2.jpg"
➥width="75" border="0">
</a>
</td>

<td>
<a href="http://cgi.ebay.com/ws/
➥eBayISAPI.dll?ViewItem&item=ITEMNUMBER3"
➥target="_self">
<img src="http://thumbs.ebay.com/pict/ITEMNUMBER3.jpg"
➥width="75" border="0">
</a>
</td>

<td>
<a href="http://cgi.ebay.com/ws/
```

```
➥eBayISAPI.dll?ViewItem&item=ITEMNUMBER4"
➥target="_self">
<img src="http://thumbs.ebay.com/pict/ITEMNUMBER4.jpg"
➥width="75" border="0">
</a>
</td>

<td>
<a href="http://cgi.ebay.com/ws/
➥eBayISAPI.dll?ViewItem&item=ITEMNUMBER5"
➥target="_self">
<img src="http://thumbs.ebay.com/pict/ITEMNUMBER5.jpg"
➥width="75" border="0">
</a>
</td>
</tr>

<tr>
<td>
<a href="http://cgi.ebay.com/ws/
➥eBayISAPI.dll?ViewItem&item=ITEMNUMBER6"
➥target="_self">
<img src="http://thumbs.ebay.com/pict/ITEMNUMBER6.jpg"
➥width="75" border="0">
</a>
</td>

<td>
<a href="http://cgi.ebay.com/ws/
➥eBayISAPI.dll?ViewItem&item=ITEMNUMBER7"
➥target="_self">
<img src="http://thumbs.ebay.com/pict/ITEMNUMBER7.jpg"
➥width="75" border="0">
</a>
</td>

<td>
<a href="http://cgi.ebay.com/ws/
➥eBayISAPI.dll?ViewItem&item=ITEMNUMBER8"
➥target="_self">
```

```
<img src="http://thumbs.ebay.com/pict/ITEMNUMBER8.jpg"
➥width="75" border="0">
</a>
</td>

<td>
<a href="http://cgi.ebay.com/ws/
➥eBayISAPI.dll?ViewItem&item=ITEMNUMBER9"
➥target="_self">
<img src="http://thumbs.ebay.com/pict/ITEMNUMBER9.jpg"
➥width="75" border="0">
</a>
</td>

<td>
<a href="http://cgi.ebay.com/ws/
➥eBayISAPI.dll?ViewItem&item=ITEMNUMBER10"
➥target="_self">
<img src="http://thumbs.ebay.com/pict/ITEMNUMBER10.jpg"
➥width="75" border="0">
</a>
</td>
</tr>

</table>
</table>
```

Adding Audio and Video to Your Listing

The final special effects in this chapter can turn any auction listing into a multimedia extravaganza, sort of. Be cautious when using these effects, however, as many users either don't have the bandwidth (due to slow dial-up connections) or patience to sit through your audio/visual add-ins.

Special Effect 9.17: Playing Background Music or Sounds

CD-ROM This is a special effect that I personally find annoying, but to each his (or her) own. What this special effect does is trigger the automatic playback of a music file when your auction listing loads.

There's actually nothing to see here, as this code embeds the audio playback into the HTML of your auction listing. The **autostart="true"** parameter is what starts the playback when the page loads; the **loop="true"** parameter forces the file to replay over and over until the visitor leaves.

Just insert the following code at the start of your template HTML:

```
<embed src="SOUND-URL" hide="true" autostart="true"
➥loop="true">
```

Special Effect 9.18: Playing a Sound or Music on Request

CD-ROM Some auction items beg to be listened to. I'm not talking about adding voice narration (although that's an interesting thought), but rather including music snippets from CDs or sound samples from vintage toys, that sort of thing. Since these audio samples aren't background music, you don't want them playing continuously when the auction page loads. Instead, you want to give visitors the option of hearing these sounds at their request. That's where this special element comes in, inserting a click-to-play sound sample in your auction listing, as shown in Figure 9.17.

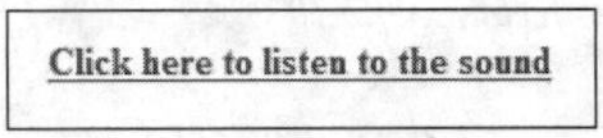

Click here to listen to the sound

FIGURE 9.17

A click-to-play sound insert.

To use this code, you first must upload the audio file to a server of your choice. Then replace *SOUND-URL* with the URL and filename of the audio file, and you're ready to go.

```
<p style="font-weight: bold; text-align: center">
<a href="SOUND-URL">
Click here to listen to the sound
</a>
</p>
```

Special Effect 9.19: Playing a Video on Request

CD-ROM Other auction items need to be demonstrated. If you have a short video of your product in action, this special effect inserts a video playback window into your auction listing, as shown in Figure 9.18. All visitors have to do is click the "play" button to initiate playback.

It's interesting to me how easy it is to insert something as fancy as a video playback window. Just insert the following code into your HTML template where you want the playback window to appear; replace *VIDEO-URL* with the full URL and filename of the video file.

```
<center>
<embed src="VIDEO-URL" hide="false" autostart="false"
➥loop="false"
width="300" height="300">
</center>
```

FIGURE 9.18

A video playback window in your auction listing.

Special Effect 9.20: Playing a Flash Animation

CD-ROM Likewise, you can insert a Flash animation into the body of your auction listing. You create Flash animations with the Macromedia Flash or Macromedia Studio programs, both available from www.macromedia.com. Most Flash animations are set to play back automatically when the web page is loaded.

Once you've created your Flash file and uploaded it to an external server, you embed it into your auction listing by inserting the following code into your HTML template where you want the animation to appear. Replace *CLASSID* with the class ID of the animation; replace *FLASH-URL* with the full URL and filename of the Flash file; and edit the **width** and **height** parameters to match the width and height of your animation.

```
<object classid="CLASSID" width="400" height="400">
<param name="movie" value="FLASH-URL">
<param name="quality" value="high">
<param name="bgcolor" value="#FFFFFF">

<!--CODE FOR NETSCAPE COMPATIBLITY-->
<embed src="FLASH-URL"
quality="high" bgcolor="#FFFFFF" width="400" height="400"
```

```
name="eBayMovie" align=""
type="application/x-shockwave-flash"
pluginpage="http://www.macromedia.com/go/getflashplayer">
</embed>
<!--END OF NETSCAPE COMPATIBLITY CODE-->

</object
```

Putting It All Together: Ten Ready-to-Use Auction Templates

In this final chapter we'll put together all the techniques presented throughout the book and use them to create 10 ready-to-use auction templates. There's very little new here; these templates use previously presented code as building blocks for these more-complex templates.

As with all the templates in this book, feel free to customize these templates for your own individual needs. There's nothing proprietary here; use the code as best you like.

Ten Sophisticated Auction Templates

The code for all 10 of these auction templates can be found on the CD that accompanies this book. Each template is located in the **Starter Kit Templates** folder, as are the graphics files necessary to present the templates as you see them here. You'll need to copy the graphics files from the CD to your computer's hard disk, and then upload the files to an external server or photo hosting service before you post the listing to eBay. Naturally, you should edit the URLs in the HTML code to reference the uploaded locations of each of the files.

Template 10.1: Colorful Borders and Background

 CD-ROM This template uses nested tables to create a very colorful multi-layer border. The outside border is a pulsating blue, with a pulsating red in the middle, and a pulsating gold as the background for the description. It's a very neat effect, quite different than what you find in a typical eBay listing.

FIGURE 10.1

A colorful template with nested borders.

The auction code itself is relatively simple, with space for two photos; the first photo can be as large as you want, the second photo is limited to a width of 150 pixels. In the code, replace the filenames for the background images (**bluestripbackground.jpg**, **redstripbackground. jpg**, and **goldstripbackground.jpg**) with the full URLs and filenames after you've uploaded the files to your own photo hosting server.

```html
<table width="80%" border="0" cellpadding="40"
cellspacing="0" align="center"
background="bluestripbackground.jpg">
<tr>
<td>

<table width="95%" border="0" cellpadding="40"
cellspacing="0" align="center"
background="redstripbackground.jpg">
<tr>
<td>

<table width="95%" border="0" cellpadding="20"
cellspacing="0" align="center"
background="goldstripbackground.jpg">
<tr>
  <td align="center">
  <h1 style="font-family: Times Roman; font-size: 36pt;
  font-weight: bold">
  Auction Title
  </h1>

  <p><img src="PICTURE1"></p>

  <p style="text-align: center; font-size: 14 pt;
  font-family: Times Roman; font-weight: bold;
  text-align: center; color: darkblue">
  This is the text for your auction's overview paragraph.
  This paragraph should be no more than 2-3
  sentences long.
  </p>

  <p><img src="PICTURE2" width="150px"></p>

  <p style="text-align: left; font-size: 12pt;
  font-family: Times Roman">
```

This is the text for the first paragraph of the
item description. The text can be as long as you like,
although 4-5 sentences is probably long enough.
You don't want to make this paragraph too long for
potential buyers to read. Include all the details you
need, but no more than necessary.
```
</p>
```

```
<p style="text-align: left; font-size: 12pt;
font-family: Times Roman">
```
This is the text for the second paragraph of the item
description. The text can be as long as you like,
although 4-5 sentences is probably long enough. You
don't want to make this paragraph too long for
potential buyers to read. Include all the details
you need, but no more than necessary.
```
</p>
</td>
</tr>
```

```
<tr>
<td align="center">
```

```
<table width="75%" cellpadding="5">
```

```
<tr>
<td colspan="2">
<p style="font-family: Times Roman; font-size: 14 pt;
font-weight: bold; color: darkblue; text-align: center">
```
Payment and Shipping Details
```
</p>
</td>
</tr>
```

```
<tr>
<td bgcolor="blue" width="25%" valign="top">
<p style="font-family: Times Roman; font-size: 10 pt;
font-weight: bold; text-align: right; color: white">
```
Payment
```
</p>
</td>
```

```
    <td bgcolor="darkblue" width="75%" valign="top">
    <p style="font-family: Times Roman; font-size: 10 pt;
    text-align: left;      color: white">
    I accept credit cards via PayPal, money orders,
    cashier's checks, and personal checks. Personal
    checks will delay shipment for ten business days.
    </p>
    </td>
</tr>

<tr>
    <td bgcolor="blue" width="25%" valign="top">
    <p style="font-family: Times Roman; font-size: 10 pt;
    font-weight: bold; text-align: right; color: white">
    Shipping
    </p>
    </td>

    <td bgcolor="darkblue" width="75%" valign="top">
    <p style="font-family: Times Roman; font-size: 10 pt;
    text-align: left;
    color: white">
    I ship via USPS Priority Mail. Shipping/handling charge
    to any location in the continental United States is
    $6.00. Email me for shipping/handling outside the U.S.
    </p>
    </td>
</tr>

<tr>
    <td bgcolor="blue" width="25%" valign="top">
    <p style="font-family: Times Roman; font-size: 10 pt;
    font-weight: bold; text-align: right; color: white">
    Returns
    </p>
    </td>

    <td bgcolor="darkblue" width="75%" valign="top">
    <p style="font-family: Times Roman; font-size: 10 pt;
    text-align: left; color: white">
    All sales are guaranteed for 30 days after receipt.
```

```
Please contact me if not satisfied. Buyer is
responsible for return postage.
</p>
</td>
</tr>
</table>

<p style="font-family: Times Roman; font-size: 12pt;
font-weight: bold; text-align: center">
<a href="http://search.ebay.com/_W0QQsassZ[USERID]QQhtZ-1">
Click here to view my other auctions
</a>
</p>

</td>
</tr>
</table>

</td>
</tr>
</table>

</td>
</tr>
</table>
```

Template 10.2: Bullets and Pictures

CD-ROM This template is ideal for any item where you need to present a lot of detailed features. The features are presented in a bulleted list in the right column, with the terms of sale at the bottom of that column. The wider left column includes the title and descriptive text, as well as a click-to-enlarge picture gallery. Visual interest is accomplished via the wide color border and the graphic banner at the top of the listing.

The click-to-enlarge picture gallery accommodates four pictures; you'll need to create both regular-sized and thumbnail versions of all your photos, and replace the *URL-BIG* and *URL-SMALL* text with the appropriate URLs and filenames. Also remember to replace *[USERID]* in the "other auctions" code with your own eBay ID. Make sure to copy the **greenbanner.jpg** file to your own photo host, and change the **<img>** reference to the new URL and filename.

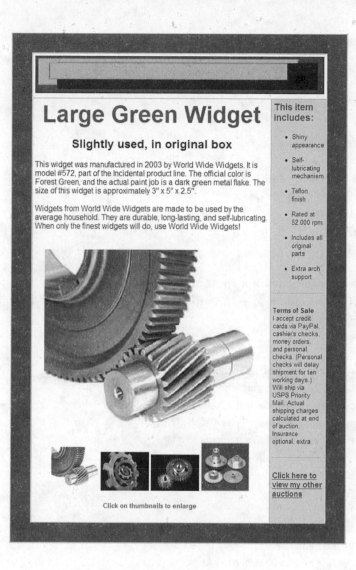

FIGURE 10.2

A template with right-column bullets, click-to-enlarge picture gallery, and graphic banner.

```
<table width="100%" cellpadding=40 cellspacing=0 border=1
bgcolor="darkgreen">
<tr>
  <td width="100%">

<table width=100% cellpadding=5 cellspacing=0 border=1
bgcolor="white">
<tr>
```

```
    <td colspan="2">
    <img src="greenbanner.jpg" width="100%">
    </td>
</tr>

<tr>
    <td width="70%" valign="top" >

    <p style="font-family: Arial; font-size: 36pt;
    font-weight: bold; color: darkgreen;
    text-align: center">
    Auction Title
    </p>

    <p style="font-family: Arial; font-size: 18pt;
    font-weight: bold; color: black; text-align: center">
    Auction Subtitle
    </p>

    <p style="font-family: Arial; text-align: left">
    This is the text for the first paragraph of the item
    description. The text can be as long as you like,
    although 4-5 sentences is probably long enough.
    You don't want to make this paragraph too long for
    potential buyers to read. Include all the details
    you need, but no more than necessary.
    </p>

    <p style="font-family: Arial; text-align: left">
    This is the text for the second paragraph of the item
    description. The text can be as long as you like,
    although 4-5 sentences is probably long enough.
    You don't want to make this paragraph too long for
    potential buyers to read. Include all the details
    you need, but no more than necessary.
    </p>

    <table align="center" cellspacing="20" height="500">
    <tr>
      <td>
      <center>
```

```
<img src="URL1-BIG" height="400" border="0"
alt name="the_pic"><br>
<a href="#"; onClick="document.the_pic.src=
➥'URL1-BIG';return false;">
<img src="URL1-SMALL" border="0"></a>
<a href="#"; onClick="document.the_pic.src=
➥'URL2-BIG';return false;">
<img src="URL2-SMALL" border="0"></a>
<a href="#"; onClick="document.the_pic.src=
➥'URL3-BIG';return false;">
<img src="URL3-SMALL" border="0"></a>
<a href="#"; onClick="document.the_pic.src=
➥'URL4-BIG';return false;">
<img src="URL4-SMALL" border="0"></a>
</center>
<p style="text-align: center; font-family: Arial;
font-weight: bold; color: darkgreen;
font-size: 10pt">
Click on thumbnails to enlarge
</p>
</td>
</tr>
</table>
</td>

<td bgcolor="#DDDDDD" width="30%" valign="top">
<p style="font-family: Arial; font-size: 14pt;
font-weight: bold; color: darkgreen">
This item includes:
</p>
<ul style="font-family: Arial; font-size: 10pt">
<li style="margin-bottom: 10pt">Bullet point</li>
<li style="margin-bottom: 10pt">Bullet point</li>
<li style="margin-bottom: 10pt">Bullet point</li>
<li style="margin-bottom: 10pt">Bullet point</li>
<li style="margin-bottom: 10pt">Bullet point</li>
<li style="margin-bottom: 10pt">Bullet point</li>
<li style="margin-bottom: 10pt">Bullet point</li>
<li style="margin-bottom: 10pt">Bullet point</li>
<li style="margin-bottom: 10pt">Bullet point</li>
<li style="margin-bottom: 10pt">Bullet point</li>
```

```
</ul>
<hr>
<p style="font-family: Arial; font-size: 10 pt">
<strong>Terms of Sale</strong><br>
I accept credit cards via PayPal, cashier's checks,
money orders, and personal checks. (Personal checks
will delay shipment for ten working days.)
Will ship via USPS Priority Mail. Actual shipping
charges calculated at end of auction.
Insurance optional, extra.
</p>

<hr>

<p style="font-weight: bold; font-family: Arial">
<a href="http://search.ebay.com/
➥_W0QQsassZ[USERID]QQhtZ-1">
Click here to view my other auctions
</a>
</p>

</td>
</tr>
</table>
</table>
```

Template 10.3: Banners and Backgrounds

CD-ROM This is a nice-looking template for when you have a single photo to present. It uses color-coordinated top and bottom banners and puts the main text against a similar color background. A white background is used behind the title (which is in the darker color) and the terms of service. Notice also the graphic links to your other auctions and About Me page.

This is relatively simple code. We start with the top banner (flush left, since it fades to white on the right), followed by centered title and subtitle in the banner color. Then it's a two-column table with background the same color as the banner and title text. After the table are the other auctions and About Me graphic links, followed by the short bottom banner, centered on the page. Remember to replace *[USERID]* and *USERID* with your eBay User ID. In addition, make sure you upload the **tealbanner.jpg**, **tealbottom.jpg**, **aboutmegraphic.jpg**, and **auctiongraphic.jpg** graphics files to your picture host, and insert the full URLs of their new locations.

FIGURE 10.3

A listing with color-coordinated banners and backgrounds.

```
<img src="tealbanner.jpg" width=95% >

<p style="font-size: 36pt; font-weight: bold;
color: teal; text-align: center">
Auction Title
</p>

<p style="font-size: 18pt; font-weight: bold;
color: teal; text-align: center">
Auction Subtitle
</p>

<table bgcolor="teal" cellpadding="10">
<tr>
  <td  width="300">
```

```
<img src="URL" width="300">
</td>

<td valign="top">
<p style="font-size: 14pt; font-weight: bold;
color: white; text-align: left">
This is the overview paragraph. It should be relatively
short, no more than 2-3 sentences long.
</p>

<p style="font-size: 12pt; color: white;
text-align: left">
This is the text for the first paragraph of the item
description. The text can be as long as you like,
although 4-5 sentences is probably long enough.
You don't want to make this paragraph too long for
potential buyers to read. Include all the details you
need, but no more than necessary.
</p>

<p style="font-size: 12pt; color: white;
text-align: left">
This is the text for the second paragraph of the item
description. The text can be as long as you like,
although 4-5 sentences is probably long enough. You
don't want to make this paragraph too long for
potential buyers to read. Include all the details
you need, but no more than necessary.
</p>

</td>
</tr>
</table>

<p style="font-size: 10pt; color: darkblue;
text-align: center; font-weight: bold">
Sold as-is. Shipment via USPS Media Mail. I accept PayPal,
cashier's check, money order, or personal check.
</p>

<center>
<p>
```

```
<a href="http://search.ebay.com/_W0QQsassZ[USERID]QQhtZ-1">
<img src="auctiongraphic.jpg" border="0">
</a>
<a href="http://cgi3.ebay.com/ws/
➥eBayISAPI.dll?ViewUserPage&userid=USERID">
<img src="aboutmegraphic.jpg" border="0">
</a>
</p>
<img src="tealbottom.jpg" width="95%" >
</center>
```

Template 10.4: Picture Column

CD-ROM Here's a nice-looking template for when you have a lot of product photos. All the photos are aligned vertically in the right column. The main text appears in the wide center column, and the photos are balanced by a vertical graphic image in the narrow left column. Each picture is a click-to-enlarge link, and the Terms of Sale goes in the bottom of the center column, under a graphic horizontal rule.

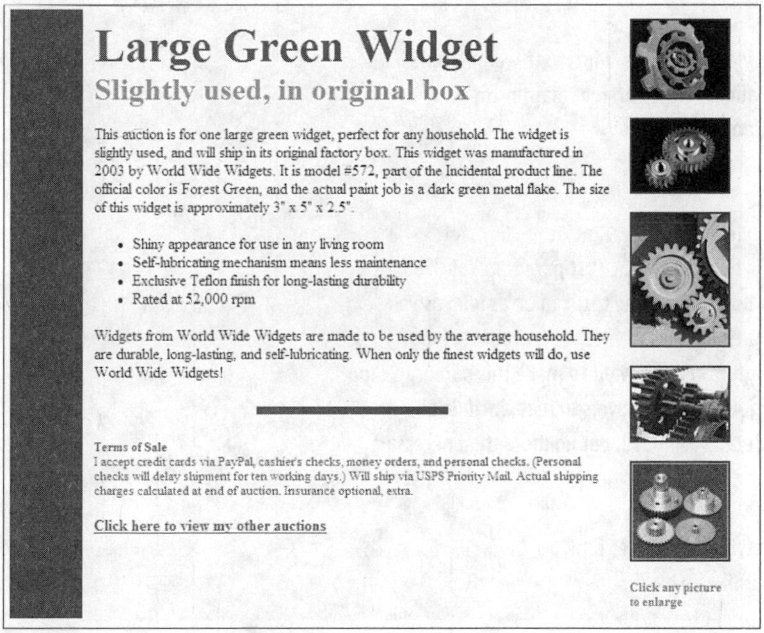

FIGURE 10.4

A template with a vertical column of small click-to-enlarge pictures.

As written, this code allows for five pictures in the right column. You can include additional photos by inserting more **<a href>** and **<img>** tags at the end of the list, or use fewer photos by deleting a line or two. Remember to replace all the *URL1*, *URL2*, and similar codes with the full URLs of your photos; you only have to link to large photos, as the code resizes the photos to a width of 100 pixels to fit within the narrow column. In addition, make sure you upload the **redside.jpg** graphics file to your picture host, and insert the full URL of its new location.

```
<table bgcolor="#FFFFCC" cellpadding="10"
width="765" align="center">


<tr>
  <td width="65" background="redside.jpg">
  </td>


  <td width="600" valign="top">
  <p style="font-size: 36pt; font-weight: bold;
  text-align: left; color: darkred; margin-bottom: 0">
  Auction Title
  </p>


  <p style="font-size: 24pt; font-weight: bold;
  text-align: left; color: red; margin-top: 0">
  Auction Subtitle
  </p>


  <p style="font-size: 12pt; text-align: left">
  This is the text for the first paragraph of the
  item description. The text can be as long as you
  like, although 4-5 sentences is probably long
  enough. You don't want to make this paragraph too
  long for potential buyers to read. Include all
  the details you need, but no more than necessary.
  </p>


  <ul style="font-size: 12pt">
  <li>Bullet text</li>
  <li>Bullet text</li>
  <li>Bullet text</li>
  <li>Bullet text</li>
  </ul>
```

```
<p style="font-size: 12pt; text-align: left">
This is the text for the second paragraph of the
item description. The text can be as long as you
like, although 4-5 sentences is probably long
enough. You don't want to make this paragraph too
long for potential buyers to read. Include all
the details you need, but no more than necessary.
</p>

<hr color="darkred" width="200" size="8">

<p style="font-size: 10pt; text-align: left;
color: darkred">
<strong>Terms of Sale</strong><br>
I accept credit cards via PayPal, cashier's checks,
money orders, and personal checks. (Personal checks
will delay shipment for ten working days.) Will
ship via USPS Priority Mail. Actual shipping
charges calculated at end of auction. Insurance
optional, extra.
</p>

<p style="font-size: 12 pt; font-weight: bold">
<a href="http://search.ebay.com/
➥_W0QQsassZ[USERID]QQhtZ-1">
Click here to view my other auctions
</a>
</p>

</td>

<td width="100" valign="top">
<p><a href="URL1" target="_blank">
<img src="URL1" width="100"></a></p>
<p><a href="URL2" target="_blank">
<img src="URL2" width="100"></a></p>
<p><a href="URL3" target="_blank">
<img src="URL3" width="100"></a></p>
<p><a href="URL4" target="_blank">
<img src="URL4" width="100"></a></p>
<p><a href="URL5" target="_blank">
```

```
<img src="URL5" width="100"></a></p>
<p style="font-size: 10pt;
font-weight: bold; color: red">
Click any picture to enlarge
</p>
</td>

</tr>
</table>
```

Template 10.5: Section Headings

 CD-ROM This is one of my favorite templates. It incorporates a single-column design for the title and description area, and a two-column design for the terms of service. Each major section features a heading with white text against a teal background—although you can change the color, of course.

FIGURE 10.5

Individual sections separated by reverse header text.

Template 10.5 is based on a simple two-column grid. Several of the rows span two columns (thanks to the **colspan="2"** attribute), but the underlying two-column grid is clearly visible in any case. This template allows for two click-to-enlarge pictures, specified at 250 pixels high each; replace *URL1* and *URL2* with the individual file URLs.

```
<table width="80%" border="0" align="center"
cellpadding="10" cellspacing="20">
<tr>
<td>

<table border="0" cellpadding="0"
cellspacing="20" width=100%>
<tr>
  <td bgcolor="teal" colspan="2">
  <p style="font-family: Verdana; font-size: 18pt;
  text-align: left;     color: white; margin-top: 0;
  margin-bottom: 0; margin-left: 5">
  <strong>Auction Title</strong><br>
  Auction Subtitle
  </p>
  </td>
</tr>

<tr>
  <td colspan="2" align="center">
  <a href="URL1" target="_blank">
  <img src="URL1" height="250">
  </a>    
  <a href="URL2" target="_blank">
  <img src="URL2" height="250">
  </a>
  </td>
</tr>

<tr>
  <td bgcolor="teal" colspan="2">
  <p style="font-family: Verdana; font-size: 14pt;
  text-align: left;     color: white; margin-top: 0;
  margin-bottom: 0; margin-left: 5">
  Item Details
  </p>
  </td>
```

```
    </tr>

    <tr>
      <td colspan="2">
      <p style="font-family: Verdana; font-size: 10pt;
      text-align: left; color: black">
      This is the text for the first paragraph of the item
      description. The text can be as long as you like,
      although 4-5 sentences is probably long enough. You
      don't want to make this paragraph too long for
      potential buyers to read. Include all the details
      you need, but no more than necessary.
      </p>
      </td>
    </tr>

    <tr>
      <td colspan="2">
      <p style="font-family: Verdana; font-size: 10pt;
      text-align: left; color: black">
      This is the text for the second paragraph of the item
      description. The text can be as long as you like,
      although 4-5 sentences is probably long enough. You
      don't want to make this paragraph too long for
      potential buyers to read. Include all the details
      you need, but no more than necessary.
      </p>
      </td>
    </tr>

    <tr>
      <td bgcolor="teal" width="50%">
      <p style="font-family: Verdana; font-size: 14pt;
      text-align: left;      color: white; margin-top: 0;
      margin-bottom: 0; margin-left: 5">
      Payment
      </p>
      </td>

      <td bgcolor="teal" width="50%">
      <p style="font-family: Verdana; font-size: 14pt;
```

```
    text-align: left; color: white; margin-top: 0;
    margin-bottom: 0; margin-left: 5">
    Shipping
    </p>
    </td>
  </tr>

  <tr>
    <td width="50%" valign="top">
    <p style="font-family: Verdana; font-size: 10pt;
    text-align: left;      color: teal; margin-top: 0">
    I accept credit cards via PayPal, money orders,
    cashier's checks, and personal checks. Personal
    checks will delay shipment for ten business days.
    </p>
    </td>

    <td width="50%" valign="top">
    <p style="font-family: Verdana; font-size: 10pt;
    text-align: left; color: teal; margin-top: 0">
    I ship via USPS Priority Mail. Shipping/handling
    charge to any location in the continental United
    States is $6.00. Email me for shipping/handling
    outside the U.S.
    </p>
    </td>
  </tr>

  <tr>

    <td colspan="2" align="center">
    <p style="font-family: Verdana; font-size: 12;
    font-weight: bold; text-align: center">
    <a href="http://search.ebay.com/
    ➥_W0QQsassZ[USERID]QQhtZ-1">
    Click here to view my other auctions
    </a>
    </p>

    </td>
  </tr>
```

```
</td>
</tr>
</table>
</td>
</tr>
</table>
```

Template 10.6: Three-Column with Block Sections

CD-ROM This template uses a modified three-column grid, each column sized at 225 pixels. The first column holds two click-to-enlarge photos, stacked vertically; the second and third columns are spanned to hold the title and descriptive text. Payment, shipping, and returns info are presented in three single-column blocks at the bottom of the listing.

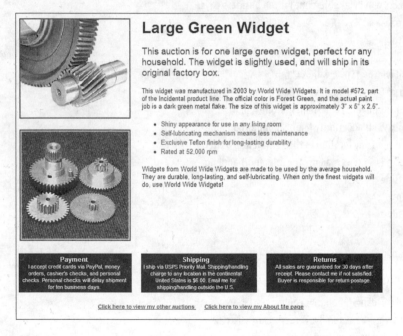

FIGURE 10.6

Block sections with a modified two-column structure.

What I like about this template is how the TOS info is presented in three horizontal blocks at the bottom of the listing. The blocks are created from table cells with a dark red background with wide white borders; the text is white reversed against the dark background.

```
<table width="870" bgcolor="white" cellspacing="20"
cellpadding="2">

<tr>
  <td width="225" valign="top">
  <p align="left">
  <a href="URL1" target="_blank">
  <img src="URL1" width="225">
  </a>
  </p>

  <p align="left">
  <a href="URL2" target="_blank">
  <img src="URL2" width="225">
  </a>
  </p>
  </td>

  <td valign="top" colspan="2">
  <p style="font-size: 24pt; font-family: Arial;
  font-weight: bold; color: darkblue; text-align: left">
  Auction Title
  </p>

  <p style="font-size: 14pt; font-family: Arial;
  color: blue; text-align: left">
  This is the text for your auction's overview paragraph.
  This paragraph should be no more than 2-3 sentences
  long.
  </p>

  <p style="font-size: 10pt; font-family: Arial;
  text-align: left; text-color: black">
  This is the text for the first paragraph of the item
  description. The text can be as long as you like,
  although 4-5 sentences is probably long enough. You
  don't want to make this paragraph too long for
  potential buyers to read. Include all the details
  you need, but no more than necessary.
  </p>
```

```
<ul style="font-family: Arial; font-size: 10pt;
color: blue">
<li>Bullet point text</li>
<li>Bullet point text</li>
<li>Bullet point text</li>
<li>Bullet point text</li>
</ul>

<p style="font-size: 10pt; font-family: Arial;
text-align: left; text-color: black">
This is the text for the second paragraph of the item
description. The text can be as long as you like,
although 4-5 sentences is probably long enough. You
don't want to make this paragraph too long for
potential buyers to read. Include all the details
you need, but no more than necessary.
</p>
</td>

</tr>

<tr>
<td width="225" valign="top" bgcolor="darkblue">
<p style="font-size: 10pt; font-family: Arial;
font-weight: bold; text-align: center; color: white;
margin-bottom: 0;  margin-top: 2; margin-left: 2;
margin-right: 2">
Payment
</p>

<p style="font-size: 8pt; font-family: Arial;
text-align: center; color: white; margin-top: 0;
margin-left: 2; margin-right: 2; margin-bottom: 2">
I accept credit cards via PayPal, money orders,
cashier's checks, and personal checks. Personal
checks will delay shipment for ten business days.
</p>
</td>
```

```
<td width="225" valign="top" bgcolor="darkblue">
<p style="font-size: 10pt; font-family: Arial;
font-weight: bold; text-align: center; color: white;
margin-bottom: 0; margin-top: 2; margin-left: 2;
margin-right: 2">
Shipping
</p>

<p style="font-size: 8pt; font-family: Arial;
text-align: center; color: white; margin-top: 0;
margin-bottom: 2; margin-left: 2; margin-right: 2">
I ship via USPS Priority Mail. Shipping/handling
charge to any location in the continental United
States is $6.00. Email me for shipping/handling
outside the U.S.
</p>
</td>

<td width="225" valign="top" bgcolor="darkblue">
<p style="font-size: 10pt; font-family: Arial;
font-weight: bold; text-align: center;
color: white; margin-bottom: 0; margin-top: 2;
margin-left: 2; margin-right: 2">
Returns
</p>

<p style="font-size: 8pt; font-family: Arial;
text-align: center; color: white; margin-top: 0;
margin-bottom: 2; margin-left: 2; margin-right: 2">
All sales are guaranteed for 30 days after receipt.
Please contact me if not satisfied. Buyer is
responsible for return postage.
</p>
</td>
</tr>
```

```
<tr>
 <td colspan="3">
 <p style="font-size: 8pt; font-family: Arial;
 font-weight: bold; text-align: center; color: darkred">
 <a href="http://search.ebay.com/
➥_W0QQsassZ[USERID]QQhtZ-1">
 Click here to view my other auctions
 </a>
      
 <a href=" http://cgi3.ebay.com/ws/
➥eBayISAPI.dll?ViewUserPage&userid=USERID">
 Click here to view my About Me page
 </a>
 </p>
 </td>
</tr>

</table>
```

Template 10.7: Table Details and Picture Show

CD-ROM Here's a template that's ideal when you're selling items with a lot of important specifications, such as consumer electronics equipment, digital cameras, and clothing. The specs are presented in tabular form, for easy scanning by potential buyers.

In addition to the table-within-a-table, this template features a manual-advance picture slideshow. This code is spec'd for four product pictures, but you can edit the code if you have more or fewer photos to display. There's also a "Check out my other auctions" drop-down menu at the bottom; be sure to customize the code with your own auction names and numbers.

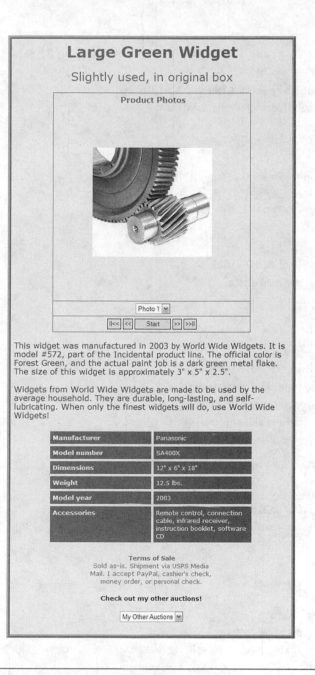

FIGURE 10.7

A template with a manual-advance slideshow and product spec table.

```
<table style="border-style: ridge; border-width: 5pt;
border-color: cyan; background-color: #CCFFCC"
align="center" width="600" cellpadding="5">
```

```
<tr>
<td>

<p style="font-family: Verdana; font-size: 24pt;
font-weight: bold; text-align: center; color: teal">
Auction Title
</p>

<p style="font-family: Verdana; font-size: 18pt;
text-align: center; color: teal">
Auction Subtitle
</p>

<!--BEGINNING OF SLIDESHOW CODE-->
<script language="JavaScript">
<!--start
var x = 0;

function rotate(num){
x=num%document.slideForm.slide.length;
if(x<0){x=document.slideForm.slide.length-1};
document.images.show.src=
➥document.slideForm.slide.options[x].value;
document.slideForm.slide.selectedIndex=x;
}

function apRotate() {
if(document.slideForm.slidebutton.value == "Stop"){
rotate(++x);window.setTimeout("apRotate()", 5000);}
}
//end -->
</script>

<form name="slideForm">
<table cellspacing=1 cellpadding=4
style="border: 1px teal solid; border-collapse: collapse"
align="center">
<tr>
<td align="center">
<strong><font face="Verdana" size="3" color="teal">
Product Photos
```

```
</font></strong>
</td>
</tr>

<tr>
<td align=center width=400 height=400>
<img src="URL1" name="show">
</td>
</tr>

<tr>
<td align=center style="border:1px teal solid;">
<select name="slide"
➥onChange="rotate(this.selectedIndex);">
<option value="URL1" selected>Photo 1
<option value="URL2">Photo 2
<option value="URL3">Photo 3
<option value="URL4">Photo 4
</select>
</td>
</tr>

<tr>
<td align=center style="border:1px teal solid;">
<input type=button onclick="rotate(0);"
value="II&lt;&lt;" title="Jump to beginning"
style="border:1px black solid;">
<input type=button onclick="rotate(x-1);"
value="&lt;&lt;" title="Last Picture"
style="border:1px black solid;">
<input type=button name="slidebutton"
onClick="this.value=
➥((this.value=='Stop')?'Start':'Stop');apRotate();"
value="Start" title="Autoplay" style="width:75px;
border:1px black solid;">
<input type=button onclick="rotate(x+1);" value="&gt;&gt;"
title="Next Picture" style="border:1px black solid;">
<input type=button
onclick="rotate(this.form.slide.length-1);"
value="&gt;&gt;II"
title="Jump to end" style="border:1px black solid;">
```

```
</td>
</tr>
</table>
</form>
<!--END OF SLIDESHOW CODE-->

<p style="font-family: Verdana; font-size: 12pt;
color: black; text-align: left">
This is the text for the first paragraph of the item
description. The text can be as long as you like,
although 4-5 sentences is probably long enough. You
don't want to make this paragraph too long for
potential buyers to read. Include all the details
you need, but no more than necessary.
</p>

<p style="font-family: Verdana; font-size: 12pt;
color: black; text-align: left">
This is the text for the second paragraph of the item
description. The text can be as long as you like,
although 4-5 sentences is probably long enough. You
don't want to make this paragraph too long for
potential buyers to read. Include all the details
you need, but no more than necessary.
</p>

<table width="75%" bordercolor="CCFFCC"
cellspacing="5" cellpadding="5" align="center">
<tr>
  <td width="50%" bgcolor="teal" valign="top">
  <p style="font-family: Verdana; font-size: 10pt;
  color: white; text-align: left; font-weight: bold">
  Manufacturer
  </p>
  </td>

  <td width="50%" bgcolor="teal" valign="top">
  <p style="font-family: Verdana; font-size: 10pt;
  color: white; text-align: left">
  Panasonic
  </p>
  </td>
```

```html
    </tr>

    <tr>
      <td width="50%" bgcolor="teal" valign="top">
      <p style="font-family: Verdana; font-size: 10pt;
      color: white; text-align: left; font-weight: bold">
      Model number
      </p>
      </td>

      <td width="50%" bgcolor="teal" valign="top">
      <p style="font-family: Verdana; font-size: 10pt;
      color: white; text-align: left">
      SA400X
      </p>
      </td>
    </tr>

    <tr>
      <td width="50%" bgcolor="teal" valign="top">
      <p style="font-family: Verdana; font-size: 10pt;
      color: white; text-align: left; font-weight: bold">
      Dimensions
      </p>
      </td>

      <td width="50%" bgcolor="teal" valign="top">
      <p style="font-family: Verdana; font-size: 10pt;
      color: white; text-align: left">
      12" x 6" x 18"
      </p>
      </td>
    </tr>

    <tr>
      <td width="50%" bgcolor="teal" valign="top">
      <p style="font-family: Verdana; font-size: 10pt;
      color: white; text-align: left; font-weight: bold">
      Weight
      </p>
      </td>
```

```
<td width="50%" bgcolor="teal" valign="top">
<p style="font-family: Verdana; font-size: 10pt;
color: white; text-align: left">
12.5 lbs.
</p>
</td>
</tr>

<tr>
<td width="50%" bgcolor="teal" valign="top">
<p style="font-family: Verdana; font-size: 10pt;
color: white; text-align: left; font-weight: bold">
Model year
</p>
</td>

<td width="50%" bgcolor="teal" valign="top">
<p style="font-family: Verdana; font-size: 10pt;
color: white; text-align: left">
2003
</p>
</td>
</tr>

<tr>
<td width="50%" bgcolor="teal" valign="top">
<p style="font-family: Verdana; font-size: 10pt;
color: white; text-align: left; font-weight: bold">
Accessories
</p>
</td>

<td width="50%" bgcolor="teal" valign="top">
<p style="font-family: Verdana; font-size: 10pt;
color: white; text-align: left">
Remote control, connection cable, infrared receiver,
instruction booklet, software CD
</p>
</td>
</tr>
</table>
```

```
<p style="font-family: Verdana; font-size: 10pt;
color: teal; text-align: center; margin-left: 150;
margin-right: 150">
<span style="font-weight: bold">Terms of Sale</span>
<br>
Sold as-is. Shipment via USPS Media Mail. I accept
PayPal, cashier's check, money order, or personal check.
</p>


<center>
<p style="font-family: Verdana; font-size: 10pt;
font-weight: bold; color: black">
Check out my other auctions!
</p>

<form>
<select name="URL"
onChange="if(options[selectedIndex].value)
window.location.href=
(options[selectedIndex].value)">
<OPTION value="">My Other Auctions</OPTION>
<OPTION value=http://cgi.ebay.com/ws/
➥eBayISAPI.dll?ViewItem&item=ITEMNUMBER1>
Auction name</OPTION>
<OPTION value=http://cgi.ebay.com/ws/
➥eBayISAPI.dll?ViewItem&item=ITEMNUMBER2>
Auction name</OPTION>
<OPTION value=http://cgi.ebay.com/ws/
➥eBayISAPI.dll?ViewItem&item=ITEMNUMBER3>
Auction name</OPTION>
<OPTION value=http://cgi.ebay.com/ws/
➥eBayISAPI.dll?ViewItem&item=ITEMNUMBER4>
Auction name</OPTION>
</select>
<noscript>
<input type=submit value="Go">
</noscript>
</input>
</form>
</center>
```

```
</td>
</tr>
</table>
```

Template 10.8: Scrolling Pictures and Text

 CD-ROM This is one scrolling, scrolling, scrolling template. We start with the item overview in a scrolling text marquee, and then continue with a scrolling slideshow of product photos. It makes for a very dynamic item listing!

The raised border effect for this template is created with nested tables; the outside table has an outset border, while the inside table has an inset border. The slideshow is set for four pictures, although you can add more. Remember to replace *URL1*, *URL2*, and so on with the full URLs of your image files.

> NOTE The code for the scrolling slideshow only works for photos stored on an external server on the Internet. If you try to use it with picture files stored on your hard disk, the photos will not display.

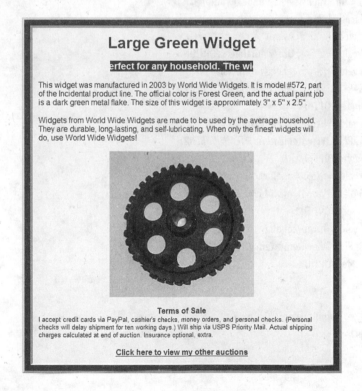

FIGURE 10.8

Template with a scrolling slideshow and text marquee.

```
<table width="75%" bgcolor="purple" cellpadding="10"
style="border-style: outset; border-width: 5px"
align="center">
<tr>
<td>

<table width="100%" bgcolor="#FFFF99" cellpadding="10"
style="border-style: inset;
border-width: 5px" align="center">
<tr>
<td>

<h1 style="color: purple; font-family: Arial;
text-align: center">
Auction Title
</h1>

<center>
<marquee behavior="scroll" width="50%">
<p style="font-family: Arial; font-weight: bold;
font-size: 14pt; color: white">
<span style="background-color: purple">
This is the overview text for the scrolling marquee.
Keep it short, no more than two sentences.
</span>
</p>
</marquee>
</center>

<p style="font-family: Arial; font-size: 12pt;
text-align: left">
This is the text for the first paragraph of the item
description. The text can be as long as you like,
although 4-5 sentences is probably long enough. You
don't want to make this paragraph too long for
potential buyers to read. Include all the details
you need, but no more than necessary.
</p>

<p style="font-family: Arial; font-size: 12pt;
text-align: left">
This is the text for the second paragraph of the item
```

description. The text can be as long as you like, although 4-5 sentences is probably long enough. You don't want to make this paragraph too long for potential buyers to read. Include all the details you need, but no more than necessary.
</p>

```
<!--BEGINNING OF SLIDESHOW CODE-->
<script language="JavaScript1.2">

var scrollerwidth='300px'
var scrollerheight='300px'
var scrollerbgcolor='white'
var pausebetweenimages=3000

var slideimages=new Array()
slideimages[0]='<img src="URL1" border=0>'
slideimages[1]='<img src="URL2" border=0>'
slideimages[2]='<img src="URL3" border=0>'
slideimages[3]='<img src="URL4" border=0>'

var ie=document.all
var dom=document.getElementById

if (slideimages.length>1)
i=2
else
i=0

function move1(whichlayer){
tlayer=eval(whichlayer)
if (tlayer.left>0&&tlayer.left<=5){
tlayer.left=0
setTimeout("move1(tlayer)",pausebetweenimages)
setTimeout("move2(document.main.document.second)",
➡pausebetweenimages)
return
}
if (tlayer.left>=tlayer.document.width*-1){
tlayer.left-=5
setTimeout("move1(tlayer)",50)
}
```

```
else{
tlayer.left=parseInt(scrollerwidth)+5
tlayer.document.write(slideimages[i])
tlayer.document.close()
if (i==slideimages.length-1)
i=0
else
i++
}
}

function move2(whichlayer){
tlayer2=eval(whichlayer)
if (tlayer2.left>0&&tlayer2.left<=5){
tlayer2.left=0
setTimeout("move2(tlayer2)",pausebetweenimages)
setTimeout("move1(document.main.document.first)",
➥pausebetweenimages)
return
}
if (tlayer2.left>=tlayer2.document.width*-1){
tlayer2.left-=5
setTimeout("move2(tlayer2)",50)
}
else{
tlayer2.left=parseInt(scrollerwidth)+5
tlayer2.document.write(slideimages[i])
tlayer2.document.close()
if (i==slideimages.length-1)
i=0
else
i++
}
}

function move3(whichdiv){
tdiv=eval(whichdiv)
if (parseInt(tdiv.style.left)>0&&parseInt
➥(tdiv.style.left)<=5){
tdiv.style.left=0+"px"
setTimeout("move3(tdiv)",pausebetweenimages)
```

```
setTimeout("move4(scrollerdiv2)",pausebetweenimages)
return
}
if (parseInt(tdiv.style.left)>=tdiv.offsetWidth*-1){
tdiv.style.left=parseInt(tdiv.style.left)-5+"px"
setTimeout("move3(tdiv)",50)
}
else{
tdiv.style.left=scrollerwidth
tdiv.innerHTML=slideimages[i]
if (i==slideimages.length-1)
i=0
else
i++
}
}

function move4(whichdiv){
tdiv2=eval(whichdiv)
if (parseInt(tdiv2.style.left)>0&&parseInt
➥(tdiv2.style.left)<=5){
tdiv2.style.left=0+"px"
setTimeout("move4(tdiv2)",pausebetweenimages)
setTimeout("move3(scrollerdiv1)",pausebetweenimages)
return
}
if (parseInt(tdiv2.style.left)>=tdiv2.offsetWidth*-1){
tdiv2.style.left=parseInt(tdiv2.style.left)-5+"px"
setTimeout("move4(scrollerdiv2)",50)
}
else{
tdiv2.style.left=scrollerwidth
tdiv2.innerHTML=slideimages[i]
if (i==slideimages.length-1)
i=0
else
i++
}
}

function startscroll(){
if (ie||dom){
```

```
scrollerdiv1=ie? first2 : document.getElementById("first2")
scrollerdiv2=ie? second2 : document.getElementById
➥("second2")
move3(scrollerdiv1)
scrollerdiv2.style.left=scrollerwidth
}
else if (document.layers){
document.main.visibility='show'
move1(document.main.document.first)
document.main.document.second.left=parseInt(scrollerwidth)+5
document.main.document.second.visibility='show'
}
}

window.onload=startscroll

</script>

<div align="center">
<script language="JavaScript1.2">
if (ie||dom){
document.writeln('<div id="main2"
➥style="position:relative;width:'+scrollerwidth+';
➥height:'+scrollerheight+';overflow:hidden;
➥background-color:'+scrollerbgcolor+'">')
document.writeln('<div style="position:absolute;
➥width:'+scrollerwidth+';height:'+scrollerheight+';
➥clip:rect(0 '+scrollerwidth+' '+scrollerheight+' 0);
➥left:0px;top:0px">')
document.writeln('<div id="first2" style="position:absolute;
➥width:'+scrollerwidth+';left:1px;top:0px;">')
document.write(slideimages[0])
document.writeln('</div>')
document.writeln('<div id="second2"
➥style="position:absolute;
➥width:'+scrollerwidth+';left:0px;top:0px">')
document.write(slideimages[1])
document.writeln('</div>')
document.writeln('</div>')
document.writeln('</div>')
}
```

```
</script>
</div>
<!--END OF SLIDESHOW CODE-->

<p style="font-family: Arial; font-size: 12pt;
font-weight: bold; text-align: center;
color: purple; margin-bottom: 0">
Terms of Sale
</p>
<p style="font-family: Arial; font-size: 10pt;
text-align: left; color: black; margin-top: 0">
I accept credit cards via PayPal, cashier's checks,
money orders, and personal checks. (Personal checks
will delay shipment for ten working days.) Will ship
via USPS Priority Mail. Actual shipping charges
calculated at end of auction. Insurance optional, extra.
</p>

<p style="font-family: Arial; font-size: 12pt;
font-weight: bold; text-align: center">
<a href="http://search.ebay.com/_W0QQsassZ[USERID]QQhtZ-1">
Click here to view my other auctions
</a>
</p>


</td>
</tr>
</table>

</td>
</tr>
</table>
```

Template 10.9: Image Border

CD-ROM What makes this template unique is that it puts an image border around the entire listing. The border is actually made up of four separate images, one each for the top, bottom, left, and right sides.

FIGURE 10.9

A template with images around all the borders.

The border images are enclosed within individual table cells. This requires the creation of a table with three rows and three columns, with the left and right columns sized to fit the thin border images. The top and bottom cells span all three columns, since the top and bottom images are sized to the full listing width (600 pixels). This template also features two click-to-enlarge pictures, displayed in-line with the description text. You should upload the **roundtop.jpg**, **roundleft.jpg**, **roundright.jpg**, and **roundbottom.jpg** files to your picture host, and insert the appropriate URLs into the code.

```
<table cellpadding="0" cellspacing="0" width="600"
bgcolor="white" align="center">

<tr>
  <td colspan="3">
  <img src="roundtop.jpg">
  </td>
</tr>

<tr>
  <td align="left" width="19" background="roundleft.jpg"
  width="20">
  </td>
```

```
<td valign="top" width="560" cellpadding="10">

<h1 style="font-family: Times Roman; color: teal;
text-align: left">
Auction Title
</h1>

<p style="font-family: Times Roman; text-align: left">
<a href="URL1" target="_blank">
<img src="URL1" align="right" hspace="5" vspace="5"
width="100; margin: 10">
</a>
This is the text for the first paragraph of the item
description. The text can be as long as you like,
although 4-5 sentences is probably long enough. You
don't want to make this paragraph too long for
potential buyers to read. Include all the details
you need, but no more than necessary.
</p>

<p style="font-family: Times Roman; text-align: left">
<a href="URL2" target="_blank">
<img src="URL2" align="left" hspace="5" vspace="5"
width="100">
</a>
This is the text for the second paragraph of the item
description. The text can be as long as you like,
although 4-5 sentences is probably long enough. You
don't want to make this paragraph too long for
potential buyers to read. Include all the details
you need, but no more than necessary.
</p>

<p style="font-family: Arial; font-size: 10pt;
text-align: left; font-weight: bold; color: teal;
margin-bottom: 0px">
Terms of Sale
</p>

<p style="font-family: Arial; font-size: 10pt;
text-align: left;      margin-top: 0 px; color: teal">
```

```
I accept credit cards via PayPal, cashier's checks,
money orders, and personal checks. (Personal checks
will delay shipment for ten working days.) Will
ship via USPS Priority Mail. Actual shipping
charges calculated at end of auction. Insurance
optional, extra.
</p>

<p style="font-family: Arial; font-weight: bold;
margin-bottom: 0px">
<a href="http://search.ebay.com/
➥_W0QQsassZ[USERID]QQhtZ-1">
Click here to view my other auctions
</a>
</p>
</td>

<td align="left" width="21" background="roundright.jpg"
width="20">
</td>
</tr>

<tr>
<td colspan="3">
<img src="roundbottom.jpg">
</td>
</tr>

</table>
```

Template 10.10: Friendly Pictures and Fonts

CD-ROM Our final template is a little different from the others in this chapter, in that it's designed to convey a homey, quite personal touch. To that end, the pictures are big and friendly, and the font (Comic Sans MS) is also a bit less professional than in the other templates. When you want to let your buyers know that you're a "small guy," just like them, this is the template to use.

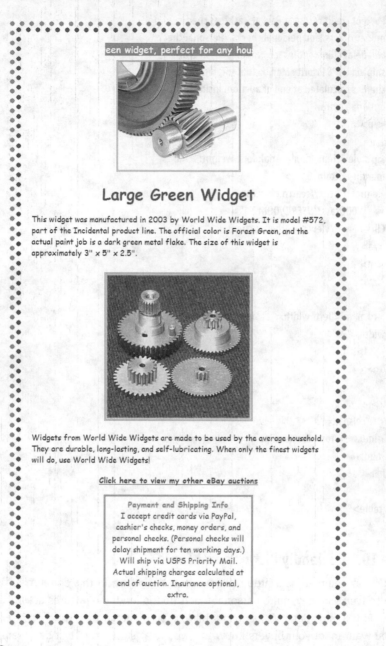

FIGURE 10.10

A less-professional-looking template—designed for that friendly touch.

By this point, there should be nothing new or startling about what we're doing here. The double border is created by nested tables, using the **dotted** border style, in two different colors. There's a scrolling marquee at the top, and everything else in the template is designed to be as homey and friendly as possible.

```html
<table width="75%" style="border-style: dotted;
border-width: 10; border-color: red" align="center">
<tr>
<td>

<table width="100%" cellpadding="20"
style="border-style: dotted; border-width: 10;
border-color: blue">
<tr>
<td>


<center>
<marquee behavior="scroll" width="50%">
<p style="font-family: Comic Sans MS; font-weight: bold;
font-size: 14pt; color: white">
<span style="background-color: red">
Insert your own personal tag line or slogan here
</span>
</p>
</marquee>
</center>


<center>
<img src="URL1" style="border-style: double;
border-color: red; border-width: 3;
margin-top: 10">
</center>


<h1 style="font-family: Comic Sans MS; color: blue;
text-align: center">
Auction Title
</h1>


<p style="font-family: Comic Sans MS;
text-align: justified">
This is the text for the first paragraph of the item
description. The text can be as long as you like,
although 4-5 sentences is probably long enough. You
don't want to make this paragraph too long for
```

potential buyers to read. Include all the details
you need, but no more than necessary.
</p>

<img src="*URL2*" style="border-style: double;
border-color: red; border-width: 3; margin-top: 10">

<p style="font-family: Comic Sans MS;
text-align: justified">
This is the text for the second paragraph of the item
description. The text can be as long as you like,
although 4-5 sentences is probably long enough. You
don't want to make this paragraph too long for
potential buyers to read. Include all the details
you need, but no more than necessary.
</p>

<p style="font-family: Comic Sans MS; font-weight: bold;
text-align: center">
<a href="http://search.ebay.com/_W0QQsassZ*[USERID]*QQhtZ-1">
Click here to view my other eBay auctions
</a>
</p>

<p style="font-family: Comic Sans MS; color: blue;
text-align: center; margin-left: 150;
margin-right: 150; border-style: double;
border-width: 3; padding: 5">

Payment and Shipping Info

I accept credit cards via PayPal, cashier's checks, money
orders, and personal checks. (Personal checks will delay
shipment for ten working days.) Will ship via USPS
Priority Mail. Actual shipping charges calculated at
end of auction. Insurance optional, extra.
</p>

```
</td>
</tr>
</table>

</td>
</tr>
</table>
```

Where to Go from Here

Template 10.10 is the last one in this book, but it doesn't have to be the last template you use in your eBay auctions. You should be able to use all the techniques I've presented to both customize the templates included on the accompanying CD, and to create your own eBay templates from scratch. Use the HTML code in this book as the building blocks for your own templates, and work to create your own personal visual identity for your eBay auctions. Ultimately, this book is just what the title says—it's a "starter kit" for all the auction templates you'll create in the future. Have fun

Appendixes

HTML for About Me and eBay Stores Pages

All of the HTML codes discussed in the body of this book can be applied to any HTML page, including but not limited to eBay auction listings. (Save for those codes that eBay prohibits, of course.) But there are also a few special HTML codes exclusive to eBay, that you can use when creating your own About Me and eBay Stores pages. These codes insert proprietary eBay information, such as your user ID and feedback rating, into your pages.

A few things to note about these special HTML tags:

- None of these special HTML codes are case-sensitive. You can write them in either uppercase or lowercase— or mixed.

- As with most HTML tags, you can gain multiple attributes together within a single tag.

- These special eBay HTML tags can only be used in About Me and eBay Stores pages. They can't be used in regular eBay auction listings.

HTML for Your About Me Page

The whole goal of an eBay About Me page is to let potential buyers and sellers learn a little about you. To that end, you may want to include some dynamic eBay-specific information, such as your current feedback rating, feedback listings, items currently for sale, and so on.

When you include these tags into the HTML code for your About Me page, the current value of the information is automatically displayed. You don't have to bother with inserting your current feedback rating manually (and keeping it constantly updated); when you insert the **<eBayFeedback>** tag, the current feedback number is inserted—and it changes automatically when your rating is updated.

Table A.1 details the special HTML tags you can use in your About Me page. You can also find a listing of these tags online at pages.ebay.com/help/account/html-tags.html. Many of these tags have additional parameters that you can add within the angle brackets. For example, to display your eBay feedback in red, you would code **<eBayFeedback COLOR="red">**.

Table A.1   eBay About Me HTML Codes

Code	Description	Parameters
<eBayFeedback>	Displays your user feedback.	SIZE="*n*" (specifies how many items you want to display
		COLOR="*color*" (displays the lower feedback line in color)
		ALTERNATECOLOR="*color*" (displays the upper feedback line in color)
		BORDER="*n*" (adds a border of *n* width around the listings)
		CAPTION="*text*" (displays a customized caption above the feedback list)
		TABLEWIDTH="*n*" (specifies the width of the feedback table, as a percentage of the available width)
		CELLPADDING="*n*" (adds spacing between the feedback comments)
<eBayItemList>	Displays the items you currently have for sale.	BIDS (displays the items you are currently bidding on)

Code	Description	Parameters
		SORT="*n*" (sorts your items by a specific method; replace *n* with 8 to sort by date newest first, with 2 to sort by date oldest first, with 3 to sort by end date of auction newest first, or 4 to sort by price in ascending order)
		CATEGORY="*n*" (lists items in the specified category; replace *n* with the category number)
		SINCE="*n*" (specifies the number of days ended auctions stay in your list)
		BORDER="*n*" (adds a border of *n* width around the listings)
		CAPTION="*text*" (puts a customized caption at the top of your items table)
		TABLEWIDTH="*n*" (specifies the width of the item table, as a percentage of the available width)
		CELLPADDING="*n*" (adds spacing between the items)
<eBayMemberSince>	Displays the date of your eBay registration.	*None*
<eBayTime>	Displays the current eBay system time.	*None*
<eBayUserID>	Displays your user ID.	BOLD (displays your user ID in bold) NOLINK (displays your user ID without a link to your Member Profile page)
		NOFEEDBACK (displays your user ID without your feedback rating)
		EMAIL (also displays your email address)
		NOMASK (hides the "shades" new user icon)

HTML for Your eBay Stores Pages

eBay also provides a similar set of custom HTML tags you can use when designing your eBay Stores pages. These tags are described in Table A.2. You can also find a listing of these tags online, at pages.ebay.com/help/specialtysites/stores-specific-tags.html. Note, however, that these tags are enclosed in curly brackets, rather than the normal angle brackets.

Table A.2   eBay Stores HTML Codes

Code	Description	Parameters
{eBayFeedback}	Displays your user feedback.	SIZE="*n*" (specifies how many items you want to display)
		COLOR="*color*" (displays the lower feedback line in color)
		ALTERNATECOLOR="*color*" (displays the upper feedback line in color)
		BORDER="*n*" (adds a border of *n* width around the listings)
		TABLEWIDTH="*n*" (specifies the width of the feedback table, as a percentage of the available width)
		CELLPADDING="*n*" (adds spacing between the feedback comments)
{eBayPromo}	Displays a promotion box that contains the text you specify.	ID="*text*" (specifies the text to display in the promo box)
{eBayStoresItem}	Displays a specific item.	ITEM="*nnn*" (specifies the item number to display)
		DISPLAY="*n*" (displays item using a numeric code to specify method: 0=list view, 1=gallery view)
		BORDER="*n*" (displays item with a border of specified size)
		TABLEWIDTH="*n*" (displays item in a table of *n* width, where *n* is a percentage of the available width)

Code	Description	Parameters
{eBayStoresItemDetail}	Displays specific details about an item in your store.	ITEM="*nnn*" (specifies the item number to display)
		PROPERTY="title" (displays the items title)
		PROPERTY="price" (displays the item's current price)
		PROPERTY="binprice" (displays the item's Buy It Now price)
		PROPERTY="time" (displays the item's remaining time)
		PROPERTY="picture" (displays the item's Gallery picture)
		PROPERTY="URL" (displays the item's URL)
{eBayStoresItemShowcase}	Displays in a special showcase display items you currently have for sale.	SORT="*n*" (sorts items using a specific numeric code: 2=ending first, 4=newly listed, 0=highest price, 1=lowest price)
		ITEM="*w,x,y,z*" (displays up to 4 items having the item numbers you manually specify)
		DISPLAY="*n*" (displays items using a numeric code to specify method: 0=list view, 1=gallery view)
		BORDER="*n*" (displays items with a border of specified size)
		TABLEWIDTH="*n*" (displays items in a table of *n* width, where *n* is a percentage of the available width)
		STORECADID="*n*" (displays items from one of your custom store categories, where *n* is the ID number of the category)
		KEYWORDS="*keyword*" (displays items that include in their titles the keywords you specify)

Code	Description	Parameters
		MINPRICE="*x*" MAXPRICE="*y*" (displays items that fall between a specified minimum and maximum price)
		LISTINGFORMAT="*n*" (displays items that use the specified listing format: 1=online auction, 6=real estate, 7=store inventory, 9=fixed price)
		SIZE="*n*" (displays a set number of items, up to 4)
		BACKFILL="*setting*" (specifies whether items you've manually selected will be automatically replaced when they are sold; values are **on** and **off**)
{eBayStoresSearchBox}	Displays a search box that shoppers can use to search for items in your eBay Store.	*None*
{eBayUserID}	Displays your user ID.	*None*

Contents of the eBay Auction Templates Starter Kit CD

The CD that accompanies this book contains a variety of eBay-related software programs and ready-to-use auction templates. You can access all the programs and templates by clicking the appropriate button on the CD's opening screen. Follow the onscreen instructions to download and use each of the programs and templates included.

Alternatively, you can bypass the CD interface and copy files directly from the folders and subfolders on the CD itself. The CD is organized into two main folders, Software and Templates, both of which contain subfolders for specific types of items. For example, to access the Auction Hawk templates, you'd go to the **templates\auctionhawk** subfolder on the CD.

Software Programs

We've included several software programs that you can use to help create your own auction templates. These include auction listing and management programs, an HTML editor, and a photo editing program.

All My Auctions

All My Auctions is an auction management program that helps you manage the auction process after you've created and launched your item listings. It lets you create and send post-auction emails, create packing slips and mailing labels, generate reports and calculate your profits, and monitor the activities of other — sellers. Learn more at www.rajeware.com/auction/.

AuctionSage

AuctionSage is a software program that lets you post and manage your eBay auction transactions. It includes a basic listing creation tool, as well as various post-auction management functions. Learn more at www.auctionsagesoftware.com.

Auction Wizard 2000

Auction Wizard 2000—that's *wizard*, not *lizard*—is an auction management software program that includes a listing creator, an image editor, a report generator, an FTP manager, and an auction database. Its biggest strength is its bulk listing capabilities, with pre-designed listing templates. Learn more at www.auctionwizard2000.com.

IrfanView

IrfanView is an easy-to-use, fully featured image editing program. You can use IrfanView to do all manner of basic editing on your eBay products photos, including cropping, adjusting brightness and contrast, sharpening fuzzy edges, and so on. Lea—ore at www.irfanview.com.

Nvu

Nvu is a full-featured HTML authoring program, based on the Mozilla Composer software, that works on any computer platform—Windows, Macintosh, even Linux. It lets you create HTML-based eBay auction templates and regular web pages in a WYSIWYG environment. Learn more at www.nvu.com.

Third-Party Auction Templates

The accompanying CD also includes a variety of ready-to-use eBay auction templates from several third-party designers. Most of these templates can be opened in any HTML or text editing program, and edited to include your own individual auction information.

AuctionSpice

AuctionSpice presents several great-looking templates, all of which can be edited to include up to 10 product photos and your choice of background colors. More templates are available at www.auctionspice.com.

Auction Hawk

Auction Hawk is a web-based auction listing/management service that also offers free-standing templates. We've included several of their freestanding templates on the accompanying CD, as well as additional templates that are usable with the Auction Hawk online service. Learn more about the Auction Hawk service and additional templates at www.auctionhawk.com.

AuctionWraps

AuctionWraps offers a wide variety of professionally designed templates. Three of these templates are included on the accompanying CD; go to www.auctionwraps.com to see other templates offered by this site.

BiggerBids/Nucite

BiggerBids and Nucite are two sites run by the same company, both offering a variety of professional-looking eBay auction templates. We've included three of their templates, free of charge, on the accompanying CD: Electric Blue (great for computers and electronics items), The Softer Side (terrific for clothing and home and garden items), and Rising Red Sun (ideal for sporting goods and apparel). All three templates link to a free online version that automates the HTML editing for you. Even more templates are available at www.biggerbids.com and members.nucite.com.

Pace Computing Limited

Pace Computing Limited (PC-Limited) offers a variety of web design services and free-standing eBay auction templates. We've included their HTML Template Pack on the accompanying CD, which includes one editable eBay auction template and an editable email template. You can see more of the company's offerings at www.pc-limited.com/web-design-templates.htm.

Templates and Special Effects from This Book

Finally, the code for all the templates and special effects presented in this book are also included on the accompanying CD. All these examples and templates are presented in plain text (TXT) files, which can be opened and edited in any text or HTML editing program, such as the Nvu editor included on the CD. The files are labeled similarly to how they're presented in the text; for example, the code for Template 10.1 (from Chapter 10) is found in the file labeled template 10-1.txt.

When using these templates, you should copy the entire text file into a text editor or HTML editing program. You can then follow the instructions in the appropriate chapter to edit the code for your individual auctions. You can then copy the edited code into a new eBay auction listing, using the HTML editor found on eBay's Describe Your Auction form.

Several of the templates in Chapter 10 have accompanying graphics files. These files are also found on the CD. To use these files with the template code, you should first copy the graphics files to your computer's hard disk, and then upload them to an external Internet server or photo hosting service. You can then reference the uploaded URL and filename in the template code.

There's More in the Readme File

In addition to all the programs and templates included on the CD, you'll also find a very important text file. The readme.txt file includes additional information about the CD's contents, as well as instructions on how to use the CD on your computer. Any changes to the CD's contents will also be noted in this file.

Index

Symbols

A

Q–R

S

U–V

W–Z

www.biggerbids.com

➡ Automated Auction Templates

➡ Integrated Image Hosting

➡ Professionally Designed Layouts

What is BiggerBids?

Our state-of-the-art system generates the HTML code you need to create top-quality, professional auction layouts. BiggerBids makes it easy for you to promote a trusted, professional image to your potential bidders.

All you have to do is fill in a few text boxes with the details of the item you are selling and BiggerBids does the rest. You can even upload your auction's images directly into any of our templates. Once you're done filling in the details and uploading images, you can see your auction in any of our template designs. Once you've found the one that works for your auction, you simply copy the code. It couldn't be easier!

BiggerBids is fast and easy!

Our system allows you to store the details that tend to stay the same for each of your auctions. Things like a business description, your company logo, selling policies, default shipping and payment details, cross-promotion of your eBay store and other details can be stored once so they don't need to be retyped with every auction layout you create.

We are FREE to join!

Auction Hawk

Make your sales soar.

Better tools for Power Sellers

eBay made eAsy.

Why use auction management tools?

Increase the number of successful transactions

There are over 7 million items on eBay. Do yours stand out?

Studies have repeatedly shown that attractive ads with higher quality photos bring higher final sale prices. In fact, items with no images or poor quality images often don't sell at all!

A professional looking listing with crisp, super-size photos is critical. People won't purchase if they can't clearly see what they are buying. That's why mail-order catalogs are always professional looking.

Maximize your profit

An increasing number of individuals and businesses are realizing the power of the eBay marketplace. Since the average price of an item sold on eBay is only about $30.00 most Power Sellers need to manage a large number of listings. Auction management is one of the most important aspects of their business.

Auction Hawk makes it simpler and less expensive to manage eBay listings. We automate the entire auction process, allowing you more time to focus on running your business.

Why choose Auction Hawk?

You get all the features you need

Manage every aspect of your eBay sales including image hosting, automated ad design and e-mail management, bulk repeatable listings, feedback management, report tracking and much more. Choose from over 300 layouts. Manage dozens or thousands of items.

Lower cost

Because of our 100% flat-fee pricing, Auction Hawk costs 50% to 80% less than the competition. Your profits won't get eaten up like they do on other listing services that charge multiple fees on each sale you make.

Easy to switch, easy to use

We'll import all of your existing listings from eBay, including descriptions. Create attractive listings in just seconds and schedule them to launch anytime. You'll get great, professional looking listings the very first time you use the service.

Uncompromised image quality

Top quality image management with crisp, clear, uncompromised images with no blurring. Fast image downloads, reliable service with easy and convenient image management.

Outstanding customer service

Auction Hawk is supported around-the-clock. Yes, everyone says they have great customer service, but don't take our word for it, listen to our customers.

> *"Your service has been phenomenal. I have come to be entirely dependent on it... Your service desk is very responsive and 100% effective with the challenges I've reported."*
> – Fred Wright

Community

Auction Hawk is a strong community of auction sellers. Use Auction Hawk discussion boards and e-mail from other Auction Hawk sellers to learn more about how they manage their sales.

If you're serious about selling on eBay, you owe it to yourself to try Auction Hawk. **Sign up at www.auctionhawk.com.**